Football in Southeastern Europe

This volume draws together scholarship across a number of disciplines – history, sociology, media and cultural studies, political science, Slavonic studies – to examine the significance of the sport of football within Southeastern Europe, with a special focus on countries of the former Yugoslavia. The volume is timely as there is growing recognition inside and beyond the academy that football is a key cultural site in which the tensions within the region have been, and continue to be, reflected. Important issues such as resurgent nationalism, ethno/religious identity construction, and collective masculine identity are played out in relation to the sport of football. The chapters within the volume explore these and other themes in detailed case studies that will be of interest to academics and policy makers concerned with wanting to know more about how football should be considered within agendas focused on reconciliation and a socially inclusive future.

This book was previously published as a special issue of *Sport in Society*.

John Hughson is Professor of Sport and Cultural Studies and Director of the International Football Institute at the University of Central Lancashire. He is author of *Making Sporting Cultures* (2009); principal author of *The Uses of Sport* (2005); co-editor of *The Containment of Soccer in Australia* (2010); co-editor of *Sport in the City: Cultural Connections* (2011); and principal editor of *The Routledge Handbook of Football Studies* (2014 forthcoming), all of which have been published by Routledge.

Fiona Skillen is Lecturer in Sport and Events at Glasgow Caledonian University. Her research interests focus on the history of sport, in particular, aspects of gender, politics, social policy and health. She is particularly interested in the influence which dominant discourses concerning gender and modernity had on women's popular culture. Dr Skillen is the author of *Women, Sport and Modernity in Interwar Britain* (Oxford: Peter Lang, 2013).

Football in Southeastern Europe

From Ethnic Homogenization to Reconciliation

Edited by
John Hughson and Fiona Skillen

Routledge
Taylor & Francis Group

LONDON AND NEW YORK

First published 2014
by Routledge
2 Park Square, Milton Park, Abingdon, Oxon, OX14 4RN, UK

and by Routledge
711 Third Avenue, New York, NY 10017, USA

Routledge is an imprint of the Taylor & Francis Group, an informa business

British Library Cataloguing in Publication Data
A catalogue record for this book is available from the British Library

ISBN 13: 978-0-415-74950-3

Typeset in Times New Roman
by Taylor & Francis Books

Publisher's Note
The publisher accepts responsibility for any inconsistencies that may have arisen during the conversion of this book from journal articles to book chapters, namely the possible inclusion of journal terminology.

Disclaimer
Every effort has been made to contact copyright holders for their permission to reprint material in this book. The publishers would be grateful to hear from any copyright holder who is not here acknowledged and will undertake to rectify any errors or omissions in future editions of this book.

Contents

SPORT IN THE GLOBAL SOCIETY – CONTEMPORARY PERSPECTIVES

Series Editors: Boria Majumdar

FOOTBALL IN SOUTHEASTERN EUROPE

From Ethnic Homogenization to Reconciliation

Sport in the Global Society – Contemporary Perspectives

Series Editor: Boria Majumdar

The social, cultural (including media) and political study of sport is an expanding area of scholarship and related research. While this area has been well served by the *Sport in the Global Society* series, the surge in quality scholarship over the last few years has necessitated the creation of *Sport in the Global Society: Contemporary Perspectives*. The series will publish the work of leading scholars in fields as diverse as sociology, cultural studies, media studies, gender studies, cultural geography and history, political science and political economy. If the social and cultural study of sport is to receive the scholarly attention and readership it warrants, a cross-disciplinary series dedicated to taking sport beyond the narrow confines of physical education and sport science academic domains is necessary. *Sport in the Global Society: Contemporary Perspectives* will answer this need.

Titles in the Series

Australian Sport
Antipodean Waves of Change
Edited by Kristine Toohey and Tracy Taylor

Australia's Asian Sporting Context
1920s and 1930s
Edited by Sean Brawley and Nick Guoth

Bearing Light: Flame Relays and the Struggle for the Olympic Movement
Edited by John J. MacAloon

'Critical Support' for Sport
Bruce Kidd

Disability in the Global Sport Arena
A Sporting Chance
Edited by Jill M. Clair

Diversity and Division – Race, Ethnicity and Sport in Australia
Christopher J. Hallinan

Diversity, Equity and Inclusion in Sport and Leisure
Edited by Katherine Dashper and Thomas Fletcher

Documenting the Beijing Olympics
Edited by D. P. Martinez and Kevin Latham

Ethnicity and Race in Association Football
Case Study analyses in Europe, Africa and the USA
Edited by David Hassan

Fan Culture in European Football and the Influence of Left Wing Ideology
Edited by Peter Kennedy and David Kennedy

Football in Brazil
Edited by Martin Curi

Football in Southeastern Europe
From Ethnic Homogenization to Reconciliation
Edited by John Hughson and Fiona Skillen

Football Supporters and the Commercialisation of Football
Comparative Responses across Europe
Edited by Peter Kennedy and David Kennedy

Football's Relationship with Art: The Beautiful Game?
John E. Hughson

Forty Years of Sport and Social Change, 1968-2008
"To Remember is to Resist"
Edited by Russell Field and Bruce Kidd

Global Perspectives on Football in Africa
Visualising the Game
Edited by Susann Baller, Giorgio Miescher and Ciraj Rassool

Global Sport Business
Community Impacts of Commercial Sport
Edited by Hans Westerbeek

Governance, Citizenship and the New European Football Championships
The European Spectacle
Edited by Wolfram Manzenreiter and Georg Spitaler

Indigenous People, Race Relations and Australian Sport
Edited by Christopher J. Hallinan and Barry Judd

Olympic Reform Ten Years Later
Edited by Heather Dichter and Bruce Kidd

Perspectives on Sport and Music
Edited by Anthony Bateman

Reflections on Process Sociology and Sport
'Walking the Line'
Joseph Maguire

Soccer in the Middle East
Edited by Issam Khalidi and Alon Raab

South Africa and the Global Game
Football, Apartheid and Beyond
Edited by Peter Alegi and Chris Bolsmann

Sport – Race, Ethnicity and Identity
Building Global Understanding
Edited by Daryl Adair

Sport and the Community
Edited by Allan Edwards and David Hassan

Sport, Culture and Identity in the State of Israel
Edited by Yair Galily and Amir Ben-Porat

Sport in Australian National Identity
Kicking Goals
Tony Ward

Sport in the City
Cultural Connections
Edited by Michael Sam and John E. Hughson

Citation Information

The chapters in this book were originally published in *Sport in Society*, volume 16, issue 8 (October 2013). When citing this material, please use the original page numbering for each article, as follows:

Chapter 1
Introduction
John Hughson
Sport in Society, volume 16, issue 8 (October 2013) pp. 943–944

Chapter 2
Fighters, footballers and nation builders: wartime football in the Serb-held territories of the former Yugoslavia, 1991–1996
Richard Mills
Sport in Society, volume 16, issue 8 (October 2013) pp. 945–972

Chapter 3
Fertile land or mined field? Peace-building and ethnic tensions in post-war Bosnian football
Davide Sterchele
Sport in Society, volume 16, issue 8 (October 2013) pp. 973–992

Chapter 4
'A lofty battle for the nation': the social roles of sport in Tudjman's Croatia
Dario Brentin
Sport in Society, volume 16, issue 8 (October 2013) pp. 993–1008

Chapter 5
'A Croatian champion with a Croatian name': national identity and uses of history in Croatian football culture – the case of Dinamo Zagreb
Tea Sindbæk
Sport in Society, volume 16, issue 8 (October 2013) pp. 1009–1024

Chapter 6
Football matches or power struggles? The Albanian case within historical conflicts and contemporary tensions
Falma Fshazi
Sport in Society, volume 16, issue 8 (October 2013) pp. 1025–1037

Chapter 7

Stronger than the state? Football hooliganism, political extremism and the Gay Pride Parades in Serbia
Christian Axboe Nielsen
Sport in Society, volume 16, issue 8 (October 2013) pp. 1038–1053

Chapter 8

Football, hooliganism and nationalism: the reaction to Serbia's gay parade in reader commentary online
Tamara Pavasovic Trost and Nikola Kovacevic
Sport in Society, volume 16, issue 8 (October 2013) pp. 1054–1076

Chapter 9

Football after Yugoslavia: conflict, reconciliation and the regional football league debate
Shay Wood
Sport in Society, volume 16, issue 8 (October 2013) pp. 1077–1090

Please direct any queries you may have about the citations to
clsuk.permissions@cengage.com

Introduction

John Hughson

International Football Institute, University of Central Lancashire, Preston, England

On 22 March 2013, the national football teams of Croatia and Serbia played against each other in Zagreb in a qualifying round match for the World Cup Finals in Brazil in 2014. Ahead of the match, much was made of the rivalry of the respective managers of the teams, former international players Igor Štimac (Croatia) and Siniša Mihajlović (Yugoslavia). A 20-year feud had existed between the two, largely based on their conflicting nationalist allegiances to the countries of the football teams for which they now have managerial responsibility. In anticipation of crowd violence, supporters of Serbia were not allowed to attend the match at the Maksimir Stadium. The absence of potential conflict between supporters saw the spotlight instead placed on the managers. Despite the promise from both Štimac and Mihajlović to 'bury the hatchet' their personal dislike for each other was feared too strong to be put aside on such an important evening. The match was won deservedly by Croatia, the result 2 goals to 0. At the conclusion of the game, as the opposing players shook hands, Štimac and Mihajlović walked to the centre of the field and embraced one another. The significance of this gesture, according to Štimac, is its sending of 'a very clear message' to 'forget the past'. He continued, 'we have a great future, we cannot build a future on the past, we are neighbours, there is plenty to live for in front of us.'[1]

Štimac's words remind me, to some extent, of what the sociologist Marina Blagojević refers to as *pozistorija*; the idea of 'positive history' in which discourses of hate and exclusion are deconstructed via reminders that behind situations of horrendous conflict and disputation, neighbourly relations and cross-community harmony remain a possibility.[2] Blagojević contends that the not so distant wars in the former Yugoslavia were not wars brought about by average people, but were produced 'from above', by political and military leaderships that fed and inflamed potential points of ethnic, religious and nationalistic tensions. But people were dragged into war via populist channels, including sport. As a number of the contributors to this special issue note, sport, especially football, played a significant symbolic role and more in association with war, particularly so the civil war between Croats and Serbs, in which the football supporter culture was manipulated by those interested in conflict for the pursuit of their own ends. Nevertheless, if we are to be hopeful for the prospects of 'positive history' taking hold in the region, then sports such as football, which constitute part of a 'common culture' (to use Raymond Williams's term) in nations of the Balkans, will play an important ongoing role towards a future of reconciliation. Štimac's words speak to this hope.

However, this is not to suggest that we should view the future of the social relations of football and sport within and between the nations of the former Yugoslavia and adjoining countries through rose-coloured glasses. Such viewing always results in distorted vision and this can involve unwarranted or, at least, overly ambitious optimism. The essays in this volume do not draw us into such complacency. Each essay is cautious in its depiction of the past and the future. I will not provide a summary discussion of the essays in this introductory note; the abstracts to the essays do a fine-enough job in that regard. Suffice to say that the ambition for the volume, when the original call for contributions was made, was to receive essays from scholars undertaking dedicated and focussed research on particular aspects of sport and the social and cultural relations relevant to matters of reconciliation in the countries and regions of the former Yugoslavia and surrounds. I am very satisfied that this ambition has been met and, as such, I thank the contributors for their essays.

Academics are these days increasingly involved in international talkfests concerning topics such as 'sport and peace', 'sport and conflict resolution' and 'sport and reconciliation'; a potentially positive development when their engagements are genuinely research-based and bringing real insights into forums, of more dubious benefit when they are just adding another voice of agreement to workshops and roundtables that provide neoliberal organizations with a means of servicing consensus rhetoric, without actually taking steps to enact meaningful change. I am not and would not make a claim for the authors of the essays in this volume to be activists or reformers, but do appeal for their research to be given serious attention by those seeking to know more about the importance of football and sport to debates about conflict and reconciliation in the countries pertinent to the author's studies. Prospective readers should include the genuinely politically active as well as symposium-attending organizational functionaries and academics.

The volume is interdisciplinary in that it carries contributions from history, sociology, media and cultural studies, political science and Slavonic Studies. It brings insights, across the essays, to a range of themes and issues, intersecting the analysis of football and sporting culture with necessary reflections upon residual and resurgent nationalisms, ethno/religious identity construction and gender concerns, most prominently homophobia. Accordingly, much of what we find in the essays may not give immediate hope for the prospects of *pozistorija* coming through sport. Yet, importantly, the essays provide insight into the challenges faced in relation to football and other sports, offering a critical dialogue essential for us to understand that the aforementioned embrace by two former footballers may, while not enabling a total forgetting of the past, nevertheless be a key signifier of positive things to come.

Notes

1. Amid 'Kill' Chants, a Peaceful Example is Set, *New York Times*, March 23, 2013, D7.
2. Blagojević, *Knowledge Production at the Semiperiphery.*.

Reference

Blagojević, M. *Knowledge Production at the Semiperiphery: A Gender Perspective*. Belgrade: Institute of Criminological and Sociological Research, 2009.

Fighters, footballers and nation builders: wartime football in the Serb-held territories of the former Yugoslavia, 1991–1996

Richard Mills

School of History, University of East Anglia, Norwich, UK

The outbreak of war in the Yugoslav republic of Croatia during 1991, and its subsequent emergence across Bosnia and Hercegovina in the following year, had a devastating effect upon cultural life. Football was no exception. Yet in spite of raging conflict, the game continued to be an important aspect of everyday life throughout the region. This paper focuses upon the newly emerging states of Republika Srpska and Republika Srpska Krajina, the Serb-held territories of Bosnia and Hercegovina and Croatia, respectively. Football served as an important morale-boosting activity, providing soldiers with a distraction from the front, but it also served a higher cause. Via league and cup competitions, it assisted in the creation of ethnically homogenous states. Alongside media coverage of them, these competitions helped 'map' the 'imagined communities' of these incipient polities. Football was also harnessed as symbolic proof that all Serbs continued to belong to Yugoslavia. The game, and the sporting press that wrote about it, also provided an ideal subject for propaganda about enemy nations and a platform from which journalists could expound the necessities of the unification of all Serb states.

On 20 December 1992, an 'international' match took place in Banja Luka, the largest city in the Serb-held territory of the former Socialist Republic of Bosnia and Hercegovina.[1] This match, better described as an 'intranational', was the first game between the incipient Serbian states of hosts Republika Srpska (RS) and their northern neighbours Republika Srpska Krajina (RSK) – a polity established on territories formerly belonging to the Socialist Republic of Croatia (Figure 1). It was played at the height of the Bosnian War and at a time when an uneasy United Nations-monitored ceasefire continued to freeze the conflict in Croatia. It was politically motivated wartime football, which 'had a much greater political meaning than a football one'.[2] As such, it is just one example of the multifaceted way in which football was harnessed, exploited and enjoyed during the war-afflicted 1990s.

The Socialist Federal Republic of Yugoslavia disintegrated along the boundaries of its ethnically constituted republics. However, ethnic and republican boundaries were rarely the same thing. In Croatia and Bosnia and Hercegovina, there were substantial numbers of Serbs who did not wish to live independently from Serbia proper. Stirred by demagogic politicians, these communities took up arms to ensure that the territories that they inhabited continued to belong to Yugoslavia. At least initially, they enjoyed both the political and military support of Belgrade.

Like the country itself, the Yugoslav First Federal Football League fell apart in stages. In the summer of 1991, clubs from seceding Croatia and Slovenia left the championship, while the war that broke out in Bosnia and Hercegovina in the following spring was the signal for another exodus. Although a modest amount of attention has been given to the role football played in the collapse of Socialist Yugoslavia – not least to the activities of

Figure 1. Banja Luka's modest Gradski Stadium, the national stadium of Republika Srpska, where the Serbian 'intranational' took place.
Note: Photograph taken by the author.

nationalist-orientated supporters' groups, members of which often became paramilitaries in the subsequent conflict – very little has been written about the game during the wars themselves.[3] Due to the nature of Yugoslavia's disintegration and the absence of previous research, this is a vast and complex topic. For this reason, this paper will focus upon wartime football in the Serb-held territories of Croatia and Bosnia and Hercegovina.

Football served as an important morale-boosting activity, providing soldiers with a distraction from the front and encouraging interaction with international peacekeepers. But the game also served a higher cause in these aspiring polities. Through the organization and execution of 'state' league and cup competitions, football served in the creation of ethnically homogenous states. Alongside media coverage of them, these competitions helped 'map' the 'imagined communities' of RS and RSK. The RSK Football League provided a rare opportunity to present the far-flung and non-contiguous territories which it was made up of as a single, unified Serbian state. By contrast, the conflict situation meant that RS had to make do with a national cup competition and various regional leagues. Yet national league and cup competitions were by no means the only tools that were harnessed in the service of Serbdom. As we will see, Borac Banja Luka Football Club was used as symbolic proof that Bosnian Serbs continued to belong to Yugoslavia, long after Bosnia and Hercegovina had declared its independence. Football, and the sporting press that wrote about it, also provided an ideal subject for propaganda about enemy nations and a platform from which journalists could expound the necessities of the unification of all Serb states.

Recreating the state daily – leagues, cups and newspapers

Michel Billig's theory of 'banal nationalism' examines the ways in which nation states are reproduced as nations on a daily basis.[4] He argues that banalities such as everyday language, flags on public buildings, the daily weather forecast and sports sections in national newspapers help maintain a strong sense of national identity and state legitimacy in the 'established nations of the west'.[5] Pilvi Torsti has demonstrated that Billig's theory can usefully be applied to states that do not easily fit his rigid category of relatively stable western societies.[6] This paper takes Torsti's proposal a step further by arguing that the processes of banal nationalism can even be seen at work during the turbulent initial years of state formation. While the Serbian polities were being forged in violent conflict, and 'invented' virtually from scratch, they nevertheless sought to develop distinct cultural spaces and reinforce their territorial scope. Moreover, while these polities were anything but 'established', the manner in which they were recreated daily in the eyes of their citizenry was not always in the form of 'overt, articulated and . . . fiercely expressed nationalism of those who battle to form new nations',[7] but could often come in banal forms, such as football competitions and weekly newspaper articles about sport. Nevertheless, it must be stated clearly that this observation in no way seeks to deny that football played a highly active role in the competing nationalisms of the former Yugoslavia, one that was frequently anything but banal.

Andrew Crampton has used Benedict Anderson's renowned 'imagined communities' theory to discuss the important role played by pilgrimages in developing national communities:

> Early pilgrimages inserted otherwise unrelated localities into a system of meaning . . . Not only did these pilgrimages have the effect of imagining a community, they also mapped that community with a particular geographical scope.[8]

Arguably, the football league and cup competitions that will be examined in this paper perform a very similar task in a modern context. In this way, statewide competitions, and media coverage of them, 'mapped' the 'imagined communities' of RS and RSK. One particular publication was perfectly suited to fulfilling this role. During 1994 and 1995, a weekly sports newspaper was produced in Banja Luka, titled *Derbi: sportski list Republike Srpske i Republike Srpske Krajine* (hereafter *Derbi*). Through its reportage on the sporting life of these two states, the newspaper facilitated the dissemination of information about 'state' league and cup competitions, helping define borders in the process. In this way, the newspaper arguably played a pivotal role in creating distinct sporting – and political – spaces for the newly emerging states. It also simultaneously encouraged the eventual integration of these polities into the Serb-dominated rump Yugoslavia.

The first issue of *Derbi* was published by its parent newspaper *Glas Srpski* in April 1994, and the editorial left the reader in little doubt about the objectives of the newspaper:

> Questioning the nation, fighters on the frontlines, school children and students, and especially sportsmen and sports workers, we know that today they need sport more than ever. Therefore we will try to be at the scene, both on Dalmatian football pitches, and in Banija, in Slavonia; on the ski slopes of Jahorina; among the Doboj rowers; in the company of Bijeljina karate experts; with the footballers of Leotar Trebinje; with 'Željo' at the Grbavica; to continue to follow Borac in Yugoslavia . . .[9]

With this mission statement, *Derbi* began to define the geographical borders of the infant RS and RSK.

This new venture faced many difficulties, including paper shortages. The second issue explained that although the publication had enjoyed an 'exceptional reception' across the territories which it encompassed, as well as in Yugoslavia, wartime conditions and a shortage of fuel prevented the distributors from reaching the northern RSK regions of Banija and Kordun.[10] However, the article triumphantly declared that a solution had been found – in future *Derbi* would be delivered to these outlying regions via the milk tankers of a local dairy! This second issue also contained a reproduction of a congratulatory telegram from the RS Football Association (*Fudbalski Savez Republike Srpske*; FSRS). It emphasized the extent to which *Derbi* was 'supplying an immeasurable contribution to the establishment of Republika Srpska, following sporting events across our young state'.[11] The newspaper was performing a similar service in equally difficult circumstances for the neighbouring state of RSK.

Republika Srpska Krajina – football and state building

RSK was established in the winter of 1991, eventually encompassing all of the Serbian Autonomous Regions (*Srpska autonomna oblast*; SAO) that had been formed previously. It encompassed a third of what had been Croatian territory in the name of 12% of the population.[12] The Croatian conflict was effectively frozen by the implementation of the Vance Agreement in January 1992, which established four United Nations Protected Areas that roughly corresponded to the territory held by Croatian Serbs.

While there were no former First Federal League clubs on the territory claimed by RSK, there were three football teams which had limited experience at the second tier of the Yugoslav league pyramid.[13] The vast majority came from the lower-level Socialist Republic of Croatia league system. In his book on the 'Serbian rebellion in Croatia', Nikica Barić provides a one and half page section on sport, but admits that he possesses 'only fragmentary information about sporting activities in the RSK'.[14] The incipient RSK Football Association (*Fudbalski Savez Republike Srpske Krajine*; FSRSK) organized the first football league in the republic for the 1992–1993 season.[15] Competition was arranged on a regional basis, with a final tournament taking place in Petrinja and Glina.[16] Co-hosts Banija Glina became the first champions of RSK. Barić notes that the regionally segmented method used for the first competition 'was prompted by difficult transport connections between the various parts' of the state.[17] Little more can be said about this inaugural competition, but the establishment of *Derbi* in April 1994 does enable a far more detailed examination of the second season of the RSK Football League.

Like its predecessor, the 1993–1994 league was organized on a regional basis and culminated in a final tournament that featured the victors from each of its constituent groups. The five regional groups were Banija and Kordun; Western Slavonia; Baranja; Eastern Slavonia/Western Srem; and South.[18] The latter group was subdivided once more into Lika and Northern Dalmatia sections, with the winners competing against one another for the South Group title and a place in the final tournament.[19] Table 1 and Figure 2 show the territorial extent of these groups and the majority of clubs that participated in the RSK Football League. The pages of *Derbi* contain relatively regular reports on the western groups of the championship, so it is possible to reconstruct these with some accuracy. However, the two eastern groups of Baranja and Eastern Slavonia/Western Srem hardly receive any attention whatsoever, presumably because of the logistical difficulties involved in getting information about these areas across the fiercely fought over corridor region of Northern Bosnia to the newspaper's base in Banja Luka. Nevertheless, the occasional article provides at least partial detail on these disconnected eastern groups.[20]

The finals were held in Baranja in July 1994 and hosts Šparta Beli Manastir were joined by their co-nationals Dinara Knin (South), Banija Glina (Banija and Kordun), Borac Bobota (Eastern Slavonia/Western Srem) and Begovača Šeovica (Western Slavonia).[21] The league, and media coverage of it, undoubtedly served as a vehicle to demonstrate the territorial integrity of RSK. Clubs from every part of the republic participated in the

Table 1. Republika Srpska Krajina League (1993–1994) (incomplete).

Regional group			South			
	Western Slavonia	Banija and Kordun	Northern Dalmatia	Lika	Eastern Slavonia and Western Srem	Baranja
Participants	Begovača Šeovica, Veteran Okučani, SRSK Ratkovac/ Smrtić, Psunj Okučani, Hajduk Pakrac, FK Bodegraj, Gradina Trnakovac, Sloboština Vrbovljani, '8. Maj' Okučani, Balkan Jasenovac	Banija Glina, Mladost Topusko, Mladost Petrinja, Petrova Gora Vojnić, OFK Vrginmost (now Gvozd), Jedinstvo Dvor na Uni, Mladost Kostajnica, FK Slunj, Kordun-Savić Krnjak, Budućnost Knežević-Kosa, PPG Šamarica Rujevac, '6. Maj' Veljun,	Dinara Knin, Bukovica Kistanje, Velebit Benkovac, Jedinstvo Islam Grčki, Kričke Drniš, Rudar Obrovac	FK Gračac, Jedinstvo Donji Lapac, Partizan Korenica, FK Krbava, Ustanik Srb, FK Plaški, FK Plitvice, Lika-mol Korenica	Borac Bobota, Sinđelić Trpinja, Vuteks Vukovar, Hajduk Mirko Mirkovci, FK Borovo, (incomplete)	Šparta Beli Manastir, FK Darda, (incomplete)
Finalists	Begovača Šeovica	Banija Glina	Dinara Knin Šparta Beli Manastir		Borac Bobota	Šparta Beli Manastir
Champion			Šparta Beli Manastir			

Figure 2. Illustrative map: Republika Srpska Krajina and its football league structure (1993–1994).
Note: Not to scale.

admittedly complex competition, helping present a vision of a united polity in the process. To borrow a construction from Benedict Anderson, newspaper articles about the league in publications such as *Derbi* brought together *this* club with *that* league, *this* cup with *that* region, assisting in creating the vision of an integrated state in the minds of readers.[22] When Anderson talked in this way, he was discussing the role of early colonial newspapers in the Americas, but this 'quite natural' process of bringing seemingly unconnected objects together, and thus creating 'an imagined community among a specific assemblage of fellow-readers', is no less valid in the case of the RSK sporting press.[23] Barić explains that the Serbian Army of Krajina (*Srpska Vojska Krajine*) was also aware that such sporting competitions aided in the 'drawing together and integration' of the state's constituent parts.[24]

However, the convoluted structure of the league, along with its final tournament, also served to highlight the disparate and non-contiguous reality of this territorially scattered polity. Favourites Dinara Knin, from the state's capital city, had to travel across the width of wartime Bosnia and Hercegovina in order to reach the finals. En route to the tournament, the club stopped off in neighbouring RS's capital, Banja Luka, playing a friendly match against Borac.[25] The Dinara player Filip Trivan explained that while he was confident that his team was the favourite for the title, 'the truth is we don't know the other teams well enough'.[26] This admission could adequately serve as a metaphor for the geographically scattered state as a whole. What is more, this fragmented league and regionally centred rivalries may well have contributed to the significant regional cleavages in RSK politics, cleavages that did so much to weaken the state.[27]

Hosts Šparta Beli Manastir went on to win the second RSK Football League in 1994.[28] Yet some of RSK's less successful teams are also of significance to this study. For example, a team called Jedinstvo (Unity) Islam Grčki, which represented a small village situated in close proximity to the Adriatic city of Zadar, actually played home matches in the town of Benkovac.[29] This is because it was effectively a refugee club after the Maslenica Offensive of January 1993, which resulted in the loss of a swathe of territory to Croat forces.[30] Jedinstvo played on regardless, its name in subsequent league tables suggesting to *Derbi* readers that the borders of RSK encompassed more territory than they actually did.

Fleeting *Derbi* match reports hint at the realities of RSK football during this period. Most league games were watched by small crowds numbering in the low hundreds, although significant matches such as the decisive final game of the Northern Dalmatia section between Dinara Knin and Bukovica Kistanje attracted 2500 spectators who created a '"hellish" football atmosphere such as … can only be seen at English First Division matches'.[31] However, it is perhaps unsurprising given the martial nature of this 'garrison society' – in which virtually every adult male belonged to either the police force or the military[32] – that matches could also be extremely violent affairs. For example, the final of the Banija and Kordun Championship was abandoned in the 43rd minute after a player 'cast a large shadow over everything which has been accomplished in football … on the territory of Republika Srpska Krajina'.[33] Having been shown a red card, the player in question 'brutally attacked' the referee, sparking an incident that involved brawling between several other players and a premature final whistle. A similar attack upon the referee occurred during a Northern Dalmatia group match in Donji Lapac. Again, the incident led to the abandonment of the fixture, only for the match to continue following 'pressure' exerted upon the referee by the home players.[34]

The first RSK Cup Final was held in the capital Knin in July 1994.[35] This state showpiece was attended by 1500 spectators, and politics were never far away. The pre-match entertainment came in the form of a friendly fixture between the police forces of RSK and Serbia proper.[36] This provided journalists with an ideal occasion on which to lavish praise upon RSK President Milan Martić. While he did not take to the field for this police friendly, he did sit on the bench of his own force throughout the match. Explaining that Martić's advice contributed massively to the 'excellent play of his protégés', a *Derbi* report went on to explain that the president 'demonstrated he is not just a brilliant politician and brave Serb warrior, but also a good football expert'.[37] For the record, the RSK police lost the match. Following the final itself, President Martić gave a speech while presenting the trophy to the victorious Bukovica Kistanje team:

> … with play on the green pitch, we have demonstrated to the whole world that we are for peace; that it matters to us. We want to live in peace with everyone, but especially with those from whom we are divided by borders. We send word to those with a military option that we are all prepared to take a stand on the battlefield. Nobody can subjugate us. Republika Srpska Krajina is ours, ours alone, and it always will be.[38]

These mixed messages from the cup's patron and head of state left those who heard or read them in little doubt that the RSK leadership was willing to continue the fight with their Croat adversaries. In this manner, the occasion of the first football final was exploited in order to convey the political stance of the increasingly isolated Krajina Serbs.

The structure of the RSK Football League was drastically simplified for the 1994–1995 season. The new system consisted of two groups, territorially divided into eastern and western sections.[39] However, the deteriorating political situation had a cataclysmic impact on all aspects of society in the spring. The western group kicked off the spring part of the championship on 22 April 1995, but on the first day of May, Croat forces launched

Operation Flash (*Bljesak*) in an effort to capture that part of Western Slavonia which fell under RSK jurisdiction.[40] Serb defences swiftly collapsed and the region was lost to Croatia in a matter of days, resulting in a mass exodus as 18,000 Serbs fled the region.[41] This territory was home to two RSK Football League clubs for this season – Psunj Okučani and Begovača Šeovica. A sudden absence of coverage on the RSK Football League in the pages of *Derbi* means that their plight is uncertain, but it is evident that the borders of RSK and its football league, if it continued at all, contracted in the first days of May. At this point, *Derbi* falls silent on developments in the most westerly Serbian republic. The final mention of specific competition in RSK appeared in April 1995 and concerned the draw for the Banija and Kordun Cup competition.[42] The semi-finals were due to be held on 3 May, with the final scheduled for the 17th. It seems extremely likely that developments in neighbouring Western Slavonia would have interrupted this competition too, not least because most footballers would have been involved in military formations.

The final issue of *Derbi* which is held in the archive dates back to 1 August 1995. By the following week, Krajina ceased to exist. Operation Storm (*Oluja*) wiped RSK off the map in a couple of days, resulting in a vast column of refugees fleeing to neighbouring RS and Yugoslavia.[43] Only the isolated sliver of territory known as Eastern Slavonia remained, but the total defeat of other Serb-held areas led to negotiations for this final region to be peacefully integrated into Croatia by 1998.[44] The RSK Football League and its cup competition were consigned to history. However, many of the participant clubs live on in the Croatian football league pyramid, albeit with airbrushed histories. For example, a modern website dedicated to NK Borovo, which participated in the eastern groups of the RSK competition, provides a detailed breakdown of the history of the club, but states that it ceased to function between 1991 and 2005.[45] Wikipedia pages for other clubs, such as that for Mladost Petrinja, also deny this active period of history for their organizations.[46] These are examples of history being deliberately rewritten in the public domain. At Dinara Knin, the club's traditional black and white emblem has been replaced with a new one that mirrors the national colours of Croatia, while a former Dinara player of Serb ethnicity notes that this historic club 'no longer has a history, even though it was founded in 1913. All history begins from 1995'.[47] Dinara's stadium, the venue for the 1994 RSK Cup Final, now serves as a parade ground for the victorious Croatian Army during annual celebrations held on the anniversary of Operation Storm.[48] Across the frontier in neighbouring RS, the worrying developments that swept away Krajina over the summer of 1995 were followed with dismay.[49]

Republika Srpska – football on the front lines

The FSRS was formed in September 1992, five months after the proclamation of the Serbian Republic of Bosnia and Hercegovina and the outbreak of war on the territory of this former Yugoslav republic.[50] At its height, RS covered up to 70% of the ill-fated Bosnia and Hercegovina.[51] In 1991, self-declared Serbs constituted 31% of the republic's population.[52] The newly founded football association began organizing matches immediately. In celebration of its establishment, two games were held featuring soldiers recalled from the front lines, for which the FSRS needed to seek special permission from the RS Army (*Vojska Republike Srpske*) in advance.[53] During the founding assembly, a Serbian Democratic Party (*Srpska Demokratska Stranka*; SDS) politician left those present in no doubt as to the importance of football to the political task of establishing RS. He stated that regardless of whether the FSRS would be recognized by international bodies, it would use football to 'demonstrate to everybody that we exist; that we are alive'.[54]

Twelve months after its formation, the FSRS deemed that conditions were sufficiently stable to hold the first RS Cup competition. Just as in the case of the RSK Football League, the conflict situation dictated that the initial rounds of the tournament be held on a regional basis, with RS territory being divided into five geographic regions.[55] This inaugural competition was plagued by difficulties. Some clubs, such as Sutjeska Srbinje (formerly and subsequently Foča) were forced to withdraw as the 'battle around Goražde', and the fact that the whole team were in military units, made it impossible for them to complete their fixtures.[56] Other clubs were displaced by the fighting, playing home matches in alternative venues. This was the case for eventual finalists Sloga Doboj, who, 'because of the daily bombardment' of their town, played their matches in Modriča and Rudanka.[57] Nevertheless, the tournament gradually proceeded towards a conclusion, and in June 1994 the first RS Cup Final was held at the Gradski Stadium in Banja Luka (Figure 3).

Kozara Gradiška became the first team to have its name engraved upon the trophy of the incipient state.[58] The occasion itself was draped in the colours of Serb nationalism and constituted part of the extensive celebrations in honour of the RS Army. While the patron of the first RSK Cup was prominent politician Milan Martić, the FSRS selected General

Figure 3.   General Milan Gvero presents the inaugural Republika Srpska Cup to the captain of Kozara Gradiška.
Source: *Derbi*, June 28, 1994.

Milan Gvero to perform ceremonial duties in their own competition.[59] The presence of generals at football matches was not unusual. For instance, General Slavko Lisica attended one of the semi-final matches in Gradiška, where he was greeted with lengthy applause from the crowd, in 'a sign of gratitude to this famous hero for all that he has done, and in truth he has done a lot for the struggle of the Serbian people'.[60] It had initially been intended that General Ratko Mladić present the trophy to the victorious cup winners, but we learn from *Derbi* that Gvero also fulfilled this function.[61] At an earlier youth football tournament, Gvero announced that while sport has always brought people together, 'its significance is especially important now, when we find ourselves defending our territory from enemies'.[62] His presentation of the RS Cup to the captain of Kozara Gradiška is reminiscent of similar military involvement in the first edition of the aptly named Generalísimo's Cup in Franco's Spain.[63] In 2005, Milan Gvero was indicted by the International Criminal Tribunal for the former Yugoslavia (ICTY) on four counts of crimes against humanity.[64] The involvement of such a high-profile military figure in this showpiece match was by no means the only reminder of the war for those present. A crowd of 5000 contained many who had 'arrived directly from the frontlines, to forget the devastation, suffering, pain . . . at least for a moment, with the assistance of football'.[65]

Derbi carried regular reports on the role played by sportsmen as soldiers in 'guarding the borders of Republika Srpska on the battlefields'.[66] In her work on music in post-1991 Croatia, Catherine Baker explains that although both high-profile musicians and athletes were conscripted into the army, they were often deployed for propaganda purposes rather than for active service by the state.[67] While this may well have been the case for certain footballers in RS, especially those of the former First League club Borac Banja Luka, the majority of ordinary players served in the armed forces alongside their fellow countrymen. Three such sportsmen-soldiers, one of whom was a first team player at FK Naprijed Banja Luka, were interviewed by a *Derbi* journalist on the Bihać Front in November 1994.[68] One of them remarked that 'we can only practice sport after our obligations on the battlefield'. An article dedicated to Leotar Trebinje Football Club explained how its footballers had 'exchanged the football for the rifle', spending the winter season break 'on the frontlines of defence'.[69] Many clubs stressed to *Derbi* that a unified RS Football League was not a possibility while first team squads were serving in the army. For example, the vice-president of FK Polet Brod emphasized the need to focus upon youth football in the prevailing circumstances: ' . . . in this time when the seniors are preoccupied with their most important task of defending the fatherland, youth should be thrust into the foreground'.[70] Indeed, in early 1994 the FSRS was informed by the Ministry of Science, Education and Culture, via the Ministry of Defence, that a league was not conceivable because of battlefield obligations. Only cup and exhibition matches were deemed appropriate.[71]

Another difficulty inhibiting the establishment of a statewide football league was the territorial situation. Like RSK to the north, Srpska was a distinctly awkward shape which, added to the fact that persistent fighting in the corridor region effectively split the state into two parts, did not bode well for an integrated competition. However, the ban on a unified league did not stifle incessant discussion about whether a competition should be established, and what format it would take. *Derbi* ran regular features on the potential competition, and even took an active role in attempts to establish a league in conjunction with the FSRS.[72] Opinion was divided upon the nature of any future RS Football League. Some clubs, such as Leotar from the southern town of Trebinje, favoured a series of regional divisions culminating in a final tournament, along the lines of the RSK Football League. The Leotar coach told *Derbi* that 'we in Hercegovina do not have another possibility, bearing in mind the drawn-out nature of the regions of Republika Srpska'.[73] Whether clubs were in favour of commencing with league competition depended largely upon their material circumstances and location in relation to the front lines at any given time. The coach of Šator Glamoč explained that the situation had deteriorated to the point where 'Glamoč is located in a peripheral war zone and it would be very dangerous to play matches'.[74] By July 1995, Damjan Pajić of the FSRS was desperate to establish a single integrated league immediately. He even gave substance to it by naming six clubs that should definitely be involved as founder members.[75] Hence, even though the competition did not exist, the promise of such a unified league in the future, along with vibrant discussion of it in the sporting press, nevertheless served the purpose of defining RS's sporting and political borders.

While a unified league was not established, a number of regional divisions were organized across Serb-held territory, serving to compliment the annual cup competition. For the 1994–1995 season, *Derbi* covered leagues including the following: the Semberija-Birač-Majevica League; the Posavsko-Ozrensko League; a Banja Luka League subdivided into Banja Luka and Gradiška groups; and a Prijedor division. These competitions faced substantial complications and disruptions as a result of the ongoing conflict. A deterioration in the political situation in November 1994 led *Derbi* to run the headline 'Weekend without Football'.[76] Noting that the weekend's fixtures had been cancelled, the article states that the regional Banja Luka and Prijedor championships were 'temporarily' postponed.[77] A couple of weeks later, *Derbi* noted that only the Posavsko-Ozrensko League remained active while mourning the fact that even in that competition many matches were being cancelled.[78] By August 1995, a drastic escalation in military activity also led to the postponement of the second RS Cup Final. Of course, August heralded the decisive Operation Storm in Croatia and an escalation of fighting across RS. On the first day of that month, before a decision had been made on the final, *Derbi* blasted that 'after the aggression of the Ustaše[79] criminals on the territory of Republika Srpska, everything changed overnight! A state of war was enforced, because the situation on the battlefield simply imposed it'.[80] Football in RS was therefore interrupted at a time when RSK, and its football milieu, was being definitively extinguished.

Logistical, personnel and military difficulties thus served to highlight the problem of creating a football league that would 'map' the 'imagined community' of RS as a whole. In this respect, in contrast to football in RSK, RS's nation builders could only look to the cup competition for reinforcement of the territorial integrity of the state. This was particularly acute when considering regions that were in contested areas near to, or on, the front lines. In certain cases, the situation was so dire that even the limited competition that did exist did not penetrate communities faced with daily combat activity. One such example of this was the town of Srbobran (formerly and subsequently Donji Vakuf). A *Derbi* feature on sport in the town noted that not a single sporting activity had taken place there for the duration of the conflict, as 'all of the sportsmen are engaged on the front lines, in defence of their ancestral hearths'.[81] The reporter emphasized that civilian and military authorities had enabled sporting activity in other 'peripheral regions' of RS and that such conditions must also be implemented in Srbobran so as to boost the morale of soldiers and make life more bearable. However, in his opinion there was also a more important, nation-building aspect to such activity:

> At this time it is necessary to involve active teams from the territories of Republika Srpska for appropriate tournaments, which would be the greatest stimulus in the organisation of sports activities in this, certainly the most endangered and poorest, Serbian region west of the Drina today. With this [Srbobran's sports associations]...could finally begin activities, without which the organisation of work and life in the creation of a new state is unthinkable. And the newly-established state of Republika Srpska is living a full sporting life which must, at least in a little stream, finally flow into the southernmost part of the broad [Bosnian] Krajina region.[82]

Such a mission statement highlights the importance of sport in the construction of the emerging polity, especially for contested 'peripheral' regions. It also highlights the critical role of geographical accessibility and patterns of conflict, not only to the establishment of stable state borders, but also to the construction of representative sporting competitions. The case of sport in Srbobran is particularly interesting because the town no longer exists, at least not in its wartime guise and not within the boundaries of RS. For this reason, the plights of peripheral football clubs serve to highlight the fluid nature of emerging sporting spheres and state borders. They underline the fact that borders can be transitory and that the identities of regions, towns and even football teams can be tailored to suit the prevailing ethnic hegemony.

By the terms of the Dayton Agreement, which brought the Bosnian War to an end in the winter of 1995, many towns with football clubs that had participated in the RS Cup fell beyond the borders of RS. However, while the FSRS haemorrhaged clubs as a result of the political compromise, the end of hostilities did enable a full resumption of sporting activities across the territory of the now clearly defined polity of RS – one of two entities in a new federal Bosnia and Hercegovina. The postponed second RS Cup Final was played almost immediately upon the conclusion of the Paris Peace Agreement, apparently demonstrating to the world that the Bosnian Serbs had a 'devotion to peace'.[83] The long-awaited inaugural RS Football League also got underway in March 1996 (see Table 2),[84] adding further clarity to the territorial settlement in the process.

Football as a tool to unite Serb lands

Dayton paved the way for eventual interethnic football integration in post-war Bosnia, but throughout the conflict there had been discussions of a very different – ethnically homogenous – future system of competition. So far, this paper has demonstrated the extent to which football was utilized in order to establish and reinforce the territorial and political contours of these incipient polities. However, while the short-term objective was to create RSK and RS, the longer-term goal was to integrate these territories into a newly constituted Federal Yugoslavia. Barrie Houlihan argues that while sport can be utilized to 'assert, both internally and externally, the territorial dimension of the state', in certain circumstances it is also 'capable of reflecting the ambiguities of the territorial basis of the nation'.[85] This assertion is certainly valid in the case of these two ethnic states, for while RSK and RS leagues assisted in giving geographic substance to the respective polities, football was also harnessed in the quest to unite all Serbs together in a single state.

In its self-assigned role as a sports newspaper for RS and RSK, *Derbi* was itself representative of the 'Greater Serbian' project. In the celebratory 50th issue of the newspaper, an editorial once again underlined its position as a publication dedicated to

Table 2. Republika Srpska First League (1996).

Group	West	East
Participants	Borac Banja Luka, BSK Banja Luka, Rudar Prijedor, Polet Srpski Brod, Sloga Doboj, Kozara Gradiška, Proleter Promtes Teslić, Borac Šamac, Ljubić Prnjavor, Sloboda Novi Grad, FK Modriča	Boksit Milići, FK Željezničar, FK Sarajevo, Slavija Srpsko Sarajevo, Romanija Pale, Jedinstvo Brčko, Mladost Rogatica, Drina Zvornik, Leotar Trebinje, Glasinac Sokolac, Panteri Bijeljina
Finalists	Rudar Prijedor	Boksit Milići
Champion		Boksit Milići

sport and sport alone: 'For sport in the two states: those west of the Drina'.[86] Its objective remained 'to contribute to the take-off of sport...to spread its wings over the whole fatherland and our brothers in Krajina; to portray...how powerful, strong, and indestructible we are'.[87] Hence, RSK and RS were portrayed as distinct, but closely related entities. The publication played a leading role in encouraging contact between the two infant football associations. For example, a 1994 *Derbi* initiative led to the holding of a 'Super Final' between the cup winners of RSK and their counterparts in RS 'to establish an overall champion of the two young states'.[88] In the final, Kozara Gradiška suffered a shock defeat at the hands of RSK representatives Bukovica Kistanje.[89] At the time Jovica Vučenović, the secretary of the FSRSK, believed that the competition would 'develop into a tradition'.[90] Following the Super Final, there were even suggestions of holding a further unofficial match against the winners of the Yugoslav Cup in order to establish an overarching champion of all 'Serbian states'. It appears as though this latter project never came to fruition as a result of reluctance on the part of the Yugoslav Football Association (*Fudbalski Savez Jugoslavije*) to break FIFA sanctions yet again.[91]

According to *Derbi* coverage, the two football associations initially signed a charter on 'fraternal Serbian cooperation' as early as February 1992.[92] This assertion is problematic as we know that the FSRS was not founded until September of that year. However, bearing in mind the tense political situation in the months prior to the outbreak of war in Bosnia and Hercegovina, it is not unlikely that FSRSK representatives did indeed travel to Banja Luka and sign an agreement with the football authorities of the Serbian Autonomous Region of Bosanska Krajina (SAO Bosanska Krajina). This polity was established in Northern Bosnia in 1991 and subsequently became a constituent part of RS.

Nevertheless, by the spring of 1995 journalists and football officials were talking openly about potential football unification. Although it is difficult to see the FSRSK as anything other than junior partners in such a merger, it was this association that strove most openly for unification. In March 1995, FSRSK President, Ljupče Mandić, sent a letter to the FSRS and the relevant ministries, in which he addressed the topic of future cooperation. He highlighted that in recent discussions between the two associations, it had been agreed to initiate two particular projects: the establishment of a unified Football Association of Serbian States and the inauguration of a shared football competition.[93] In a subsequent interview with *Derbi*, FSRS President Branko Lazarević appeared to be slightly more hesitant, noting that the proposal was worth considering, but that while 'we support the initiative of the people from the Republika Srpska Krajina FA...a lot also depends on other factors'.[94] By contrast, his opposite number in the neighbouring association once again underlined his organization's commitment to unification:

> We are a single whole, so we must also behave this way in sport. The two Krajinas are integral Serbian territory, and when it is already like that it is normal to have shared league competitions.[95]

He also expressed an opinion that, should peace reign, joint leagues could be in place by spring 1995. Speaking the following month, FSRSK Secretary Jovica Vučenović echoed the support of his president, stating: 'In my opinion, the match between the winner of the Republika Srpska Cup, Kozara, and our Cup victor, Bukovica Kistanje, was the beginning of the merger'.[96] RSK footballers also voiced favourable opinions about the potential joint league.[97] Bukovica Kistanje player Željko Tošić raised the valid point that examples of sporting integration were already in evidence in other sports, noting that the handball teams Željezničar Knin and Petrinja both competed in RS competitions.[98]

These discussions did not take place in a political vacuum, but occurred at a time when the politicians of the beleaguered RSK were also talking about full political unification. The idea of merging the two Serbian states west of the Drina was by no means a novel one. Back in the summer of 1990, Croatian Serb politician Jovan Rašković advocated the unification of the Croatian and Bosnian Krajinas in order to create an entity with a Serb majority.[99] During the war itself, the prospect of the political unification of RSK and RS became a salient issue. According to Nina Caspersen, the project was often little more than a rhetorical mechanism by which the leaders of the two states could engineer 'greater space for manoeuvre', be this in their dealings with enemy nations or the Yugoslav 'kin-state'.[100] Nevertheless, while Bosnian Serb leaders were 'reluctant alliance partners', their vulnerable counterparts in RSK played a far more active role in championing the virtues of a political union. A 1993 RSK referendum returned the dubious outcome of 99% in favour of unification with RS, with a 97% turnout.[101]

Of course, in the martial climates of RSK and RS, these political questions impacted significantly on society as a whole. Football was no exception. Realizing that RSK was in a perilous position, Milan Martić and other leaders threw their support behind the proposed union in the spring of 1995.[102] Indeed, the RSK parliament unanimously adopted a decision to join RS in June, but this was thwarted by political infighting between regional leaders across the disparate state.[103] The project for 'football unification' was escalated concurrently. In the aftermath of the fall of Western Slavonia, *Derbi* ran a vociferous article advocating the immediate amalgamation of the two football associations and the establishment of joint leagues.[104] The piece noted that the republics were extremely close to achieving their shared political goal of unification, with just 'one more small step left until that which all proud Serbs west of the Drina have been waiting for impatiently for so long'. It was stated that 'political unification will open the door to football unification'.[105] Once again, the publication gave substance to a future league by naming potential participants from both states. Noting that the selection of constituent teams would cause substantial infighting, along with attempts to utilize political pressure in order to secure places for certain favoured teams, the journalist nevertheless noted:

> In it, without dilemma, there is a place for Borac Banja Luka, the former Second League clubs Rudar-Prijedor, Jedinstvo (Brčko), Radnik (Bijeljina), Leotar (Trebinje), Kozara (Gradiška), and then Dinara (Knin), Mladost (Petrinja), Velebit (Benkovac), Bukovica (Kistanje) ...[106]

This summoned a competing vision of a new Serbian state west of the Drina, with discussions over the embryonic football league giving the proposed new polity territorial dimensions, just as football competitions had done earlier for RSK and RS. However, the closing lines of the article offered a premonition of what was to come: 'If, God forbid, an inflaming of war clashes takes place in the coming months, then it will be shelved and will await better, more peaceful times'.[107] The routing of RSK in August 1995 brought an abrupt end to discussions about unification – both political and sporting.

There was also significant sporting cooperation between the two states west of the Drina and the 'kin-state' of Federal Yugoslavia. At least in terms of spoken intentions, there was willingness for the eventual re-integration of clubs from RS and RSK into the federal league system. For example, in February 1995 the secretary of the Serbian Football Association informed *Derbi* that 'the Serbian FA is prepared to immediately welcome clubs from Republika Srpska and Republika Srpska Krajina, when and if they are incorporated into a federation with the Federal Republic of Yugoslavia'.[108] A year earlier, Branko Lazarević, FSRS president, expressed his opinion that in a future united Serbian state, clubs from RS would be integrated into the leagues of Yugoslavia or Serbia 'according to the principle of the former inter-republican leagues'.[109] Nevertheless, he hoped that some teams would be 'incorporated into the Yugoslav leagues by administrative channels, because it is not only sport. The participation of our clubs is a significant political and national question'.[110]

During the war itself, there were examples of football cooperation between the two states and Yugoslavia. For example, the Montenegrin Football Association invited the youths of Leotar Trebinje to participate in their competitions,[111] while RSK clubs held preparatory training camps in Vojvodina.[112] However, the most significant wartime football cooperation of all was undoubtedly the continued presence of Borac Banja Luka in the federal league system of competition.

Borac Banja Luka – 'On Two Fronts'

Borac (fighter) Banja Luka, from what became the largest city in RS, enjoyed a prominent history in Socialist Yugoslavia. It spent several seasons competing in the First Federal League and even lifted the Marshal Tito Cup in 1988. Despite the outbreak of war across Bosnia and Hercegovina, the club continued to participate in the federal leagues of the rump Yugoslavia for the duration of the conflict. This was only made possible by registering it as Borac Belgrade in 1992, a measure which, according to the president of the Yugoslav Football Association, was necessary in order for FIFA and UEFA to allow Borac to participate in the Yugoslav leagues.[113] The war had an adverse effect on the club's ability to fulfil its home fixtures. Following a FIFA ban on playing football on the territories of the former Bosnia and Hercegovina, which, to the obvious disappointment of the FSRS president, 'Yugoslav clubs and the Yugoslav Football Association are firmly conforming to', Borac needed to leave its native Banja Luka in order to continue as a Yugoslav club.[114] Consequently, Borac began playing home matches at various stadiums across Yugoslavia. Nevertheless, it continued to represent the territories which became RS, symbolically integrating them into Federal Yugoslavia in the process.

FSRS President Branko Lazarević made it clear that in terms of football, Borac 'was the only one which managed to survive' in the Yugoslav federal structure.[115] As the sole representative from RS and RSK territory, the flagship Borac received constant attention in the pages of *Derbi*. A February 1995 article stated that the club would undoubtedly 'enter into the history of European sport' as it had spent the last three years doing nothing but travelling in order to fulfil its matches.[116] The squad had to make the perilous journey out of Banja Luka and 'across the Drina' every Friday or Saturday.[117] For a long time, Borac did not have a fixed venue for home games, hosting teams in 'Senta, Šid, Valjevo, Sremska Mitrovica, Kostolac ...'.[118] However, the club eventually found a more stable and welcoming base in the small Vojvodinian town of Bač. Club President Anđelko Grahovac spoke with great affection for his team's temporary home, explaining that they had become 'kindred spirits' with the local population:

> There are many people from our region there. They accepted us as their own. I must mention our sponsor Marko Jovešić, the director of Bačvanska Arma, a man who animates people in that wonderful Vojvodinian place. He was, as we say it, our president in the diaspora. ... I think that for everything that they did for the club, Bač and Marko Jovešić should be written in golden letters into the history of Borac.[119]

From its 'exceptionally comfortable' base in Serbia's northern province, Borac fought on in the Yugoslav Federal Leagues. The hosting Vojvodina Football Association made it clear that it would 'make extra efforts so that the team feel comfortable in our jurisdiction'.[120] The Vojvodina FA went on to explain that 'we will continue to make allowance for Borac, as we have done up until now', promising the club 'special support'.[121] As mentioned, Vojvodina also hosted the training camps of a number of RSK clubs, while another RS team – Radnik Bijeljina – also considered relocating to the Serbian province in order to participate in the provincial Vojvodinian League, following in the footsteps of the town's basketball club.[122]

On the pitch, Borac did not enjoy a great deal of success during this turbulent and unsettled period. Relegation from the First Federal League in 1993 was followed by steady decline in subsequent seasons. The whole wartime period witnessed the ceaseless loss of first team players to other, more stable clubs.[123] However, in the circumstances mere survival at the federal level was seen as a huge success by everyone involved. When Borac managed to avoid relegation from the federal-level Second League 'B' (the fourth tier of competition) in the spring of 1994, the president considered it 'a huge success for the club and also for the city of Banja Luka, and our young state of Republika Srpska'.[124] Nevertheless, Borac was finally relegated from the federal level of competition in the following season. This meant that it was faced with the difficult decision of whether to retire from Yugoslavia all together and return to the incipient world of RS football or to battle on in the lower-level republican leagues.[125]

This decision was not as clear-cut as it appears. As soon as organized football returned to RS in 1994, Borac, as the vanguard club of the emerging state, found itself competing 'on two fronts'.[126] While the senior first team squad continued to play in Yugoslavia, the junior team defended the club's colours (at senior level) in the inaugural RS Cup and also in the regional Banja Luka League. As a result of this desire to be in two places at once, *Derbi* frequently contained two separate match reports from the same afternoon for 'Borac Banja Luka'. For example, on the last weekend of October 1994, while the 'Yugoslav' Borac faced Priština in Kosovo, the juniors of the Republika Srpska Borac played BSK at the Gradski Stadium.[127]

The senior team was prohibited by the FSRS from competing in the inaugural RS Cup.[128] However, by 1995 the strongest 'Yugoslav' Borac was permitted to take to the field in this competition. So it comes as no surprise that the club lifted the trophy when the end of conflict at last allowed the final matches to be played in December of that year.

Borac's continued presence in Yugoslav competition can be viewed as a symbolic act for Bosnian Serbs wishing to remain within the federation. Of course, such a potentially controversial measure had significance for the political leaderships of the polities in question. In the summer of 1994, Borac President Anđelko Grahovac fielded the perennial politically loaded question on where his club would play its football the following season:

> Next season we will play where we belong, in the Yugoslav Federal League. In truth, that will also depend upon a political solution and resolution. But we will endeavour with all of our powers to be together with Yugoslav clubs.[129]

Borac served as a concrete example of the use of football to reflect a desirable political union with Federal Yugoslavia. Grahovac discussed the political implications of his club's activities:

> ... this is more than football, more than sport. Because Borac playing in the Yugoslav League, together with clubs from Serbia and Montenegro, is a unique case in the world. And in that way we are practically demonstrating that we are together.[130]

While Borac's participation symbolically presented RS as an integral part of Federal Yugoslavia, the phenomenon of clubs playing in leagues beyond their own state borders is by no means unique. For example, after repeated sectarian complications prevented Derry City Football Club from competing in the domestic Northern Irish league, it was finally given permission by FIFA to participate in the football leagues of the Republic of Ireland,

Figure 4.   Today, Republika Srpska government buildings tower over Borac Banja Luka's Gradski Stadium.
Note: Photograph taken by the author.

across an internationally recognized border.[131] The club has been competing in another state since 1985. A situation comparable to that surrounding Borac can also be found in the recent history of Georgian football, where Spartak Tskhinvali and Dinamo Sukhumi – from the disputed territories of South Ossetia and Abkhazia, respectively – withdrew from the domestic championship in 1990, with the latter going on to compete in the neighbouring Commonwealth of Independent States league.[132] Yet, the fact that Borac's conduct is not unique in world football does little to diminish the significance of the political capital that could be derived from its activities. The club not only represented a desire for Bosnian Serbs to remain within a Federal Yugoslav state, but also served as an open denial of the independence of Bosnia and Hercegovina (Figure 4).

It is clear that football elites in both Yugoslavia and RS viewed the club's uncertain status as a temporary situation. Despite its relegation from the federal levels of competition, by August 1995 Borac claimed to have a promise in writing from Yugoslav Football Association president Miljan Miljanić that it was guaranteed a place in the First Federal League as soon as the war ended.[133] Talk of this so-called 'frozen status' is reminiscent of the aforementioned vision of FSRS President Branko Lazarević, who hoped RS teams would be incorporated via 'administrative channels' because of political and national motivations.

As a result of its wartime role, Borac quickly became an important element of Bosnian Serb identity. Indeed, for certain *Derbi* journalists the club was viewed as a war hero. One article, which trumpets the club's achievements, plays upon its name (fighter) when asserting that 'Borac is a hero':

> ... for all three wartime years, it has shown and proved how strong it is, even when 'condemned' and forgotten by everybody. Borac is our genuine hero. To lose around seventy first team players in three years; to lose all of the best who are of value; to come face to face

19

with deserters of this and that variety – this would have made much bigger and more developed [clubs] fall to their knees.[134]

Derbi also highlighted the fact that players from the senior 'Yugoslav' Borac were doing their duty by literally defending the borders of RS during breaks in the football season. This piece of sporting propaganda noted that 'all of those who have completed their military service took rifles in their hands and are now guarding the borders of Republika Srpska somewhere on the battlefields of Vlašić'.[135] According to the article, 'the arrival of footballers, even for a short period, represents a huge stimulus' for the excited 'fighters' (*borci*) who welcomed them to the front lines.[136]

Like many institutions in RS, the political situation surrounding Borac also reflected prevalent wartime disunity among Bosnian Serbs. For example, club President Grahovac was highly critical of RS's political leadership, castigating it for its lack of support for Borac's highly symbolic activity in Yugoslavia.[137] He noted that the political importance of his club's continued presence in federal competitions warranted far more significant engagement from Pale-based politicians: 'But they are pallid characters and it is not worth mentioning them any longer'.[138] This evokes the considerable political tensions that were present between northern Banja Luka and the isolated wartime capital.[139] Certain journalists from the Banja Luka-based *Derbi* were also keen to point out factionalism and opportunism which targeted the club. While emphasizing Borac's wartime achievements, the newspaper condemned what others were saying about it:

> ... that it is a third-rate team; that it only disgraces us around Yugoslavia; that Šator, Kozara, Naprijed, and also Panteri, would play much better there. These football 'experts' have forgotten that on every occasion Borac is always the visiting team; that both referees and functionaries are 'sharpened' against it; that it is bearing the brunt of everyone: both of small scale local strongmen, party leaders, and the football gods from the FSJ [Fudbalski Savez Jugoslavije, Football Association of Yugoslavia].[140]

The journalist in question went on to condemn the 'morbidly ambitious types' who seek to gain from Borac's misfortune. Highlighting the fact that the senior team thrashed rivals Naprijed in the RS Cup, he questioned whether pretenders to its throne became 'ashamed when they slandered, maligned and belittled Borac's games in Yugoslavia'.[141] The same article concludes that among all of RS's clubs, only Borac was capable of attracting support from cities across the polity.

It was not until the end of the war that Borac's national and political value really became apparent. Since the Dayton Accords brought the conflict to an end, the club – which during the socialist era served as a representative of a multiethnic Banja Luka – has continued to stand as a symbol of Serbian nationalism. This is in spite of the fact that the peace agreement also marked the end of Borac's participation in Yugoslav competitions. In 2001, a series of friendly matches were played in order to celebrate this institution's 75th anniversary.[142] Over the course of the year, all of Federal Yugoslavia's biggest teams visited the capital of neighbouring RS. Borac played high-profile matches against Red Star and Partizan Belgrade, Vojvodina and Obilić – the club of assassinated paramilitary leader Željko 'Arkan' Ražnatović. However, the largest celebration took place when the Yugoslav national team travelled to Banja Luka for a match against Borac. Chants of 'Yugoslavia, Yugoslavia' thundered from a packed crowd of 20,000 spectators, while journalists used the game as proof that 'Republika Srpska loves Yugoslavia!'[143] Alongside these prominent relations to Yugoslav football, post-war Borac is also draped in Serbian iconography. The club's badge was altered to echo the colours of the RS flag, while its Vultures (*Lešinari*) supporters' group revels in national symbolism and chanting. The group is twinned with supporters of FK Vojvodina Novi Sad, and the two organizations

Figure 5. Serbian national symbolism on the walls of Borac Banja Luka's stadium.
Note: Photograph taken by the author.

socialize and cooperate on a regular basis.[144] The Gradski Stadium, located in the shadow of RS's new parliament building, is covered with Serbian nationalist graffiti (Figure 5).

Football beyond the frontiers – through a Serb lens

While football in other parts of wartime Bosnia and Hercegovina, and Croatia, must be the subject of future research, Serbian perceptions of the game in those territories are of significance here. It has been demonstrated that *Derbi* and the football leagues which it covered served in the imagining of homogeneous Serb territory on the relevant side of the front lines. However, it can also be argued that RS sport and media organizations concurrently sought to discredit the 'former' Bosnia and Hercegovina as a viable state.[145] To some extent, *Derbi* was no different from the broader media in its tactics, frequently referring to the territory of ethnic opponents in derogatory terms. For example, a belittling 1994 article, written in the aftermath of UEFA's recognition of the Bosnia and Hercegovina national football team, referred to it as the representation of the '*Fildžan-State*'.[146] A *Fildžan* is a traditional handleless coffee cup of Turkish origin that has come to be associated with Bosnia's Muslims. Here it is metaphorically used to signify a tiny 'tin pot' Muslim state. Another article disparagingly referred to the inaugural football championship of 'the wannabe *Džamahirija*', a word that denotes an Islamic state of the masses.[147] The same piece also invokes Bosnia's Ottoman past, echoing a metaphor popularized by writers such as Ivo Andrić, by calling Muslim territory the '*tamni vilajet*' or 'dark province'.[148] Revelling in the fact that a second war had broken out between Bosnian Muslims and Croats in the 'so-called Bosnia and Hercegovina', *Derbi* was quick to gloat that this territory's football league would encompass a very small area:

> The amount of Hercegovina left over for the Muslims is – nothing, and of Bosnia just a little more – a slice over which they are squabbling with their Croat 'brothers'.[149]

A subsequent article on the 'muslim' [*sic*] national team called it 'Alija's representation', a reference to Bosnian President Alija Izetbegović.[150] The journalist went on to discuss the proceeds from the representation's friendly match against the German club Fortuna Düsseldorf:

> ...proceeds of 80,000 Deutsche Marks allegedly went to the children of the former Bosnia (how funny that sounds), but most probably it was used for the purchasing of weapons. You never know with muslims [*sic*].[151]

However, cheap propaganda shots against ethnic opponents were by no means the only method by which football was exploited in the service of the Serbian war effort in RS and RSK. The right to inherit the legacy of the pre-war game was also a fiercely disputed terrain. Moves to discredit opposing claims to particular football clubs can be seen as a direct assertion of ownership of specific territories and settlements. The case of the two Željezničar Sarajevos is indicative in this respect.

The first wartime championship in government-controlled Bosnia and Hercegovina was held in September 1994 – conditions imposing the familiar regional format – with a final tournament taking place in Zenica. One of the four teams to reach the final stage was former First League side Željezničar Sarajevo.[152] Željo, as the club is affectionately nicknamed, is based in the Sarajevo suburb of Grbavica, which was held by RS forces for the duration of the war. The club's stadium was located on the front line.[153] Nevertheless, Željo re-emerged in government-held besieged Sarajevo, initially training in school halls and beset by all manner of difficulties.[154] Football was played extensively in the city during the conflict, with indoor tournaments taking place as early as 1993, while serious competition resumed during the ceasefires of 1994.[155] According to a history of Željezničar, the club's participation in the final tournament of the inaugural Bosnia and Hercegovina Championship 'was definite confirmation of its survival'.[156] However, on the other side of the front lines, sports journalists held a very different opinion. Discussing the tournament, *Derbi* was incredulous at the idea that Željezničar was one of the participants.[157] The reason for such hysteric astonishment was that a parallel 'Serbian' club had been established under the same name and laid claim to the legacy of the Yugoslav era Željezničar, along with its Grbavica Stadium:

> They know – they know well – that Željo is located on this, our, Serbian side. They know. How can they not know that Željo participated in the Republika Srpska Cup? But they have still, even alongside everything else, usurped the club. Without regard to the fact that the famous Grbavica belongs to Republika Srpska. They are disguising themselves, evidently, in somebody else's clothes.[158]

The Serbian Željezničar Sarajevo was apparently founded in 1993 – although it continued to use the 1922 foundation year of the original Željo – but because of the fighting in Grbavica, it played home games elsewhere, basing itself in Vlasenica for matches of the 1994 RS Cup.[159] The club featured regularly in the pages of *Derbi* and became a founder member of the RS First League when it began in 1996.[160] Yet, as a result of the peace settlement reached at Dayton, Grbavica was allocated to the Federation of Bosnia and Hercegovina, meaning that RS was forced to surrender its grip on the suburb. This meant that while the Bosnian Željezničar was able to return to the Grbavica Stadium, its Serbian counterpart was forced to continue in 'exile'.[161] On the pitch, the latter did not enjoy much success, and it was disbanded following relegation to the RS Second League in 1998.[162] Regarding this Serbian incarnation, a club history of the other, Bosnian, Željezničar notes that 'another Željo was even formed in the surrounding districts of Sarajevo, but that artificial creation vanished in the rubbish dump of history after a few years'.[163] A comment below a recent article on an RS sport website about Serbian Željo also made a similar remark from the Bosnian perspective: 'Everything which is artificial only lasts a short time . . . there is only One'.[164]

A comparable but far more tenuous claim was also made for Željo's city rivals FK Sarajevo. The Serbian incarnation 'continued the tradition of the Sarajevo Football Club founded in 1946, and resumed its work in . . . free Serbian territory'.[165] Unlike the Grbavica, Sarajevo's Koševo Stadium always remained within government-controlled territory – and was used to stage the Sarajevo group matches of the 1994 Championship – while the original FK Sarajevo continued to function throughout the war, participating in Bosnian competitions and also playing numerous friendly matches abroad in order to raise awareness of the situation in the besieged city.[166] Much like Serbian Željo, 'Srpsko' Sarajevo competed in the inaugural RS First League of 1996 and reached the RS Cup Final in the following season. Following Dayton, the club 'relocated' to the small town of Višegrad, located in RS, and played its home fixtures there (Figure 6).[167] This Serbian incarnation of the famous FK Sarajevo suffered the same fate as Serbian Željo, ceasing to function as a club following relegation in 1999.[168]

Similar cases of haggling over the legacies of formerly non-ethnically exclusive clubs can also be observed in RSK. The ethnically motivated post-war rewriting of club histories following the collapse of RSK has already been documented above, but disputes over ownership of prominent sports organizations also took place during the war years. For example, *Derbi* made much out of the fact that a team named Borovo Vukovar was participating in the final of the Croatian Chess Cup of 1994.[169] In much the same way as Željo was used to emphasize the fact that Grbavica was integral RS territory, the case of Borovo Vukovar was trumpeted in order to underline that these towns came under Serbian jurisdiction as integral parts of RSK. The article, titled 'Croats do not know geography well – Where is Vukovar?' went on to explain:

Figure 6.   A long way from the Koševo. The picturesque Višegrad Stadium, home to the Serbian incarnation of FK Sarajevo in post-Dayton Republika Srpska.
Note: Photograph taken by the author.

> They still – after so many years – do not know where Borovo and Vukovar are located. To them it still appears a vision that these two hero-cities remain in: Croatia. Really! Since we are certain that at least one copy of *Derbi* will make it to SR Croatia [sic], we are pertinently notifying the local population that Borovo and Vukovar are located in: Republika Srpska Krajina. The inhabitants of those cities are living peacefully, trying to repair what is destroyed, playing chess, football, volleyball, etc. and a long time ago they sent word to everyone, even to Croats: 'never again under the same roof ...'[170]

Just as the Borovo Vukovar chess team was formed on Croatian territory, the football club Vukovar '91, founded in Zagreb at the height of the war, also participated in Croatian leagues while the town remained within the borders of RSK.[171] This is another example of the role sport and sports journalism played in the establishment of disputed territorial boundaries, both physical and imaginary.

The disappearance of ethnically opposed incarnations such as Željezničar Srpsko Sarajevo and FK Srpsko Sarajevo aided the eventual re-integration of football on the territories of post-war Bosnia and Hercegovina. While the FSRS continues to hold its own league and cup competitions as one entity within the federal state, since 2002 clubs from RS have participated in a united Bosnia and Hercegovina Premier League alongside clubs from Bosnian Muslim and Croatian-held territory.[172] Below the top-flight, the game continues to be divided along ethnic lines. Serbian clubs have enjoyed some notable success in this shared competition, although football continues to serve as a forum for ethnically exclusive politics in the unstable federation. Nevertheless, the re-integration of Serbian teams into federal Bosnian competitions signalled an end, at least for the foreseeable future, to the project of uniting all Serbian clubs into a single greater Serbian system of competition.

There was also a far darker side to football in the Serb-held territories under examination. The transcripts of the ICTY expose the use of stadium infrastructure in Bosnia and Hercegovina as makeshift detention facilities and even execution sites.[173] Venues such as the Bratunac football stadium, which was utilized during the 1995 Srebrenica massacre, played host to RS Football League and Cup matches. Football grounds were also harnessed as detention facilities in the short-lived Croat state of Herceg-Bosna.[174] In terms of the game, numerous players were forced to flee their homes, and clubs were ethnically homogenized. Alongside these violent methods of ethnic cleansing, this paper highlights that ostensibly innocuous cultural activities such as football were also harnessed in the construction of ethnically homogenous polities.

Both of the states in question demonstrate the extent to which football was exploited in the service of state building, aiding in the imagining of these incipient polities. It is clear that football journalism acted as a conduit for such ideas, reporting upon 'national' league and cup competitions and banally 'mapping' their geographical scope in the process. Disputed territory was also claimed via football and the journalists who wrote about it, be that the front-line settlements of Srbobran and Grbavica in RS or the 'liberated' town of Vukovar in RSK. The creation of 'national' representations can be viewed as an additional tool in the state-building process, as well as in the fruitless quest for international recognition. In all of these respects, the game was exploited in order to show that these territories wished to remain part of a Yugoslavia that encompassed all Serbs. This came at the expense of the territorial integrity of seceding republics. On the other hand, the game also occasionally became a forum for intranational rivalries within the two polities, echoing concurrent developments in politics.

Alongside the task of recreating the state daily, journalists and politicians simultaneously harnessed football for additional propaganda purposes. Regular, statewide competition implied stability, while the involvement of footballers in the defence of Serbdom's borders served as an example to fellow citizens. The example of Borac Banja Luka, among others, shows that even after the war, football persists as a forum for the championing of nationalism, albeit in the delicate multiethnic federation of Bosnia and Hercegovina. The post-war ethnic remodelling of other clubs – such as Dinara Knin – illustrates that the history of the game continues to be a highly charged political sphere, in which rival national groups seek to establish legitimate pasts for the clubs in question. These processes mirror developments in wider society. While the other polities that emerged from Yugoslavia's demise are beyond the scope of this paper, it is possible to see remarkably similar processes at work across the territories of the ill-fated federation. But, at least in Serb-held areas of the disputed territories of the former Yugoslavia, the wartime game did indeed have 'a much greater political meaning than a football one'.[175]

Notes

1. Tica, Babić and Basara, *10. Godina Fudbalskog Saveza*, 23–4.
2. Ibid., 23.
3. Work on the role of football in the collapse of Yugoslavia includes the following: Čolović, *Politics of Identity*, 259–86; Vrcan and Lalić, 'From Ends to Trenches'; and Sack and Suster, 'Soccer and Croatian Nationalism'. Previous research on Yugoslav football in wartime examines the plight of a single club during the conflict: Mills, 'Velež Mostar Football Club'. The unrelenting playing of sport during times of intense armed conflict has been documented in many historical and territorial circumstances. For example, Veitch, 'Play Up! Play Up! and Win the War!'; Collins, 'English Rugby Union'; Rollin, *Soccer at War*; Nielsen, 'Sport at the Front'; Kuper, *Ajax, the Dutch*; Riordan, *Sport in Soviet Society*, 153–60; and Edelman, *Spartak Moscow*, 133–4.
4. Billig, *Banal Nationalism*.
5. Ibid., 6.
6. Torsti, 'History Culture and Banal Nationalism', 143.
7. Billig, *Banal Nationalism*, 16.
8. Andrew Crampton, cited in Mitchell, 'Monuments, Memorials, and the Politics', 447.
9. Momo Joksimović, 'Vrijeme povratka', *Derbi*, April 19, 1994. The problems inherent in producing sporting publications during times of wartime shortages are addressed in the British context of the First World War in Osborne, 'To keep the life', 141–3.
10. 'Promocije na sve strane', *Derbi*, April 26, 1994.
11. Rodoljub Petković, General Secretary of the (RS) Football Association, telegram reproduced in *Derbi*, April 26, 1994.
12. Caspersen, *Contested Nationalism*, 100. A considerable proportion of Croatia's ethnic Serb population did not live in the areas claimed by RSK, but in urban centres beyond its borders.
13. These clubs were NK Borovo, Mladost Petrinja and Šparta Beli Manastir. Dragoljub Jovanović, Igor Kramarsić and Misha Miladinovich, 'All-Time Table Yugoslavia Second Division 1947-1992', *Rec.Sport.Soccer Statistics Foundation*, 2004, http://www.rsssf.com/tablesj/joeg2alltime.html#yug.
14. Barić, *Srpska Pobuna u Hrvatskoj*, 458.
15. Ibid.; and Dragoljub Petrović, 'Selo koje je izgradila "Oluja"', *Danas.rs*, August 4, 2010, http://www.danas.rs/danasrs/drustvo/terazije/selo_koje_je_izgradila_oluja.14.html?news_id=196398.
16. Stanko Križanić, 'Naš tip – Banija', *Derbi*, July 19, 1994.
17. Barić, *Srpska Pobuna u Hrvatskoj*, 458–9.
18. Željko Đekić, 'Jedan trofej – pet želja', *Derbi*, July 19, 1994.
19. Mile Sovilj, 'Tuča, Prekid, Nastavak', *Derbi*, April 26, 1994.
20. For example, the 19 July 1994 issue contained two paragraphs about the Eastern Slavonia/Western Srem Group, mentioning five constituent clubs: J.B., 'FK "Borac" (Bobota) – Bolji od Borova', *Derbi*, July 19, 1994.
21. Željko Đekić, 'Jedan trofej – pet želja', *Derbi*, July 19, 1994.
22. Anderson, *Imagined Communities*, 62.

23. Ibid.
24. Barić, *Srpska Pobuna u Hrvatskoj*, 459.
25. Tatjana Papić, 'Morao sam otići', *Derbi*, July 26, 1994.
26. Ibid.
27. For more on prevalent political infighting among the RSK elite, see Caspersen, *Contested Nationalism*, 99–129.
28. Željko Tica, 'Šampionski dar za rođendan', *Derbi*, August 2, 1994.
29. '"Knindže" gaze ka tituli', *Derbi*, November 15, 1994. The history of this settlement and its unusual name is discussed in Mayhew, 'Behind Zara', 86.
30. Silber and Little, *The Death of Yugoslavia*, 353; and Goldstein, *Croatia: A History*, 250.
31. Stevo Grkinić, 'Remi za titulu', *Derbi*, June 14, 1994.
32. Silber and Little, *The Death of Yugoslavia*, 355.
33. Stevo Križanić, 'Šolić crveni i – udara', *Derbi*, June 14, 1994.
34. Mile Sovilj, 'Tuča, Prekid, Nastavak', *Derbi*, April 26, 1994.
35. Željko Tica, Željko Đekić and Jovica Vučenović, 'Kistanje u Vinu', *Derbi*, July 5, 1994.
36. Željko Tica, Željko Đekić and Jovica Vučenović, 'Čočević "uhapsio" Knindže', *Derbi*, July 5, 1994.
37. 'Ratnik, Političar i Fudbalski Stručnjak', *Derbi*, July 5, 1994.
38. Željko Tica, Željko Đekić and Jovica Vučenović, 'Mi smo za mir', *Derbi*, July 5, 1994.
39. Jovan Vučenović, 'Dinara Rafalno', *Derbi*, September 6, 1994.
40. Tatjana Papić, 'Juriš na peto mjesto', *Derbi*, April 4, 1995; and Silber and Little, *The Death of Yugoslavia*, 355.
41. Silber and Little, *The Death of Yugoslavia*, 355; and Goldstein, *Croatia: A History*, 252–3.
42. Tatjana Papić, 'Banija u Vrginmostu', *Derbi*, April 4, 1995.
43. Goldstein, *Croatia: A History*, 253.
44. Ibid., 263; and Caspersen, *Contested Nationalism*, 110.
45. HNK Borovo website, hnkborovo.webs.com/druga.htm.
46. *Wikipedia.org*, 'NK Mladost Petrinja', http://hr.wikipedia.org/wiki/NK_Mladost_Petrinja.
47. Dragoljub Petrović, 'Selo koje je izgradila "Oluja"', *Danas.rs*, August 4, 2010, http://www.danas.rs/danasrs/drustvo/terazije/selo_koje_je_izgradila_oluja.14.html?news_id=196398.
48. Turistička Zajednica Grada Knina, 'Dan Zahvalnosti', http://www.tz-knin.hr/index.php?option=com_content&task=blogcategory&id=38&Itemid=64 (accessed July 4, 2011).
49. Silber and Little, *The Death of Yugoslavia*, 360.
50. Tica, Babić and Basara, *10. Godina Fudbalskog Saveza*, 9.
51. Caspersen, *Contested Nationalism*, 100.
52. Ibid., 23.
53. Tica, Babić and Basara, *10. Godina Fudbalskog Saveza*, 9 and 17–8.
54. Dr Radosav Vukić, president of the SDS regional committee, cited in 'Prvi korak na velikom putu', *Glas Srpski*, September 6, 1992.
55. 'Odluku o sistemu takmičenja za Fudbalski Kup FSRS', Fudbalski Savez Republike Srpske, September 9, 1993. Reproduced in full in Tica, Babić and Basara, *10. Godina Fudbalskog Saveza*, 136.
56. 'U Slavu Fudbala', *Derbi*, June 14, 1994.
57. Ibid.
58. 'Kup u Gradišci', *Derbi*, June 28, 1994. See also Tica, Babić and Basara, *10. Godina Fudbalskog Saveza*, 135–9.
59. M.J., 'General Gvero Presjednik', *Derbi*, June 14, 1994.
60. Željko Tica and Zoran Vajkić, 'General na tribinama', *Derbi*, June 7, 1994.
61. 'General Mladić predaje pehar', *Derbi*, June 14, 1994; and Tatjana Papić, 'Kup je naš, Kup je naš …', *Derbi*, June 28, 1994.
62. General Milan Gvero, cited in Brane Radulović, 'Potencijal za fudbalsku orbitu', *Derbi*, May 3, 1994.
63. Ball, *Morbo*, 151.
64. ICTY, 'Charges against Milan Gvero and Radivoje Miletic Released to the Public – Press Release', February 24, 2005, www.icty.org/sid/8643. Gvero was sentenced to five years' imprisonment in June 2010, but was granted early release later the following month: The Hague Justice Portal, 'Gvero, Milan', www.haguejusticeportal.net/index.php?id=6063.
65. Tica, Babić and Basara, *10. Godina Fudbalskog Saveza*, 135.

66. 'Prvotimci na ratištu!', *Derbi*, July 12, 1994.
67. Baker, 'Popular Music and Narratives', 65–6 and 224.
68. 'Sport u slobodno vrijeme', *Derbi*, November 1, 1994.
69. Dragan Kisin, 'Odmora na "čukama"', *Derbi*, January 10, 1995.
70. Nenad Šukurma, cited in Željko Tica, Slobodan Babić and Dragan Kisin, 'Vrijeme (ni)je za fudbal', *Derbi*, February 14, 1995.
71. Momo Joksimović, 'Umjesto prve lige – Liga "Derbija"', *Derbi*, April 26, 1994.
72. Ibid.
73. Slavko Šarović, cited in Željko Tica, Slobodan Babić and Dragan Kisin, 'Vrijeme (ni)je za fudbal', *Derbi*, February 14, 1995.
74. Mile Jovičić, cited in ibid.
75. Željko Tica, 'Liga mora krenuti', *Derbi*, July 11, 1995.
76. 'Vikend bez fudbala', *Derbi*, November 8, 1994.
77. Ibid.
78. Željko Tica, 'Fudbal čeka bolja vremena', *Derbi*, November 29, 1994.
79. Derogatory term for Croats, dating back to the fascist Ustaše regime of the Second World War Independent State of Croatia.
80. L.P., 'Finale, da ili ne?', *Derbi*, August 1, 1995.
81. Dragan Kisin, 'Radnik prekršten u Jug', *Derbi*, September 13, 1994.
82. Ibid.
83. Tica, Babić and Basara, *10. Godina Fudbalskog Saveza*, 141.
84. Ibid., 41.
85. Houlihan, 'Sport, National Identity and Public Policy', 120–1.
86. Editorial Board, 'Jubilej', *Derbi*, April 4, 1995.
87. Ibid.
88. Željko Tica, Željko Đekić and Jovica Vučenović, 'Superfinale Kozara – Bukovica', *Derbi*, July 5, 1994.
89. Željko Tica, 'Superkup u Avgustu', *Derbi*, July 12, 1994; 'Žal za superkupom', *Derbi*, November 8, 1994; and Dragoljub Petrović, 'Selo koje je izgradila "Oluja"', *Danas.rs*, August 4, 2010, http://www.danas.rs/danasrs/drustvo/terazije/selo_koje_je_izgradila_oluja.14.html?news_id=196398.
90. Željko Tica, 'Superkup u Avgustu', *Derbi*, July 12, 1994.
91. 'Kozara – Partizan u Gradišci', *Derbi*, July 12, 1994; and Dragoljub Petrović, 'Selo koje je izgradila "Oluja"', *Danas.rs*, August 4, 2010, http://www.danas.rs/danasrs/drustvo/terazije/selo_koje_je_izgradila_oluja.14.html?news_id=196398.
92. Željko Tica, 'Liga Dvije Krajine', *Derbi*, March 21, 1995; and Željko Tica, 'Fudbalsko Ujedinjenje', *Derbi*, May 30, 1995.
93. Željko Tica, 'Liga Dvije Krajine', *Derbi*, March 21, 1995.
94. 'Prijedlog za razmišljanje', *Derbi*, March 21, 1995.
95. Željko Tica, 'Od jeseni jedinstveno', *Derbi*, March 21, 1995.
96. Tatjana Papić, 'Zajedno je bolje', *Derbi*, April 18, 1995.
97. Ibid.
98. Ibid. Reports on the RS Handball League confirm that football was lagging behind in this respect: Darko Grabovac, 'Prva Liga Republike Srpske za muškarce – grupa zapad – start 24. septembra', *Derbi*, September 6, 1994.
99. Caspersen, *Contested Nationalism*, 69.
100. Ibid., 122.
101. Ibid., 117–8 and 122.
102. Ibid., 109–10.
103. Ibid.
104. Željko Tica, 'Fudbalsko Ujedinjenje', *Derbi*, May 30, 1995.
105. Ibid.
106. Ibid.
107. Ibid.
108. 'Srbija čeka Krajišnike', *Derbi*, February 14, 1995.
109. Momo Joksimović, 'Umjesto Prve Lige – Liga "Derbija"', *Derbi*, April 26, 1994.
110. Ibid.
111. Dragan Kisin, 'Bez liga – propast', *Derbi*, February 14, 1995.

112. R.D., '"Sinđelić" neuhvatljiv?', *Derbi*, February 28, 1995; and Tatjana Papić, 'Juriš na peto mjesto', *Derbi*, April 4, 1995.
113. Milan Fulurija, 'Borac čemo sačuvati', *Derbi*, June 27, 1995.
114. Branko Lazarević, cited in Momo Joksimović, 'Umjesto Prve Lige – Liga "Derbija"', *Derbi*, April 26, 1994.
115. Momo Joksimović, 'Vrijeme povratka', *Derbi*, April 19, 1994.
116. 'Vrijeme putovanja', *Derbi*, February 7, 1995.
117. Ibid.
118. Željko Tica, 'Borcu je mjesto u jugo-eliti!', *Derbi*, June 14, 1994.
119. Ibid.
120. Slobodan Babić, 'Uspješan dogovor čelnika FS Vojvodine i Republike Srpske', *Derbi*, March 21, 1995.
121. Ibid.
122. D. Tešić, 'Radnik se seli u Vojvodinu', *Derbi*, April 26, 1994.
123. Momo Joksimović, 'FK Borac "eksport-import"', *Derbi*, December 27, 1994.
124. Željko Tica, 'Borcu je mjesto u jugo-eliti!', *Derbi*, June 14, 1994.
125. 'Na dva fronta', *Derbi*, August 1, 1995.
126. Ibid.
127. *Derbi*, November 1, 1994.
128. 'U Slavu Fudbala', *Derbi*, June 14, 1994.
129. Željko Tica, 'Borcu je mjesto u jugo-eliti!', *Derbi*, June 14, 1994.
130. Ibid.
131. Cronin, 'Playing Away from Home', 72–5.
132. Allison, 'Sport among the Soviet Ruins', 178.
133. 'Na dva fronta', *Derbi*, August 1, 1995.
134. Momo Joksimović, 'Borac je Heroj', *Derbi*, November 1, 1994.
135. 'Prvotimci na ratištu!', *Derbi*, July 12, 1994.
136. Ibid.
137. Željko Tica, 'Borcu je mjesto u jugo-eliti!', *Derbi*, June 14, 1994.
138. Ibid.
139. Caspersen, *Contested Nationalism*, 135–7.
140. Momo Joksimović, 'Borac je Heroj', *Derbi*, November 1, 1994.
141. Ibid.
142. Tica, Babić and Basara, *10. Godina Fudbalskog Saveza*, 267–82.
143. Ibid., 267–9.
144. 'Intervju: Lešinari Banja Luka', *Navijačke Informativne Novine*, No. 13, February, 2009.
145. G.V., 'Osim na tribinama', *Derbi*, July 25, 1995.
146. 'Reprezentacija "Fildžan-Države"', *Derbi*, April 26, 1994.
147. 'Prisvojili "Želju"', *Derbi*, September 13, 1994.
148. Ibid.
149. Ibid.
150. V.G. 'Osim na tribinama', *Derbi*, July 25, 1995.
151. Ibid.
152. Kajan, *Sarajevski Derbi*, 160–1; and Hadžialić, *Fudbalski Klub Željezničar*, 58–9.
153. Hadžialić, *Fudbalski Klub Željezničar*, 55–6; ICTY, Stanislav Galić Case IT-98-29, 'Public Transcript of Hearing January 22 2002', 2028; and ICTY, Dragomir Milošević Case IT-98-29/1, 'Public Transcript of Hearing 19 April 2007' 4742.
154. Hadžialić, *Fudbalski Klub Željezničar*, 18.
155. Untitled material signed by the President of Mjesna Zajednica 'Adem Buć' regarding the indoor tournament 'Bitka za Žuč', scheduled to be played at SC 'Skenderija' in June 1993. May 24, 1993. Displayed at the Historical Museum of Bosnia and Hercegovina (Historijski Muzej Bosne i Hercegovine); and Hadžialić, *Fudbalski Klub Željezničar*, 116.
156. Hadžialić, *Fudbalski Klub Željezničar*, 55.
157. 'Prisvojili "Želju"', *Derbi*, September 13, 1994.
158. Ibid.
159. Milan Đorđić, 'RS-Sport vremeplov: FK Željezničar, Srpsko Sarajevo', *RS-Sport.org*, January 24, 2011, http://www.rs-sport.org/index.php?s=novosti_citaj&vise=888; and Željko Tica, '"Željo" juri među sedam', *Derbi*, April 26, 1994.

160. Tica, Babić and Basara, *10. Godina Fudbalskog Saveza*, 41–2.
161. Hadžialić, *Fudbalski Klub Željezničar*, 61.
162. Milan Đorđić, 'RS-Sport vremeplov: FK Željezničar, Srpsko Sarajevo', *RS-Sport.org*, January 24, 2011, http://www.rs-sport.org/index.php?s=novosti_citaj&vise=888.
163. Hadžialić, *Fudbalski Klub Željezničar*, 18.
164. 'Manijak' comment on Milan Đorđić, 'RS-Sport vremeplov: FK Željezničar, Srpsko Sarajevo', *RS-Sport.org*, January 24, 2011, http://www.rs-sport.org/index.php?s=novosti_citaj&vise = 888.
165. Milan Đorđić, 'RS-Sport vremeplov: FK Srpsko Sarajevo', *RS-Sport.org*, January 7, 2011, http://www.rs-sport.org/novosti.php?vise=832.
166. For example, in the winter of 1994, FK Sarajevo played matches in Italy and Turkey 'at the end of a world tour': 'Valentić, Repuh i Pita pobjegli', *Oslobođenje: Evropsko Nedjeljno Izdanje*, December 8, 1994; 'Bravo, usprkos porazu', *Oslobođenje: Evropsko Nedjeljno Izdanje*, November 17, 1994; and 'Bursa, grad prijatelja Bosne', *Oslobođenje: Evropsko Nedjeljno Izdanje*, December 29, 1994. For more on wartime FK Sarajevo, see Wilson, *Behind the Curtain*, 172–4.
167. Milan Đorđić, 'RS-Sport vremeplov: FK Srpsko Sarajevo', *RS-Sport.org*, January 7, 2011, http://www.rs-sport.org/novosti.php?vise=832; and Tica, Babić and Basara, *10. Godina Fudbalskog Saveza*, 41–2 and 153.
168. Milan Đorđić, 'RS-Sport vremeplov: FK Srpsko Sarajevo', *RS-Sport.org*, January 7, 2011, http://www.rs-sport.org/novosti.php?vise=832.
169. 'Gdje je Vukovar?', *Derbi*, June 14, 1994.
170. Ibid.
171. HNK Vukovar '91 website, 'O nama', www.hnk-vukovar91.com/index.php?option=com_content&view=article&id=1&Itemid=1 (accessed March 20, 2012).
172. Tica, Babić and Basara, *10. Godina Fudbalskog Saveza*, 311–8; and Hadžialić, *Fudbalski Klub Željezničar*, 85–7.
173. ICTY, 'Momčilo Krajišnik and Biljana Plavšić Amended Consolidated Indictment', Case IT-00-39 & 40-PT, March 7, 2002; ICTY, Momčilo Krajišnik Case IT-00-39-T, 'Public Transcript of Hearing April 21, 2004' 2385; and Honig and Both, *Srebrenica*, 59–60.
174. Mills, 'Velež Mostar Football Club', 1123–4.
175. Tica, Babić and Basara, *10. Godina Fudbalskog Saveza*, 23.

References

Allison, Lincoln. 'Sport among the Soviet Ruins: The Republic of Georgia'. In *Sport in Divided Societies*, ed. John Sugden and Alan Bairner, 167–81. Oxford: Meyer & Meyer Sport, 2000.

Anderson, Benedict. *Imagined Communities: Reflections on the Origin and Spread of Nationalism*. London: Verso, 2006.

Baker, Catherine. 'Popular Music and Narratives of Identity in Croatia since 1991'. PhD diss., University College London 2008.

Ball, Phil. *Morbo: The Story of Spanish Football*. London: When Saturday Comes Books, 2003.

Barić, Nikica. *Srpska Pobuna u Hrvatskoj*. Zagreb: Golden marketing-Tehnička knjiga, 2005.

Billig, Michel. *Banal Nationalism*. London: Sage, 1995.

Caspersen, Nina. *Contested Nationalism: Serb Elite Rivalry in Croatia and Bosnia in the 1990s*. New York: Berghahn, 2010.

Collins, Tony. 'English Rugby Union and the First World War'. *The Historical Journal* 45, no. 4 (2002): 797–817.

Čolović, Ivan. *Politics of Identity in Serbia: Essays in Political Anthropology*. London: Hurst, 2002.

Cronin, Mike. 'Playing Away from Home: Identity in Northern Ireland and the Experience of Derry City Football Club'. *National Identities* 2, no. 1 (2000): 65–79.

Edelman, Robert. *Spartak Moscow: A History of the People's Team in the Worker's State*. Ithaca, NY: Cornell University Press, 2009.

Goldstein, Ivo. *Croatia: A History*. London: Hurst, 1999.

Hadžialić, Nedžad. *Fudbalski Klub Željezničar 1982–2007*. Sarajevo: Nedžad Hadžialić, 2007.

Honig, Jan Willem, and Norbert Both. *Srebrenica: Record of a War Crime*. London: Penguin, 1997.

Houlihan, Barrie. 'Sport, National Identity and Public Policy'. *Nations and Nationalism* 3, no. 1 (1997): 113–37.

Kajan, Dževad. *Sarajevski Derbi: 74 prvenstvene utakmice, 1954–1999*. Sarajevo: Mediapress, 1999.

Kuper, Simon. *Ajax, the Dutch, the War: Football in Europe during the Second World War*. London: Orion, 2003.

Mayhew, Tea. 'Behind Zara – Zara's *contado* between Ottoman and Venetian Rules 1645–1718'. PhD diss., University of Padova, 2008.

Mills, Richard. 'Velež Mostar Football Club and the Demise of "Brotherhood and Unity" in Yugoslavia, 1922–2009'. *Europe-Asia Studies* 62, no. 7 (2010): 1107–33.

Mitchell, Katharyne. 'Monuments, Memorials, and the Politics of Memory'. *Urban Geography* 24, no. 5 (2003): 442–59.

Nielsen, Niels Kayser. 'Sport at the Front: Football in Finland during the Second World War'. *Sport in History* 24, no. 1 (2004): 63–76.

Osborne, John M. '"To Keep the Life of the Nation on the Old Lines": *The Athletic News* and the First World War'. *Journal of Sport History* 14, no. 2 (1987): 137–50.

Riordan, James. *Sport in Soviet Society: Development of Sport and Physical Education in Russia and the USSR*. Cambridge: Cambridge University Press, 1978.

Rollin, Jack. *Soccer at War 1939–45: The Complete Record of British Football and Footballers during the Second World War*. London: Headline, 2005.

Sack, Allen L., and Zeljan Suster. 'Soccer and Croatian Nationalism: A Prelude to War'. *Journal of Sport and Social Issues* 24, no. 3 (2000): 305–20.

Silber, Laura, and Allan Little. *The Death of Yugoslavia*. London: Penguin, 1996.

Tica, Željko, Slobodan Babić, and Slavko Basara. *10. Godina Fudbalskog Saveza Republike Srpske*. Banja Luka: Fudbalski Savez Republike Srpske, 2002.

Torsti, Pilvi. 'History Culture and Banal Nationalism in Post-War Bosnia'. *Southeast European Politics* 5, no. 2–3 (2004): 142–57.

Veitch, Colin. '"Play Up! Play Up! and Win the War!" Football, the Nation and the First World War 1914–1915'. *Journal of Contemporary History* 20, no. 3 (1985): 363–78.

Vrcan, Srdjan, and Dražen Lalić. 'From Ends to Trenches, and Back: Football in the Former Yugoslavia'. In *Football Cultures and Identities*, ed. Gary Armstrong and Richard Giulianotti, 176–85. London: Macmillan, 1999.

Wilson, Jonathan. *Behind the Curtain: Travels in Eastern European Football*. London: Orion, 2006.

Fertile land or mined field? Peace-building and ethnic tensions in post-war Bosnian football

Davide Sterchele

Department of Philosophy, Sociology, Education and Applied Psychology, University of Padua, Padua, Italy

With the outbreak of the war in Bosnia and Herzegovina (BiH), each ethno-national group – Bosnian Muslims (Bosniaks), Bosnian Serbs and Bosnian Croats – set up its own football federation and began to organize its own competitions separately. Nevertheless, under strong pressure from FIFA, UEFA and the IOC, the three football establishments finally agreed to merge into a unified Bosnian Football Federation in 2002 and to organize the Premijer Liga, the first united Bosnian post-war championship. Drawing on ethnographic studies conducted in BiH since 2003, the paper examines the consequences of such a revamped inter-ethnic competition both in terms of the re-integration of the Bosnian population, on the one hand, and the possible exacerbation of ethnic tensions, on the other. It is concluded that the reunification of the Bosnian football's landscape helps to demonstrate how ethnicity is instrumentally used by the post-war élites to exploit the common good for private enrichment.

Introduction

Oh, if the people had their way, there wouldn't be any problem at all! People are already ready to play all together in mixed championships. We already play friendly matches with Serb or Croat teams, indeed. The problem is only a political one: it is at the top of the political level that they make every effort to maintain the separations.

With these words, a Bosniak coach introduced me into the controversial world of football in Bosnia and Herzegovina (henceforth BiH) at the beginning of my fieldwork in 2003, confirming how sport, and notably football, functions as a contentious site for social, cultural and political representations[1] in the interplay between territory, politics and identity.[2] Although sport has usually provided some space for the expression of resistance in former communist regimes,[3] the new political apparatuses emerging from the breakdown of the latter seem to have inherited and maintained, especially in the Balkans, the old capacity to ignore the claims coming from the sporting sphere, thereby limiting its allegedly transformative potential.

Towards the end of the 1980s, Yugoslavian football had undergone a progressive politicization. The emerging nationalist élites utilized the sport as a basis for personal enrichment, construction of power at the local level and political self-legitimization in the eyes of their own national groups. With the outbreak of the war in BiH, each ethno-national group – Bosniaks (Bosnian Muslims), Bosnian Croats and Bosnian Serbs – set up its own football federation and began to organize its own competitions separately. After the war, Bosnian football was in a catastrophic condition, divided between three separate mono-ethnic federations, lacking financial and structural resources and controlled by incompetent speculators coming from outside the world of sport itself.

Nevertheless, strong pressures from international sport governing bodies convinced the football establishments of the three ethno-national groups to finally merge into a unified Bosnian Football Federation (NFSBiH) in 2002 and to organize the first united Bosnian post-war championship, named the Premijer Liga. This paper examines the consequences of such a revamped inter-ethnic competition both in terms of the re-integration of the Bosnian population, on the one hand, and the possible exacerbation of ethnic tensions, on the other.

Several studies have analysed the role of sport in promoting social integration and development,[4] particularly in conflicting societies,[5] highlighting both the alter-globalist[6] and neo-colonialist[7] potential of sport as a civilizing medium. Many scholars have warned about the difficulties in assessing sport's impact on social regeneration,[8] which are also due to the complexity of the field and the variety of actors involved.[9] As noted by Gasser and Levinsen while analysing the Open Fun Football Schools programme in BiH, the achievements of sport-based interventions depend heavily 'on the interactions between local, national and international players as they struggle to advance their multiple agendas in both the little game (football) and the big one (winning the peace)'. Hence, 'OFFS long-term success hinges on the successes of the local officials, international organizations, international and national sporting bodies and others who work to develop Bosnia and Herzegovina as a multiethnic nation'.[10] The impact of 'bottom-up' sport initiatives at the ground level in polarized communities strictly depends on the consequences of 'top-down' interventions and governance dynamics on the overall context. While the former are often intentionally designed to generate social integration, the latter affect peace-building processes also through the indirect fallout of their own functional and organizational logics. This is the case, for example, of the partial discrepancy between the criteria adopted by FIFA, UEFA and the IOC to accept new member federations, on the one hand, and those embraced by the UN to recognize state sovereignties, on the other. By examining the reunification of Bosnian football after the bloody wars of the 1990s, the paper seeks to explore this multi-layered interplay.

Since an exclusive focus on ethnicity would run the risk of reifying ethnic-based representations, the role of Bosnian football will be analysed in relation to the broader interaction order and power system which such representations serve to hide and/or legitimize. Indeed, a key issue in BiH is the way social distrust is nourished and ethnicized by the ruling élites. According to Bieber, 'ethnic distrust is both a way to channel broader frustration and a mechanism to re-produce distrust'. Such a mechanism causes 'disengagement from politics and helps to sustain parties that re-affirm low trust politics and, while not being particularly trusted themselves, direct high levels of distrust elsewhere'.[11]

The paper draws on ethnographic research conducted in BiH since 2003 through participant observation, in-depth interviews and informal conversations, complemented with the study of other secondary data, notably content analysis of various media sources. The fieldwork was carried out with a primary focus on football practitioners (players, coaches, officials, supporters) from semi-professional to grass-roots level, while simultaneously sharing everyday interaction with various kinds of other ordinary people.[12] The secondary data were collected both directly in the field and by monitoring a wide range of online sources, thus ensuring a broad and differentiated access to information, in order to partly offset the bias of the involved and situated perspective.[13]

Moving from Gasser and Levinsen's remark that 'as a terrain for re-integrating communities polarized by war, football is something like frontline farmland: fertile, but likely to be mined',[14] the paper is divided into three main parts. The first part illustrates the condition of football in the post-war Bosnian context by analysing the interplay between ethnicity, socio-economic inequalities and power relations. The second part explores the connections between the growing unification of the Bosnian football community, the qualitative development of Bosnian football and the potential overcoming of the particularistic system hidden behind ethnic division. The third part analyses the enduring capacity of the criminal élites who lead Bosnian football to preserve the status quo, thus demonstrating how the first decade of a partly unified Bosnian championship – besides providing opportunities to downplay the relevance of ethnicity – has also generated a 'mined field' where ethno-national tensions continue to be fostered.

Ethno-nationalist profiteers: the exploitation of Bosnian football

In contrast to what happened to other ex-Communist countries, the Yugoslavian breakdown took place through armed conflict. Ethno-nationalist politics guided by Milosevic and Tudjman led to the war between Croats and Serbs, which quickly spread to the territory of BiH, involving its multiethnic population.

The tremendous conflicts of 1992–1995 accelerated the ethnic polarization in BiH, thus forcing the people to side with one or the other ethnic group.[15] The country's social landscape drastically changed after 97,207 people died or disappeared (2.2% of the population)[16] and half the population of 4.4 million was displaced (1.2 million emigrated outside the boundaries of the state and another million left their places of origin remaining within BiH).[17]

While stopping the fighting, the US-brokered Dayton Peace Agreement of November1995 froze and legitimized the situation generated by the war after more than three years of violence, atrocities and ethnic cleansing. The formal integrity of the state was preserved by making ethnic differences integral to the new Bosnian institutional design.[18] BiH was established as a single country with two separated entities: the Republika Srpska (RS) and the Federacija[19] BiH, the latter comprising Croats and Bosniaks, who were themselves actually divided at the cantonal level.

A complex administrative system guaranteed equal representation to the three Bosnian 'constitutive peoples' by trebling every political seat, thus creating hypertrophic, but weak and inefficient central institutions, while leaving great autonomy and power at the local level (entities, cantons, municipalities). This was partially balanced by establishing the UN Office for the High Representative, endowed with the so-called Bonn powers to impose a wide range of decision over the local politicians and even to dismiss some of them, thus making BiH a semi-protectorate.[20]

Reflecting the country's general situation, the condition of post-war Bosnian football was disastrous: inept speculators with no passion for sport capitalized on the ethnic rhetoric to rule three distinct federations, exploiting the few available resources and causing further impoverishment of the game's quality. As each ethno-national group began to organize its own competition separately, post-war football was played into mono-ethnic areas.

Nevertheless, following strong pressures from FIFA, UEFA and the IOC, the football establishments of the three ethno-national groups finally consented to come together into a unified Bosnian Football Federation[21] in 2002. The new Federation was shaped following the Dayton model, with a tripartite presidency and a seats-rotation system between the representatives of each ethno-national sub-federation, which continued to exist separately. Although intended to be a temporary solution, this structure operated until April 2011, when the UEFA suspended the NFSBiH and replaced its board with a 'normalization committee' in charge of mediating between the Federation's members, and finally amended the statute by replacing the current tripartite-rotational structure with a single-member presidency (the consequences of this change will be discussed later in this paper).

The first united Bosnian post-war championship named Premijer Liga was organized in 2002, while the lower divisions remained ethnically separated at the entity and regional/cantonal levels (with the Prva Liga Federacije BiH and the Prva Liga RS henceforth serving as the second national leagues). A united championship was also organized at the youth level since the 2003–2004 season, but only for the country's U-18 best teams, while all the other youth tournaments remained separated.

When the Premijer Liga started, just seven years after the end of the armed conflict, there were many concerns about its possible negative consequences in terms of inter-ethnic tensions. Actually, by putting teams and fans from different ethnic backgrounds into contact, the football world became a potential 'mined field', giving room both to physical and (mainly) verbal/symbolical/psychological violence. Nonetheless, a deeper understanding of the role played by ethnicity in shaping the Bosnian context during and after the war helps to highlight also the integrative potential of a unified Bosnian football world.

Ethnicity, particularism, clientelism

Following the Yugoslavian breakdown, ethnicity and nationalism became the main basis to gain political legitimacy and economic power in BiH. The ethno-nationalist ideology, characterized by the claim to establish new nation-states based on ethnic dominance or homogeneity, was rhetorically used to hide and reshape the symbiotic relationship between political power and organized crime structures.[22] Inter-ethnic trust was broken by creating separated (mono-ethnic) life-worlds, thus fuelling tensions and feeding the war through the propagandistic demonization of the 'others'. Such a separation has been maintained and reinforced in post-war everyday life, within each of the three life-worlds, by strengthening the symbolic representations of distinctive imagined communities through the antagonist reconstruction of physical symbols (notably religious buildings and cultural monuments)[23] and the differentiation of flags, school textbooks and programs, streets names and signs, tourist guides, etc. In this way, the newly reshaped physical, cognitive and emotional landscapes have been further embodied into visibly displayed banal nationalism, thus rewriting Bosnians' history culture.[24] Ethnic hatred, hostility and intolerance therefore have to be considered both as a *tool* used by the local political and criminal entrepreneurs to feed the war, and as a *result* of the war itself, rather than simply the *cause* of the conflict.[25]

In the post-war BiH, local élites were often composed of people who had gained power positions through illegality and crimes during the conflict while championing the ethnic cause. Victorious nationalists continued the Balkan tradition of patronage[26] by replacing the communist ideology with the ethno-national one. Ethnicity became the recognition criteria used by the local élites to legitimize particularistic allocations and parasitic use of social power. Furthermore, it was (and continues to be) used to deny responsibilities by laying the blame on the other groups. As the allocation of resources is mainly based on cronyism and ethnic affiliation rather than redistributive justice and professional qualifications, in each field of Bosnian society, many competent people have been relegated to the lowest ranks of the social hierarchy.[27]

Those people who reject the exclusive hegemony of the ethnic self-representation in favour of more universalistic and meritocratic criteria of recognition can be considered as a liminal group composed of individuals who share a marginal position within the power structure[28] and would therefore have an interest in acting collectively to improve their condition. Nonetheless, they tend to remain a quasi-group until they do not find the conditions for their aggregation and mobilization[29] alongside different cleavages, alternative to those defined by the ethno-national belongings.

Meanwhile, at the top of the social pyramid, the nationalist élites of the three groups stage the ethnic struggle in front of public opinion, only to then partake in the advantages of such an 'ethnic sharing' of power and exploited resources, when they are backstage.[30] Being tacitly allied and mutually concerned with maintaining the relevance of the ethno-national cleavage, they prevent a large part of the population – disadvantaged by this socio-political order – from coalescing against them alongside the ethnically cross-cutting socio-economical cleavages.[31]

Inverting the route?

Such a vicious circle is also evident in Bosnian football, exploited by incompetent (and sometimes criminal) élites who do not care about the decreasing standards of the game. Especially in the first post-war years, the leaders at the NFSBiH utilized the national team to pocket money from useless friendly matches, as well as to cap unknown low-quality players, thus increasing their value and selling them internationally through their agents (BiH has a higher proportion of FIFA players' agents for its footballers than any other country).[32] Local championships have also been habitually exploited through match fixing, clientelism and illegal misappropriation of Federation's funds. Similar attitudes characterize the practices of many club officials who manage public resources for private enrichment without making any personal investment, as football clubs in BiH are not private companies, rather public associations predominantly funded out of municipal budgets. This situation reduces the spectators' interest and the public relevance and visibility of Bosnian football, thus removing it from the public view and favouring its privatistic and parasitic management by the incompetent élites, while further disempowering the competent operators and football enthusiasts.

Therefore, the unification of Bosnian football can be considered to be a 'fertile land' mainly if (and insomuch) it helps to break such a vicious circle, i.e. to (1) settle the ethno-national separations by enabling a wider imagined community, (2) re-publicize football by restoring its visibility and accountability and (3) enhance the quality of football by promoting meritocracy. This virtuous circle would foster a 'displacement of conflicts',[33] downplaying the relevance of the ethno-national cleavage (Bosniaks vs. Croats vs. Serbs) while highlighting the meritocratic confrontation (competent/enthusiasts vs. criminals/profiteers). It is therefore important to assess if and how the development of a united Bosnian football community provides an arena in which the dominance/relevance of ethnicity as a recognition criteria can be questioned by counter-discourses that celebrate alternative criteria.

Fertile land?

This section explores the connections between the widening/unification of the Bosnian football community, the qualitative development of Bosnian football and the potential overcoming of the particularistic system hidden behind the ethnic separations.

Settling the ethno-national separations: towards a wider imagined community?

In football, as in other spheres of Bosnian everyday life, the armed conflict has created three separated worlds, which are still persisting long after the end of the war. This is highlighted by the following comment of a young Bosnian Serb in 2004:

Do people in Republika Srpska follow the Bosnian Premijer Liga?

Well . . . we do follow it, yeah, but . . . not as much as we follow or read what happens in Serbia – 'cause the Serbian are our 'brother-people'. I mean, in Republika Srpska you don't have enough information at your disposal to be able to follow what happens in BiH, for instance about football . . . at least if we consider the news that reach us in Republika Srpska. I mean, everybody read Serbian media, everybody eat food made in Serbia, and so on . . . Do you understand what I mean? Although there is also something coming from BiH . . . But we mainly read the Serbian mass media. You read stuffs coming from Belgrade: Večernji Novosti, Sport, and so on. We read their newspapers, you understand? Otherwise, when I read a Bosnian newspaper . . . we only read about our own teams, those from the Republika Srpska. I may read something about Sarajevo and Željježničar, but nothing about the other teams . . . (P., 22, from the Bosnian Serb town of Šipovo)

The unification of Bosnian football has contributed to bringing these separated worlds together, at least in part, by stimulating the football enthusiasts to travel to the former 'enemy territory' to attend matches of the newly established Premijer Liga.[34]

Now we have it here very close, in Modriča [Serb town] – I mean, the Premijer Liga – and a lot of people comes from the neighbourhood. A lot of players from Gradačac [Bosniak town] went to attend the last match, but I've also noticed many people from Šamac, from Ođak [Croat town] . . . Among the neighbouring towns, only Modriča and Orašje have a team in Premijer Liga at the moment, so everybody want to come here to watch Želj, Sarajevo, Čelik, Borac, Leotar . . . (S., 37, from the Bosnian Serb town of Modriča)

For many of them, this was their first and only motivation to cross the old front lines and set foot in what was 'enemy territory':

Do you travel to Modriča sometimes?

Well, yeah . . . Recently we've been there to attend a match of Premijer Liga, and we'll surely go to watch other matches . . .

And . . . what apart from football? Are you used to go to Modriča also for other reasons?

No, just therefore, just therefore. Well, now I and my friends – those I usually go to the football matches with – have planned to go there also to attend some volleyball match, when the championship will begin. You know, Modriča is close to Gradačac, it's not far. (I., 34, from the Bosniak town of Gradačac)

The unification of Bosnian football has increased the occasions for encounters, especially among people who already knew each other before the war, but had been separated by the conflict.[35] This is particularly the case for many people who are actively involved in football as trainers and athletes, especially at grass-roots level. Eager to get out of a self-referential mono-ethnic football world that limits the possibilities for constructive confrontation, which is necessary to sporting improvement, many sport enthusiasts welcome the enlargement of the Bosnian football landscape as an occasion for comparison and reflexivity. For instance, just after getting to know a Bosniak colleague from a neighbouring town, a Bosnian Serb youth coach told me:

I've just got to know Alija. He has immediately invited me to play some friendly match in their town, and I don't back down, this is what I want to do with the children that I'm coaching. I'm in favour of such initiatives, because . . . I want to support the club I work for, and create a good football school. Therefore . . . I take this upon myself, so that I can see which teams from Federacija BiH have more money, and which of them are working better with the children. There, the first goal at the moment is to reach them, see where we are positioned when compared to them, try to play with them. It's neither that easy, nor that quick, but . . . this is our first goal . . . So far, we have achieved very good results with our youth teams in Republika Srpska playing against the youth teams of Leotar, Slavija, Glasinac, Sokolac, which are all clubs from Premijer Liga or Prva Liga. But we don't know where we are positioned, when compared to the teams from the Federacija . . . (R., 43, youth coach from the Bosnian Serb town of Nevesinje)

Another important element contributing to the widening of the Bosnian imagined community is the increasing mobility of players, especially at the professional level. While teams used to be mono-ethnic when the Premijer Liga began in 2002, they are now increasingly becoming mixed. Similar to other professional activities, football enables the development of weak ties among people who downplay ethnicity while focusing on the pursuit of common achievements/interests.[36] At the same time, such a process enhances the relevance of the team's sporting identity while reducing, at least in part, its ethnic representativeness[37]:

> At the very beginning of the new Premijer Liga the teams were mainly mono-ethnic, but now, say, a Muslim guards the goal of Borac [the team of Banja Luka, the main Bosnian Serb town], a Serb is the main striker of Željo ['Bosniak' team from Sarajevo], a Muslim goes to play for Zrinjski [the 'Croat' team of Mostar], the coaches . . . the coaches go and interchange, the players interchange as well . . . I think that it [the Premijer Liga] has had quite a good influence on this exchange between people. (E., 42, youth coach from the Bosniak town of Bosanska Krupa)

Further steps towards the normalization of Bosnian football can be noticed from the progressive shift from ethnic rivalries to traditional local and sport rivalries. Classic matches between famous teams catalyse more interest than others, no matter what the ethnic backgrounds of the teams are. For instance, the match between the Bosniak team Željezničar and their Bosniak city rivals Sarajevo is much more thrilling than the match between Željezničar and the Croat team Orašje, or the Serb team Leotar.

Also, the classical rural/urban cleavage[38] often becomes more relevant than the ethno-national one in the unified Bosnian football arena. For instance, when the Croat team of Široki Brijeg from Herzegovina complained about being damaged by the NFSBiH in favour of the biggest teams Željezničar and Zrinski in 2004, they did not relate the discrimination to ethnic reasons – Zrinski is a Croat team as well, indeed – rather to the fact that Široki Brijeg was penalized for being a small peripheral town while Željezničar and Zrinski benefited from representing the main cities of Sarajevo and Mostar, respectively.[39] Common urban roots and belonging can become more relevant than ethno-national affiliations, as indicated by the director of Slavija, the club of the Bosnian Serb part of Sarajevo:

> Let me tell you this: even nowadays our football team Slavija has far better relationships with Željo and Sarajevo than with Borac of Banja Luka! Now, someone might probably ask 'Wait, how is this possible?', but . . . it has nothing to do with the usual ethnic antipathy, it is not the reason why we are in good terms with someone rather than others, in this case. We are in better terms with someone simply because . . . sport circumstances require that we are in better terms with them rather than with Borac. And when we come to Modriča . . . we couldn't stand each other's sights, we couldn't even look in each other's eyes . . .

> *Before the war or after it?*

> Before the war they didn't even exist! We were like Bundesliga to them! They were really kind of a peasant-team . . .

Re-publicizing football by restoring its visibility and accountability

Another crucial issue to be examined is whether the unification of the Bosnian championships, by promoting a wider imagined community out of the three separated mono-ethnic worlds, can contribute to re-publicization of football as a public good, rescuing it from the hands of the current incompetent élites.

The connection between the visibility and accountability of football can be explored by analysing the perceptions of the Bosnian enthusiasts about the quality of refereeing after the first two seasons of the new Premijer Liga:

> Well . . . since they have made a unified Premijer Liga the level is increasing. The fact that referees come from different areas has enhanced the quality of refereeing. Quite a selection

has been made, preventing some people from refereeing, whom I don't know how had been included in those lists: there were some refs here...people who were outside the world of sport before the war, but then the war – I don't know how – has helped to fly very high. However, the way they flew high, the same way they've fallen down! In short, the level has improved. I follow the Premijer Liga, as far as I can, in Tuzla, now in Modriča, sometimes I go to Sarajevo, and I can tell that the level of refereeing is much better than it was just after the war. (N., 37, youth coach from the Bosniak town of Gradačac)

These narratives, collected in 2004, tend to connect football accountability to the increase of both its national and (potentially) international visibility:

I think that now the situation with the referees has improved, but only at the level of Premijer Liga, the unified one, because now those refs aspire to referee in the European Cups – they can't referee in the Champions League yet, we haven't that level yet, but they could referee for instance in the UEFA Cup. Yeah, I think that now the refereeing has a bit improved there, but in the lower categories I think that things are not going well yet... (D., 39, from the Bosnian Serb town of Modriča)

The difference between the Premijer Liga and lower leagues seems to further confirm the impact of the new enlarged tournament in connecting football visibility and accountability:

Now I tell you how it works here. It doesn't matter if you're in the first team, or in the youth sector: at home, most of the referees help you, while when you play away...Ok, now the Premijer Liga is a little changing; but apart from that, if you look at all these lower categories, lower than the Premijer Liga...Anyway, in the Premijer Liga they can't referee dishonestly because there are the cameras, you know, one can see it...there are controls. (H., 22, from the Bosniak town of Gradačac)

However, despite these initial signs of change, in the last decade, football has continued to be exploited by criminals and unqualified profiteers. At the same time, the unified football landscape has also provided an arena for the Bosnian enthusiasts' protest and resistance, aiming to restore the public value of football.

Since its first season in 2002, many clubs participating in the Premijer Liga – often led by the country's most historically important clubs Željezničar, Sarajevo and Borac – coalesced across ethnic divides against the Federation's officers, appealing all the other clubs to formally associate in order to better defend their rights, and sometimes even threatening to retire from the tournament. Although contingent clubs' interests were obviously often behind the protests, trans-ethnic collective arguments were used to support the dissent, such as 'the salvation of Bosnian football' and 'cleaning the football house up from corruption'.

Similar arguments were used by the organized fans of the different clubs, who often arranged several trans-ethnic collective protests in front of the NFSBiH seat in Sarajevo, as well as by the BHFanaticos, mainly composed of supporters from the Bosnian diaspora, who usually display their 'Rat savezu!' (War to the Federation!) banners at the national team games.

Along with the fans, famous players and other public personages are vocal about their opposition to the football establishment. For example, on 30 October 2006, 13 Bosnian national team players (Bajramović, Bartolović, Berberović, Bešlija, Grlić, Grujić, Hasagić, Hrgović, Milenković, Misimović, Papac, Spahić and Tolja) published a letter of protest in the *Dnevni Avaz* daily after some corruption scandal involving the officials of the NFSBiH in 2004, announcing that they would boycott all national team matches until the Federation's leaders resigned:

Regarding all that have happened around our national team, we, football players who currently fight in the pitch for the blazon of the country, feel the need to announce our stances to the public opinion...We've had enough that the members of the Presidency Milan Jelić,

Iljo Dominković i Sulejman Čolaković, as well as the national team director Ahmet Pašalić, seal the destiny of our football and national team. We will no longer accept call-ups to the national team while these people are performing these functions, hoping that our gesture will mark the first step in the healing of this cancer in our soccer and a new beginning for the national team for which our hearts beat.[40]

Nevertheless, not even this sensational stand changed the situation, and the immovable Federation's leaders continued with their unaccountable management, raising further frustration and dissent.

In 2008, the well-known former striker Meho Kodro, who had been appointed as the national team manager in January being guaranteed full independence in the technical management of the side, quickly broke his relationship with the NFSBiH in just a few months after refusing to take charge of the team for a game against Iran in Tehran, arranged by the Federation without his knowledge. On 1 June 2008, while the BiH national side was facing Azerbaijan in a friendly match in Zenica in front of just 50 spectators, a friendly humanitarian game between former Bosnian football legends, organized by Kodro and Elvir Bolić to protest against the NFSBiH, was played in Sarajevo at the same time in front of 15,000 people and broadcasted by the FTV.[41]

In November 2009, the former NFSBiH secretary general Munib Ušanović, together with the finance and marketing secretary Miodrag Kureš, were sentenced to five years in jail over tax evasion and illegal misappropriation of the NFSBiH funds.[42] However, despite continual scandals, the Federation's officers never resigned and persisted with their criminal management until 1 April 2011, when FIFA and UEFA suspended all Bosnian teams from international competition to punish the unwillingness of the NFSBiH to amend its statute. The tripartite presidency was considered no longer acceptable by the main governing bodies of international football, and the Bosnian federation was required to finally have a single president.

Such a measure roused further important statements to support the re-publicization of Bosnian football. Worried that the national team would be prevented from playing the last decisive matches of the Euro 2012 qualification,[43] the Bosniak member of the BiH joint presidency Bakir Izetbegović addressed a letter to Joseph Blatter and Michel Platini, the FIFA and UEFA presidents, respectively, appealing for a solution:

> Without wishing to interfere . . . in your activities, I voice my sincere conviction that you will find an adequate solution to establish in Bosnia a football organisation of the best quality to allow Bosnia's national team and our clubs to continue taking part in European competition . . . You certainly know that Bosnia-Hercegovina is a complex country . . . It would be unfortunate that irresponsible behaviour of members of our (football) federation prevents our international and local football players from taking part in international matches. Hundreds of thousands of their fans do not deserve that.[44]

Even the Dean of the Sarajevo University wrote a letter to the UEFA President Michel Platini:

> Dear Mr. Platini, I've decided to address you on behalf of teachers, associates and more than 40,000 students of the University of Sarajevo, from all over Bosnia and Herzegovina and abroad . . . Personally, this is the first time to me to write a letter to any sport organizations. The reason behind my addressing to you is my concern for the football in B&H, and thus extending to the B&H society as well . . . Essentially, I want you to recognize the real culprits, no matter from which milieu they come and regardless of their names, and to punish them most severely, and to open a path of healthy development for the football in Bosnia and Herzegovina and without the impact of politics, living in and living from the football, and the same time undermining the system of a country that is allowing them to do so.[45]

The talented midfielder of the Bosnian National team Miralem Pjanić, interviewed by the French newspaper *L'Equipe*, confirmed:

> It's very serious. It's a huge shock for the players and those that love Bosnian football. The people to be blamed are the federation's officials. We are simply hostage to incompetent people, who think only of making profit on the back of our efforts rather than about the team. I hope UEFA and FIFA now take the right decisions. We love our country and we always want to wear its colours. It's not us who should pay. The country is already poor – they cannot take football away from us. Today, lots of people demonstrated outside the hotel where the meeting took place. We will discuss it among (the team) but if there is anything that can be done to help our cause, it must be done.[46]

A temporary solution was found by dismissing the past officials and establishing a normalization committee working under the hugely respected former Yugoslavia coach Ivica Osim, who gained the trust of the ethno-national representatives and worked out a compromise involving a single-member presidency.[47] This welcome change led to the suspension being overturned on 28 May and the normalization committee, initially set up only to manage the emergency phase, was confirmed as being in charge on 29 October until the end of 2012.

Enhancing the quality of football by promoting meritocracy

Since the very first seasons of the Premijer Liga, the quest for transparency and accountability in Bosnian football has been linked to the quest for fair competition, meritocracy and improving the playing standards. This connection is well expressed by the words of a Bosniak football enthusiast interviewed in 2003:

> In the last round of the championship we went to Modriča, to watch Modriča-Zrinški. But it was an ugly match. You see, while watching that match we recalled the matches that ones we used to play in the late 80s, and I think those team that played in the then Regional League were much stronger than the ones currently playing in today's Premijer Liga. Nowadays the quality is . . . nothing. Nothing when compared to how it should be, if you look at the English Premier League, or the Italian championship, or the Spanish one, and so on . . . You know, a desire would be that one could see something similar in our country as well. I would like to go to Tuzla, at the Tušanj stadium, to watch Sloboda playing against, say, Željo, or Sarajevo, or whatever, and see just that level, that football. And not to see, on the contrary, a . . . war between two teams! (A., 32, from the Bosniak town of Gradačac)

Also, the increasing mobility of practitioners and followers slowly generated by the normalization of Bosnian football, by providing occasions for comparison and reflexivity, has contributed to encourage the quest for fair competition, meritocracy and improving playing standards. This link is well exemplified by the words of a Bosniak non-professional player interviewed in 2004, just after he signed his first transfer to a neighbouring Serb team in the RS' Second League. The quote shows how, by attending a match of his future team, he had the occasion to compare the standards of football (notably refereeing) in the two Bosnian entities and develop some self-critical reflections, thus eluding the usual ethno-national sanctification of 'us' and demonization of 'them':

> Last time that they *(my forthcoming teammates)* played away I went to watch the match. The referee really looked like someone coming from a higher category . . . and I was really surprised from the way he refereed. 'Cause both teams were competitive and wanted to win, and the match was balanced. He even disallowed a goal to the home team, a goal that I wouldn't have disallowed. He said he had seen a foul, and that's how he decided . . . The refereeing was excellent, and also the players were fair; if someone got injured, they kicked the ball out to break the game, they apologized . . . In our matches it is not like that. Well, I would like that . . . if we are better, we win 10:0, and if you are better, you win 10:0. But it's not like that, unfortunately. (E., 31, amateur footballer from the Bosniak town of Gradačac)

While initially almost all the matches in the BiH Premijer Liga were won by the home teams, such a trend has recently changed and victories of the guest teams are more frequent.[48] However, the situation has not improved in the lower leagues. Still in 2011, some players of the Prva Liga Federacije BiH publicly asserted that 'Refs are the Bosnian football's greatest evil' and 'Playing under these conditions doesn't make any sense'[49]; eight teams of the same league jointly protested that 'Time for change has come, 'cause we cannot tolerate such a situation, with Prva Liga FBiH no more being a place for correct people and football enthusiasts'.[50]

However, the recent establishment of the normalization committee has fostered the hope for professional competence and passion to finally become the main criteria when appointing people in the leading positions, as exemplified by this quote from a Bosniak youth coach interviewed during the summer of 2011:

> It will be much more difficult than people expect. It can't easily happen, now, that some Osim, Hadžibegić, Bajević, who are all worldwide well-known people, suddenly order: 'You will be here, you will be there' . . . I believe in some 3–4 years they will build a good system, so that worthy and competent people, who above of all love football, will float to surface. I myself have had many problems in football because of my stances, and I've been relegated to the margins, so that I've been forced to work with some smaller club, and so on. However, I believe in 3–4 years the right people will reach their deserved place. (E., 42, youth coach from the Bosniak town of Bosanska Krupa)

Nonetheless, many Bosnian enthusiasts remain sceptical about the possibility of eradicating the incompetent élites, as they fear that former officials will use their patronage (clientelar) power to quickly regain charge by manipulating the future elections, after the normalization committee finishes its job.

Mined field?

The high conservative capability of the criminal élites who lead Bosnian football by hiding behind ethno-national masks exposes the ambivalent potential of the sporting arena. Besides providing opportunities to downplay the relevance of ethnicity, indeed, the first decade of (partially) unified Bosnian championships has also generated a 'mined field' where the ethno-national tensions can be fostered, giving room both to physical and – mainly – verbal/symbolical/psychological violence.

Verbal/symbolic violence

Since the first Premijer Liga season, slogans and offences have been emphasized through the use of war symbolisms, particularly by the – relatively small, but vociferous – groups of organized supporters. Drawing on derogatory terminology of war, the Serb fans were called 'četnik' by the Croat or Bosniak opponents, the Croat fans were called 'ustaša' by the others, while the Bosniaks were called 'balija'.[51]

Serb fans occasionally welcomed Bosniak supporters brandishing banners stating 'Nož, žica, Srebrenica' (Knife, barbed wire, Srebrenica), thus celebrating the Srebrenica massacre in which approximately 7000 Bosniaks were killed by Ratko Mladić's paramilitary bands. This obviously offended many Bosniaks; for instance, supporters of Željezničar from Sarajevo once retaliated by making their own banner stating 'Od Sarajeva do Borika, nigdije neće biti četnika!' (From Sarajevo to Borik, there won't be no chetnik), and displaying it to the Bosnian Serb fans of Borac Banja Luka.

Croat banners have been displayed to celebrate 'Ante Gotovina' (a Croat war criminal)* and 'Oluja' ('Storm', a huge retaliatory operation against Serbs in 1995). Both Croats and

Serbs occasionally use the 'Ubij Turčina' (Kill the Turk) and 'Mrzim Bosno' (I hate Bosnia) banners, while exclusively Serbs use the banners hymning 'Ratko Mladić' and 'Radovan Karadžić'. As far as they are concerned, Bosniak extremist supporters welcome their Croat and Serb opponents by waving Turk flags, thus enforcing the representation of their stadium and the Bosniak-majority area as a hostile Islamized territory.

Nonetheless, a very controversial aspect of the transformations characterizing the unified Bosnian football can be noticed in the trans-ethnic use of ethno-nationalistic offences. Indeed, nationalist symbolisms are sometimes curiously used not to reaffirm one's own ethnic belonging, rather to outrage the opponents as much as possible.

In order to achieve such a goal, some supporters go as far as borrowing symbols and slogans from the other ethnic groups. For example, during the match between two Bosnian Serb teams – Modriča and Slavija – in May 2003, the fans of both teams addressed each other with the following offensive terms: 'Stupid chetniks!', 'You love Alija (Izetbegović)', 'Also Radovan Karadžić roots for us!'. In the first case, the term 'chetnik' was used – by Serbs against Serbs – in the same derogatory way in which it is usually used by Bosniaks and Croats against Serbs. In the second case, the opponents were offended by equating them to Bosniaks. In the third case, by claiming to be backed by Karadžić's support, one group's members classified themselves as 'first-class-Serbs' and the opponents as 'second-class-Serbs'.

Another example occurred when Široki Brijeg (Croats) played against Željezničar (Bosniaks) in May 2003. Besides chanting 'Burn the balija!' and 'Kill the Turk!', the supporters of Široki Brijeg also chanted 'Knife, barbed wire, Srebrenica', thus implicitly celebrating the Serbs – who are not exactly supposed to be the Croats' role models! – for the massacre they orchestrated against the Bosniaks. Even more surprisingly, while doing so, they also raised the three-fingers salute,[52] usually flashed by Serbian soldiers as a nationalist sign during military operations and therefore perceived as highly offensive by the Bosnian Croats themselves.

A third example is even more paradoxical. During the match between two Bosniak teams in August 2003 – Sloboda of Tuzla and Željezničar from Sarajevo – a banner of the Sloboda's supporters stated 'Why didn't the Serbs kill you as well?'. In this case, it was the Bosniaks supporters who went as far as celebrating the Serbs just to outrage the Bosniak rivals. Despite the severity of such an outrage, it came from people of the same ethnic group and was therefore perceived as a purely sporty offence, instead of an ethnic one.

Insults linked to ethno-national belongings and memories of the recent war have therefore ambivalent consequences. On the one hand, the transformation of the ethno-national outrages into normal provocations between rival fans groups may change their original function and meaning, partially reducing their relevance in terms of ethnic opposition. On the other hand, they provide the Bosnian fans groups more opportunity to provoke one another, making the Bosnian matches more flammable.

Riots and physical violence

Football riots involving physical aggression have been less common than expected in the unified Premijer Liga, although a number of serious incidents did occur during these 10 years. One of the main reasons for the relatively low intensity of fights is the small number of fans attending the Bosnian championship, with core groups of organized supporters usually numbering just dozens or, at most, hundreds of people.[53] Furthermore, a strong police presence has helped to reduce riots (according to some of my interviewees, there are sometimes more policemen than fans in the stadium). On the other hand, especially in the first Premijer Liga seasons, the police have been criticized for unfair treatment of visiting supporters, thereby contributing to make the stadium a hostile territory for the guest teams and their followers.

Although thousands of matches have proceeded quite peacefully in the Premijer Liga since its beginning in 2002, the relatively few incidents ending up in physical confrontation and damage immediately attract the attention of the mass media. One of the most discussed cases was the death of Vedran Puljić, a Sarajevo fan killed before a match in Široki Brijeg in 2009. More recently, much attention was also paid to three important incidents that happened within a couple of weeks between September and October 2011: the fans of Borac attacking those of Željezničar in Banja Luka, the supporters of Zrinski assaulting the players of Velež during the derby in Mostar and the (supposed) fans of Hajduk Split fighting followers of Željezničar before a friendly match in Sarajevo.

The increased frequency of the riots appeared to reflect a rise in inter-ethnic intolerance, thus recalling the Yugoslavian football clashes which preceded the war in the early 1990s.[54] Yet, many observers highlighted that the incidents happened – in close succession and in all the three main ethno-national cities (Banja Luka, Sarajevo and Mostar) – in the very week when a delegation of UEFA and FIFA was awaited in Sarajevo to discuss the possible extension of the normalization committee's mandate.[55] The incidents might therefore have been devised and orchestrated by former members of the football establishment who had been dismissed and marginalized after the settlement of the normalization committee. According to this interpretation, they aimed at undermining the positive atmosphere of inter-ethnic cooperation already established by the committee in just a few months, thereby 'proving' its ineffectiveness and leading to its removal.[56]

Media amplification

The impact of all these forms of physical and verbal/symbolic violence on the Bosnian public opinion depends very much on the way they reverberate through the usually factious media coverage. Indeed, despite several heroic stories of extremely qualified editors and journalists who paid high personal prices for impartially reporting about the social and political events before, during and after the Yugoslavian breakdown, the majority of the mass media are presently controlled by the ruling ethno-nationalist élites.[57]

Bosnian media coverage of football riots contributes to intensify ethnic separation in three main ways, i.e. through out-groups denigration, inter-ethnic fights amplification and out-groups misrecognition.

The first and most common way consists highlighting and stigmatizing the outrages perpetrated by the out-group fans, while downplaying those committed by in-group supporters. For example, after the riots between the Široki Brijeg fans (the Škripari) and those of Sarajevo (the Horde Zla), Bosniak media celebrated the killed Sarajevian fan Vedran Puljić as a victim of the Croat hooligans, while Croatian media portrayed the alleged murderer Oliver Knenzović as the defender of the city from the predetermined attack launched by Horde Zla.

The second way consists the very amplification of inter-ethnic fights between football fans, which, even when non-factiously accounted, plays into the hands of those arguing for the impossibility of inter-ethnic peaceful cohabitation. As bad football stories are generally considered more newsworthy than good ones, football stadia are more frequently depicted as 'mined fields' rather than fertile lands. It follows that mass media, by simply reporting about football riots, serve as a megaphone for messages and gestures spreading nationalistic hatred, even independently from any politically driven editorial line.[58]

A third contribution to enforce the ethno-national partition is made by the majority of the Croat and Serb media through their agenda setting, which pays more attention to the sport news regarding athletes and teams from Croatia and Serbia, while only marginally reporting BiH sport by presenting it together with (or even after) international sport news. Such an approach is more evident in the Serb media, which take advantage of RS being a formal administrative entity with high territorial autonomy to ambiguously present the sporting news about BiH as if they regard it as a foreign country.

The impact of mass media on inter-ethnic relations and power networks can thus vary from extremely direct and explicit to more indirect and unintentional forms. As an example of the first pole, mediated statements about sport can be used by the ethno-national leaders to increase social distrust, as the RS President Milorad Dodik did by publicly declaring that he supports the Serbian football team and would only cheer for BiH if they were playing Turkey, or that the RS will accept to further stay within BiH only if, among other things, it will be allowed to have its own sport representative team at international competitions.[59] On the other hand, given the link between ethnicity and patronage networks in the Bosnian power system, by simply highlighting football riots, mass media contribute to nourish the social distrust which feeds patronage relations and corruption dynamics in Bosnian football and society at large.[60]

Conclusion

This paper has sought to illustrate the complex role played by the reunification of the Bosnian football landscape in affecting socio-political identities and power relations in the post-war environment. On the one hand, football reunification has surely contributed to further unveil how ethnicity is instrumentally used by the Bosnian élites to exploit the common good for their private enrichment. To use Hirschmann's words,[61] in a country where people are mainly divided between the loyalty option (i.e. accepting and actively supporting ethno-national politics) and the exit one (i.e. passively giving up after experiencing frustration and resignation), the football world becomes, at least in part, an arena where those who are disempowered by the current status quo can express their voice. At the same time, while confirming football's potential for the mobilization of public opinion, the Bosnian case shows how it can also be easily used by the establishment to preserve the status quo.

A distinction can be made between the public sphere, built upon ordinary interactions among football practitioners and enthusiasts, which provides fragments of normalization and de-ethnicization of the everyday life, and the far more visible media space which spreads to a broader audience mainly negative news about incidents and fights, rather than positive reports regarding spectacular matches, local football stars or the festive atmosphere in crowded stadia.

Hence the quest for fair competition, meritocracy and improved playing standards, implicit in the inner logics and rhetoric of sport, and supported by many Bosnians keen on football, had only limited success in advocating transparency and accountability. To a large extent, the football world has mirrored the country's social and political evolution, going from a partial normalization of inter-ethnic relations in the early 2000s to an increasing impasse in the later years, nourished and capitalized on by the ruling parties. The partial autonomy of football from other social spheres, based on both its inner logics and its reliance on international independent governing bodies, still seems too weak in BiH to challenge the hegemony of the political and criminal élites. The constitution of a professional clubs association in charge of directly running the championships (so far managed by the NFSBiH), together with the transformation of football clubs from public (municipal) associations into private companies, would plausibly increase officials' accountability and motivate them to assume their own responsibilities.

Nonetheless, whereas changes 'from below' find it hard to emerge, the partial autonomy of sport displays its effects 'from above' through decisions imposed by FIFA and UEFA. Breaking away from the Dayton model, the new NFSBiH is becoming the first Bosnian institution to be headed by a single president, i.e. without the rotational balance system which is usually claimed to guarantee each 'constituent people' not to be overpowered by the others. However, this very system has so far paralysed BiH, since the fear of becoming a minority was used – sometimes with good reason, sometimes speciously – to impose vetoes on any kind of political, social and economic reform. Hence, the new Federation could serve as a testing ground for possible transformations of the broader institutional apparatus, providing insightful answers to some crucial questions: What will happen to the Croats and Serbs in Bosnian football henceforth? Will things work better – both generally and for them – or will they be overcome by the Bosniaks? Moreover, in the event that it works better, will this experience constitute an example also suitable for the BiH politics, or will it simply be attributed to the peculiarity of the sport world?

Although this last question recalls once again the unsettled scientific challenge of isolating sport's impact from the many other societal influences (politics, media, economy, judiciary and police will certainly play a great role either in supporting or boycotting the work of the normalization committee), the Bosnian context surely represents an insightful case for further research and observation.

Acknowledgements

Part of the research for this paper was funded by the University of Padua, Italy, through a PhD grant and a subsequent senior research grant. The author is also indebted to Alan Bairner and Oliver S. Williams for their precious support and valuable remarks.

Notes

* Gotovina was exonerated by the International Criminal Tribunal for the Former Yugoslavia on 16 November 2012.
1. Bradley, 'In-Groups, Out-Groups'.
2. Bairner and Shirlow, 'Territory, Politics and Soccer Fandom'.
3. Numerato, 'Between Small Everyday Practices'.
4. For some examples, see Beutler, 'Sport Serving Development and Peace'; Jarvie, 'Sport, Development and Aid'; Kay, 'Developing through Sport'; Spaaij, 'Social Impact of Sport'; Vermeulen and Verweel, 'Participation in Sport'.
5. Sugden and Bairner, *Sport in Divided Societies*; Gasser and Levinsen, 'Breaking Post-War Ice'; Rookwood, *Social Development in Post-Conflict Communities*; Schulenkorf, 'Sport Events and Ethnic Reconciliation'; Armstrong, 'Lords of Misrule'; and Sorek, *Arab Soccer in a Jewish State*.
6. Kidd, 'A New Social Movement'.
7. Darnell, 'Power, Politics and Sport'. See also Giulianotti, 'Human Rights, Globalization and Sentimental Education'.
8. Coalter, 'Sports Clubs, Social Capital'.
9. Giulianotti, 'Sport, Peacemaking and Conflict Resolution'.
10. Gasser and Levinsen, 'Breaking Post-War Ice', 471.
11. Bieber, 'Negotiating Division and Co-operation'.
12. Most of the fieldwork was realized in Gradačac, a Bosniak town in the Tuzla canton, very close to the Republika Srpska (the Bosnian Serb majority entity) and the Posavina canton (with Bosnian Croat majority). I spent eight continuous months with a Bosniak family in 2003, training with the local football team Zvijezda (which was playing in the semi-professional third Bosnian league at that time) and broadly sharing the ordinary people's everyday life. The fieldwork was continued through further periods of several weeks between 2004 and 2006, and is currently being followed up in 2011–2012. The bias of such an in-depth involvement with a Bosniak majority community was partly balanced both by frequently visiting the neighbouring

towns with Croat and Serb majority, chiefly Modriča, and by attending the seminars and activities of the Open Fun Football Schools humanitarian project, which provided numerous opportunities to visit non-Bosniak areas while observing, interviewing and playing with many Bosnian Croat and Serb football practitioners and enthusiasts.

13. The in-depth knowledge accumulated during the fieldwork proved to be a crucial asset to filter the monitored news by better recognizing the degree and quality of their bias, and consequently their author's social, ethnic and political orientation. A wide range of sources was consulted, from highly factious to independent ones, based in all the three ethno-national areas.

14. Gasser and Levinsen, 'Breaking Post-War Ice', 471.

15. Oberschall, 'Manipulation of Ethnicity'.

16. The dead and missing are 66% Bosniaks, 26% Serbs and 8% Croats. 41% of the dead and missing are civilians, 83% of whom are Bosniaks (Belloni and Hemmer, 'Bosnia-Herzegovina', 131).

17. Sekulić, 'Forced Migration and Perception', 84.

18. Belloni, *State Building and International Intervention*, 3. See also Campbell, *National Deconstruction*.

19. Following the Bosnian grammatical rules, the term will change throughout the text being spelled either Federacija or Federacije according to its accusative or genitive form.

20. Bieber, *Post-War Bosnia*.

21. Namely, Nogometni/Fudbalski Savez Bosna i Hercegovina, including both the 'Croat' and 'Serb' words for football ('nogomet' and 'fudbal', respectively) in order to avoid disputes.

22. Far from being a Bosnian (or Balkan) peculiarity, this evolution of the political/criminal relationship simply highlights how 'the global neo-liberal economy de-structures traditional organizational models, empowers intermediation, and gives organized crime a formidable opportunity to emancipate itself from the traditional role of provider, often allowing direct intervention in the management of political violence and in the moulding of state structures' (Strazzari, 'Decade Horribilis', 185).

23. See Hayden, 'Antagonistic Tolerance'.

24. For a detailed description, see Torsti, 'History Culture'. For the concept of banal nationalism – i.e. the ways in which a nation is symbolically 'flagged' in the habitual, everyday life practices of ordinary people – see Billig, *Banal Nationalism*.

25. This interpretation does not deny the existence of ethnic differences and tensions (see, for instance, Hayden, 'Antagonistic Tolerance'), but highlights how they are emphasized and instrumentally used in the Bosnian context as a pretext and cloak for a clientelist patronage system. See Bose, *Bosnia after Dayton*; Burg and Shoup, *War in Bosnia-Herzegovina*; Chandler, *Bosnia: Faking Democracy*; Pickering, 'Generating Social Capital'; and Sekulić, Massey, and Hodson, 'Ethnic Intolerance and Ethnic Conflict'.

26. See Woodward, 'Bosnia after Dayton'.

27. Discriminatory hiring and firing was accelerated during the war and immediately following it (OSCE, *Employment Discrimination*), but clientelism and patronage keep on dominating Bosnians' life nowadays.

28. See Turner, *Ritual Process*.

29. See Dahrendorf, *Class and Class Conflict*.

30. Such a power system is based on the disenchantment of the most competent, educated and cosmopolitan part of the Bosnian population, which contributes to push the electoral abstention up to 50%. It is mainly the rural population that votes, which is more easily manipulated by the ethno-nationalist through politics of fear, as 'fear of how the other sides will vote drives voters to choose the party of security for their own ethnicity' (Belloni and Hemmer, 'Bosnia-Herzegovina', 133).

31. Although often hidden by the dominant ethno-national representation, many other social cleavages are displayed in the Bosnian context, cross-cutting the barriers of ethnic identity. They regard prevalently the problems not only of distribution of restricted material resources, but also of differences related to attitudes, mentality, customs, culture in general and political choice. The fluxes of refugees and internal displaced persons further increases this inter-, intra- and trans-ethnic complexity (Sekulić, 'Forced Migration and Perception', 92).

32. There are 123 FIFA licensed players' agents in BiH, more than in the Netherlands, Portugal, Russia or Turkey, for instance. Only Italy, Spain, UK, Germany, Brazil, France and Argentina have more agents and also far more players than BiH (see Dautbegović, 'BiH osma u svijetu'; see also http://www.fifa.com/aboutfifa/organisation/footballgovernance/playeragents/list.html).

33. Schattschneider, *Semisovereign People*.

34. As shown by other researches in different polarized communities, fear often prevents people to cross old front lines despite an ongoing peace process (see, for instance, Bairner and Shirlow, 'When Leisure Turns to Fear').

35. Recent researches assess that 'by virtue of the nature of pre-war Bosnia-Herzegovina with more mixed communities and histories of relative tolerance, older people (. . .) have more friends from different nationalities', although 'younger people show a higher preference for mixed friendships' (O'Loughlin, 'Inter-Ethnic Friendships', 48).

36. See Pickering, 'Generating Social Capital'.

37. This would be in line with the broader tendency of contemporary sport to contribute to de-ethnicize nations and to de-territorialize identities (see Poli, 'Denationalization of Sport').

38. About the primacy of the urban–rural factor for questions on current friendship networks, see O'Loughlin, 'Inter-Ethnic Friendships'.

39. 'Sport', *Avaz*, May 27, 2003.

40. See http://www.sarajevo-x.com/sport/reprezentativci-bih-nece-igrati-dok-ne-odu-jelic-domi nkovic-colakovic-i-pasalic/061031019

41. Babić, 'Svi na Koševo'.

42. Zuvela, 'Bosnia Soccer Officials'.

43. As the suspension threatened to damage the then-seemingly-likely qualification of the national team to the European championship in 2012, most of the appeals came from the Bosniaks, who mainly identify with the Bosnian side (while the great majority of the Bosnian Croats and Bosnian Serbs root for Croatia and Serbia, respectively). Nonetheless, pleas also came from the representatives and fans of the Bosnian Serb club Borac from Banja Luka, having just won their first Premijer Liga and therefore expecting to play the UEFA Champions League's preliminaries.

44. See 'Bosnian Leader Appeals to UEFA over Ban'. http://www.kickoff.com/european-league/ 31735/bosnian-leader-appeals-to-uefa-over-ban.php

45. Retrieved from unsa.ba/s/images/stories/pdf/a1-n/uefa.pdf

46. E.T. 'Pjanic: "'Un énorme choc"', *L'Equipe*. http://www.lequipe.fr/Football/breves2011/20110329_ 180655_pjanic-un-enorme-choc.html (accessed March 29, 2011).

47. Wilson, 'Bosnia-Herzegovina's United Return'.

48. Although this does not necessarily mean that match fixing has disappeared – as it rather became more subtle and complex, detaching from the simple rule that 'the home team has to (be made) win' – now results are a little less predictable and therefore the matches are more interesting to the spectators.

49. Škorić, 'Sudije su najveće zlo'.

50. Škorić, 'Osam klubova'.

51. During the WWII, the četniks were the Serbian royalist paramilitary combatants, while the ustaša were the soldiers of the Croatian fascist anti-Yugoslav separatist movement. Both names have been recalled during the recent Yugoslav wars in the 1990s and are mutually used as derogatory terms. The word balija, once used to describe descendants of Turks of Ottoman Empire in the Balkans, has become a slang name used for Bosniaks as an insult or description by Croats or Serbs.

52. The three-finger salute is almost exclusively used by Serbs. Apart from having religious meanings, it had also been used as a nationalist sign before and during the Yugoslav wars, and was often flashed by Serbian soldiers during military operations. Therefore, among Serb opponents in the Yugoslav wars – Croats, Bosniaks and Albanians – the three-finger salute is usually perceived as a provocation, especially when directed at them personally.

53. In the first half of the 2010–2011 season, the average attendance in Premijer Liga was 1563 spectator per match (from the 4167 of the Sarajevo team to the 607 of Olimpik). The highest attendance was 15,000 spectators for Sarajevo, 8000 for both Željezničar and Borac, and 5000 for Celik (http://www.european-football-statistics.co.uk/attn/avebih.htm).

54. Radenović and Karać, 'Sportski tereni'.

55. Dautbegović, 'Huligani u službi'.

56. Hasić, 'Navijački izgredi'.

57. After the decline of the once respected newspaper *Oslobodjenje* (Liberation) – which managed to maintain a multiethnic staff with high professional standards and impartiality even under the tremendous war conditions, but was not able to 'survive the peace' – independent journalism could be mainly found in the two Sarajevian weekly *Dani* and *Slobodna Bosna*, and the newspaper *Nezavisne Novine* from Banja Luka (whose editor-in-chief Željko Kopanja lost both of his legs in a car-bomb assassination attempt in 1999). For a detailed and touching account of

the media's role in the Yugoslavian breakdown, see Kurspahić, *Prime Time Crime*, partially summarized in Kurspahić, 'Missed Opportunities'.

58. See Skaka, 'BHT1 kao megafon'.
59. *Dnevni Avaz*, 'Dodik: Spremni smo'.
60. For a deeper reflection on the complex interplay between mass media, sport and corruption – of which the Bosnian case represents an indirect example – see Numerato, 'Media and Sports Corruption'.
61. Hirschmann, *Exit, Voice, and Loyalty*.

References

Armstrong, Gary. 'The Lords of Misrule: Football and the Rights of the Child in Liberia, West Africa'. *Sport in Society* 7 (2004): 473–502.

Babić, I. 'Svi na Koševo – Spasimo BH. Fudbal' [Everybody to the Koševo stadium – Let's save Bosnian football]. *Sportsport.ba*. http://sportsport.ba/bh_fudbal/svi-na-kosevo--spasimo-bh-fudbal/2980

Bairner, Alan, and Peter Shirlow. 'Territory, Politics and Soccer Fandom in Northern Ireland and Sweden'. *Football Studies* 3 (2000): 5–27.

Bairner, Alan, and Peter Shirlow. 'When Leisure Turns to Fear: Fear, Mobility, and Ethno-Sectarianism in Belfast'. *Leisure Studies* 22 (2003): 203–21.

Belloni, Roberto. *State Building and International Intervention in Bosnia*. London: Routledge, 2008.

Belloni, Roberto, and Bruce Hemmer. 'Bosnia-Herzegovina: Constructing Civil Society under a Semi-Protectorate'. In *Civil Society and Peacebuilding: A Critical Assessment*, ed. T. Paffenholz, 129–52. Boulder, CO: Lynne Rienner, 2010.

Beutler, Ingrid. 'Sport Serving Development and Peace: Achieving the Goals of the United Nations through Sport'. *Sport in Society* 11 (2008): 359–69.

Bieber, Florian. *Post-War Bosnia: Ethnic Structure, Inequality and Governance of the Public Sector*. London: Palgrave Macmillan, 2006.

Bieber, Florian. 'Negotiating Division and Co-operation in Today's Bosnia'. http://fbieber.wordpress.com/2011/05/31/negotiating-division-and-cooperation-in-today%E2%80%99s-bosnia/ (accessed May 31, 2011).

Billig, Michael. *Banal Nationalism*. London: Sage, 1995.

Bose, Sumantra. *Bosnia after Dayton: Nationalist Partition and International Intervention*. London: Hurst, 2002.

Bradley, Joseph M. 'In-Groups, Out-Groups and Contested Identities in Scottish International Football'. *Sport in Society* 14 (2011): 818–32.

Burg, Steven L., and Paul S. Shoup. *The War in Bosnia-Herzegovina*. Armonk, NY: M.E. Sharpe, 1999.

Campbell, David. *National Deconstruction: Violence, Identity and Justice in Bosnia*. Minneapolis: University of Minnesota Press, 1998.

Chandler, David. *Bosnia: Faking Democracy after Dayton*. London: Pluto Press, 2000.

Coalter, Fred. 'Sports Clubs, Social Capital and Social Regeneration: "Ill-Defined Interventions with Hard to Follow Outcomes"?' *Sport in Society* 10 (2007): 537–59.

Dahrendorf, Ralf. *Class and Class Conflict in Industrial Society*, 241–8. Stanford, CA: Stanford University Press, 1959.

Darnell, Simon. 'Power, Politics and Sport for Development and Peace: Investigating the Utility of Sport for International Development'. *Sociology of Sport Journal* 27 (2010): 54–75.

Dautbegović, Mirza. 'BiH osma u svijetu po broju menadžera?' [BiH ranks eighth in the world in number of players managers?]. *Sportsport.ba*. http://www.sportsport.ba/bh_fudbal/bih-osma-u-svijetu-po-broju-menadzera/70396

Dautbegović, Mirza. 'Huligani u službi rušenja Komiteta?' [Hooligans to serve Committee's demolition?]. *Sportsport.ba*. http://sportsport.ba/bh_fudbal/huligani-u-sluzbi-rusenja-komiteta/65275

Dnevni Avaz. 'Dodik: Spremni smo ostati ako dobijemo svoju reprezentaciju, a od BiH uzmemo što nam treba'. [Dodik: We are ready to stay if we get our national team, and if we can take from BiH what we need] http://www.dnevniavaz.ba/vijesti/iz-minute-u-minutu/70862-milorad-dodik-bih-je-u-fazi-raspadanja-i-niko-joj-ne-moze-pomoci-cak-ni-amerikanci.html (accessed December 16, 2011).

Gasser, Patrick K., and Anders Levinsen. 'Breaking Post-War Ice: Open Fun Football Schools in Bosnia and Herzegovina'. *Sport in Society* 7 (2004): 457–72.

Giulianotti, Richard. 'Human Rights, Globalization and Sentimental Education: The Case of Sport'. *Sport in Society* 7 (2004): 355–69.

Giulianotti, Richard. 'Sport, Peacemaking and Conflict Resolution: A Contextual Analysis and Modelling of the Sport, Development and Peace Sector'. *Ethnic and Racial Studies* 34 (2011): 50–71.

Hasić, Nedim. 'Navijački izgredi u Banja Luci i Mostaru izrežirani kako bi se sazvala izvanredna Skupština NS BiH?' [Fans' rows in Banja Luka and Mostar devised in order to have an extraordinary assembly of the NFSBiH convened?]. *Slobodna Bosna*, September 30, 2011.

Hayden, Robert. 'Antagonistic Tolerance: Competitive Sharing of Religious Sites in South Asia and the Balkans'. *Current Anthropology* 43 (2002): 205–31.

Hirschmann, Albert O. *Exit, Voice, and Loyalty: Responses to Decline in Firms, Organizations, and States*. Cambridge, MA: Harvard University Press, 1970.

Jarvie, Grant. 'Sport, Development and Aid: Can Sport Make a Difference?' *Sport in Society* 14 (2011): 241–52.

Kay, Tess. 'Developing through Sport: Evidencing Sport Impacts on Young People'. *Sport in Society* 12 (2009): 1177–91.

Kidd, Bruce. 'A New Social Movement: Sport for Development and Peace'. *Sport in Society* 11 (2008): 370–80.

Kurspahić, Kemal. *Prime Time Crime: Balkan Media in War and Peace*. Washington, DC: United States Institute of Peace Press, 2003.

Kurspahić, Kemal. 'Missed Opportunities in Post-War Bosnia'. In *Media and Glocal Change: Rethinking Communication for Development*, edited by Oscar Hemer and Thomas Tufte, 335–48. Buenos Aires: CLACSO, 2005.

Numerato, Dino. 'The Media and Sports Corruption: An Outline of Sociological Understanding'. *International Journal of Sport Communication*, 2 (2009): 261–73.

Numerato, Dino. 'Between Small Everyday Practices and Glorious Symbolic Acts: Sport-Based Resistance against the Communist Regime in Czechoslovakia'. *Sport in Society* 13 (2010): 107–20.

Oberschall, Anthony. 'The Manipulation of Ethnicity: From Ethnic Cooperation to Violence and War in Yugoslavia'. *Ethnic and Racial Studies* 23 (2000): 982–1001.

O'Loughlin, John. 'Inter-Ethnic Friendships in Post-War Bosnia-Herzegovina: Sociodemographic and Place Influences'. *Ethnicities* 10 (2010): 26–53.

OSCE (Organization for Security and Co-operation in Europe). *Employment Discrimination in Bosnia and Herzegovina*. Sarajevo: OSCE, June 1999.

Pickering, Paula. 'Generating Social Capital for Bridging Ethnic Divisions in the Balkans: Case Studies of Two Bosniak Cities'. *Ethnic and Racial Studies* 29 (2006): 79–103.

Poli, Raffaele. 'The Denationalization of Sport: De-Ethnicization of the Nation and Identity Deterritorialization'. *Sport in Society* 10 (2007): 646–61.

Radenović, Vedran, and Goran Karać. 'Sportski tereni ogledalo situacije u BiH' [Sport pitches mirror the situation in BiH]. *Nezavisne Novine*. http://www.nezavisne.com/sport/fudbal/Sportski-tereni-ogledalo-situacije-u-BiH-108319.html

Rookwood, Joel. *Social Development in Post-Conflict Communities: Building Peace through Sport in Africa and the Middle East*. Saarbrücken: VDM, 2009.

Schattschneider, Elmer Eric. *The Semisovereign People: A Realist's View of Democracy in America*. New York: Holt, Rinehart and Winston, 1960.

Schulenkorf, Nico. 'Sport Events and Ethnic Reconciliation: Attempting to Create Social Change in War-Torn Sri Lanka'. *International Review for the Sociology of Sport* 45 (2010): 273–94.

Sekulić, Duško, Garth Massey, and Randy Hodson. 'Ethnic Intolerance and Ethnic Conflict in the Dissolution of Yugoslavia'. *Ethnic and Racial Studies* 29 (2006): 797–827.

Sekulić, Tatjana. 'Forced Migration and Perception of Borders: War-Migrant Associations as a Resource of Integration'. In *The Borders of the Polity: Migration and Security across the EU and the Balkans*, ed. L. Chiodi, 81–100. Ravenna: Longo Editore, 2005.

Skaka, M. 'BHT1 kao megafon za glas nacionalne mržnje' [BHT1 as a megaphone for the voice of national hatred]. *Sportsport.ba*. http://sportsport.ba/bh_fudbal/bht1-kao-megafon-za-glas-nacionalne-mrznje/63154 (accessed August 25, 2011).

Škorić, E. 'Sudije su najveće zlo bih. fudbala' [Referees are the greatest evil in Bosnian football]. *Sportsport.ba*. http://www.sportsport.ba/bh_fudbal/sudije-su-najvece-zlo-bh-nogometa/67279 (accessed October 31, 2011).

Škorić, E.. 'Osam klubova se bori za bolje sutra'. [Eight clubs fight for a better tomorrow] http://www.sportsport.ba/bh_fudbal/osam-klubova-se-bori-za-bolje-sutra/68160 *Sportsport.ba*. (accessed November 14, 2011).

Sorek, Tamir. *Arab Soccer in a Jewish State: The Integrative Enclave*. Cambridge: Cambridge University Press, 2007.

Spaaij, Ramón. 'The Social Impact of Sport: Diversities, Complexities and Contexts'. *Sport in Society* 12 (2009): 1109–17.

Strazzari, Francesco. 'The Decade Horribilis: Organized Violence and Organized Crime along the Balkan Peripheries, 1991–2001'. *Mediterranean Politics* 12 (2007): 185–209.

Sugden, John and Bairner, Alan, eds. *Sport in Divided Societies*. Aachen: Meyer & Meyer Sport, 1999.

Torsti, Pilvi. 'History Culture and Banal Nationalism in Post-War Bosnia'. *Southeast European Politics* 5 (2004): 142–57.

Turner, Victor. *The Ritual Process: Structure and Anti-Structure*. Chicago, IL: Aldine, 1969.

Vermeulen, Jeroen, and Paul Verweel. 'Participation in Sport: Bonding and Bridging as Identity Work'. *Sport in Society* 12 (2009): 1206–19.

Wilson, Jonathan. 'Bosnia-Herzegovina's United Return to International Football'. *The Guardian*. http://www.guardian.co.uk/football/blog/2011/jun/03/bosnia-herzegovina-fifa- euro-2012 (accessed June 3, 2011).

Woodward, Susan L. 'Bosnia after Dayton'. In *After the Peace: Resistance and Reconciliation*, ed. Robert L. Rothstein, 139–66. Boulder, CO: Lynne Rienner, 1999.

Zuvela, Maja. 'Bosnia Soccer Officials Jailed for 5 Years Over Tax'. *Reuters.com*. http://uk.reuters.com/article/2009/11/23/bosnia-court-soccer-idUKGEE5AM1E020091123 (accessed November 23, 2009).

'A lofty battle for the nation': the social roles of sport in Tudjman's Croatia

Dario Brentin

School of Slavonic and Eastern European Studies, University College London, London, UK

In post-socialist Croatia, sport can be described as a unique source of social knowledge contributing greatly to the formation, establishment and conservation of the emerging national identity after the country's secession from socialist Yugoslavia in 1990–1991. Throughout the 1990s, sport, including interpretation, images, metaphors and actual events, proved to be a highly politicized form of national expression in which narratives of nation, identity and culture were intensely articulated. After all, the country's first president, Franjo Tudjman, proclaimed that 'football victories shape a nation's identity as much as wars do', showing a remarkable awareness of the galvanizing effect sport can have in times of crisis. This paper examines narratives expressed within the field, pointing out how ideological contents were transmitted through sport events, media reports and fan culture in order to show what functions and social roles sport had taken during the first 10 years of Croatian independence.

Introduction

The starting point for this research is the general assumption expressed by Sack and Suster that 'given the intensity of ethnic and nationalist sentiments in the Balkans and the importance of sport [. . .] in this region, the former Yugoslav Republic provides a natural laboratory for examining the intimate connections between sport, religion, ethnicity, and nationalism'.[1] A closer look at the relevant literature reveals that in the case of post-socialist Croatia, sport can be described as a unique and malleable source of social knowledge contributing greatly to the formation, establishment and conservation of emerging national identity after the country's secession from Yugoslavia in 1990–1991. Moreover, scholars agree that throughout the 1990s, sport, including interpretation, images, metaphors and actual events, proved to be a highly politicized form of Croatian national expression in which narratives of nation, identity and culture were intensely articulated.[2] Yet, sport has remained a peripheral research topic within the (post-)Yugoslav context, with the existing scholarship largely focusing on isolated and 'sporadic outbursts of ethnic hatred in sport arenas',[3] leaving its other significant social functions – i.e. strengthening national defence, endorsing social control, influencing foreign or economic policies, (re-)producing traditional gender roles, etc. – as an under-researched aspect of the region's nation- and identity-building processes.

Throughout this time, the Croatian state and society experienced extensive political, economic, cultural and social changes. While the introduction of multiparty elections in 1990 ultimately resulted in secession from the Socialist Federative Republic of Yugoslavia, the establishment of statehood and international recognition, the post-socialist transition remains predominantly characterized by the *Homeland War*,[4] ethnic polarization, societal deterioration, severe economic disruption and authoritarian regime policies.[5] The first democratic elections in April and May 1990 saw Franjo Tudjman and his party, the Croatian Democratic Union (*Hrvatska Demokratska Zajednica* – HDZ), win a two-thirds majority in parliament and set the ground for the president's political hegemony over the next decade. Although the political success of the 'state-building forces' (*državotvorne snage*) initially unleashed an outpour of national euphoria and consequently led Croatia into independence, Tudjman's autocratic style of government – evident in his influence on state institutions and organizations, the expansion of presidential authorities, his interventions in civil society and popular culture or the firm control of the media – triggered international isolation and often only exacerbated inherited social and political problems. During his presidency, ethno-nationalist ideology became the prism through which Croatian politics of identity were conceptualized and promulgated, resulting in the dominance of nationalist narratives in almost all fields of life and everyday parlance.[6] As the self-proclaimed *spiritus rector* of the Croatian nationalist movement and 'father of the nation', Tudjman operated as the main ideologist and sole political leader presiding over Croatia in an increasingly undemocratic manner as his regime lingered.

In such a political culture, the field of sport repeatedly epitomized central ideological narratives imposed by the government – often the president himself[7] – functioning as an 'icebreaker'[8] for future political developments and an influential transmitter of political and symbolic messages. This paper's objectives are therefore to reconstruct how Croatian sport was (mis-)used as a mobilizing tool to generate popular support for Tudjman's 'national idea' and to legitimize his rule, as well as to illustrate when the limits of exploitation would be reached. Shifting the analytical focus away from single and/or de-contextualized sporting events, this approach will offer a more balanced perspective of sport's symbolic significance in the country's nation- and identity-building processes.

Sporting nationalism, identity and nation-building

Over the past two decades, several influential nationalism scholars have argued that modern sport has become one of the major rituals of popular culture, substantiating concepts of the nation as an 'imagined community'.[9] By encompassing social axioms, structures, norms and values, it significantly contributes to their reproduction and therefore qualifies as an 'integral part of society [...] which may be used as a means of *reflecting on society*'.[10] The ceremonial and ritual surroundings of sporting competitions represent 'arenas for the display of national symbols and the alignment of national allegiances'[11] functioning as moments of national crystallization. Expressed through an array of cultural symbols – national flags, anthems, songs, chants, colours and folklore – which signal preferred conceptions of national unity and powerfully invoke feelings of identity, representative sport conveys a public expression of national identity. While uniting people domestically, these symbols simultaneously project national distinctiveness and individuality on an international stage drawing external boundaries against others.

For post-socialist Croatia, Alex Bellamy writes that due to the disastrous conditions in other areas of everyday life affected by the *Homeland War*, sport played a significant role in 'forging Croatian unity, promoting Croatia internationally and creating a popular homogenising sense of national pride'.[12] Generally, we can observe that, particularly in times of crisis and conflict, the cultural domain of sport often becomes a highly politicized terrain enabling the ruling government to 'enhance prestige, secure legitimacy, compensate for deficiencies in other areas of life [or] pursue international rivalry by peaceful means'.[13] John Hoberman describes this 'sportive nationalism' as the 'ambition to see a nation's athlete excel in the international arena [which] may be promoted by a political elite or [...] may be felt by many citizens without the promptings of national leaders'.[14] It gains its strongest momentum in its elusive opposition towards official forms of nationalism orchestrated by government propaganda, appearing to foster a purely emotional and 'passionate nationalism' which transcends political, social and ideological boundaries. The phenomenon of 'sporting nationalism' has consequently received considerable academic attention,[15] often being emphasized as an ambiguous social phenomenon due to its capacity to legitimize and undermine political authority at the same time.

However, in the first decade of Croatian independence – although offering some spaces for agency – sport generally proved to be a social field where alternative political standpoints remained marginalized and almost non-existent. The country's president, Franjo Tudjman, stated that 'after war, sport is the first thing by which you can distinguish nations'[16] and as such a salient national habitus code, it needed close monitoring and political guidance. Experienced in how quickly sport can turn into a contestation of political power, the HDZ government was adamant in keeping Croatian sport strictly centralized with the president himself, or politically loyal *nomenklatura*, in control of 'sporting associations, clubs, coaches, referees, delegates for international tournaments' all the way to 'sport editors and commentators'.[17] Tudjman later often emphasized that during the war, he 'knew about the importance of sport [and] personally governed the procurement of some people into sport'. He continued asserting that:

> it is politics, which [should] decisively influences sport [because] everything is politics [and while] they say sport should be separated from politics, that economy should be separated from politics [...] I am telling you, such a thing does not exist.[18]

The president's extensive personal involvement enabled him to interfere in clubs' financial matters and to appoint coaches, reaching comic levels at times with him 'dictating' who should play for the national team or indicating what scoreline 'he would like to see' for certain games.[19] An arguable pinnacle of political interventions in sport was disclosed in the summer of 1999, when the political weekly *Nacional* published documents proving that Croatian football league referees were systematically put under pressure by people close to the president's office in order to secure *Dinamo Zagreb* – which had the name *Croatia Zagreb* back then (the name change will be detailed later) – the win of the 1998–1999 Croatian football championship.[20]

Sport as a 'national motor'

In the late 1980s, Yugoslav sport and in particular Yugoslav football rapidly deteriorated into an ideologically contested terrain with supporters increasingly demonstrating a strong sense of national allegiance. Expressions of nationalist sentiments – the appearance of 'national' flags and various *Ustaša* and *Četnik* symbols, the singing of 'forbidden and nationalistic song' and the open pronouncement of anti-Yugoslav sentiments or hatred against 'other' republics – were repeatedly articulated, transforming sport stadia into 'stands of free will'[21] open to otherwise rigorously sanctioned political standpoints. Although predominantly visible within the relatively small and socially marginalized community of 'football fan tribes',[22] the tense situation in sporting arenas resulted in reoccurring and brutal violence emblematizing the critical and fragile condition of the Yugoslav state system in the late 1980s and early 1990s. Manifested through acute economic problems, hyperinflation and a drastic rise in unemployment, the inability of Yugoslavia's communist regime to resolve the crisis gradually aggravated social problems across the federation accompanied by the rise of nationalist politics and demands for stronger autonomy in some republics. The diverse political standpoints on how to solve the crisis eventually culminated at the extraordinary 14th Congress of the League of Communists of Yugoslavia (LCY) in January 1990 when the Croatian and Slovenian delegation walked out as a sign of protest against the Serbian standpoint. This political statement ultimately resulted in the dissolution of a unitary LCY and the establishment of a multiparty system.

In this phase of political turmoil and general insecurity, football-related violence peaked on 13 May 1990 when the game between the 'eternal' rivals in the Yugoslav football league *Dinamo Zagreb* and *Crvena Zvezda Beograd* at Zagreb's *Maksimir* stadium had to be suspended due to violent clashes between the opposing set of fans, who turned the stadium into a 'gladiatorial arena of madness and hate, danger and rage'.[23] Two decades later, the dominant narratives in Yugoslav successor states suggest that the riots represent the 'symbolic date when the Yugoslav dissolution began' – 'the day, the war started'.[24] Only two weeks after Tudjman's election as president, the tensely awaited game escalated into wild stadium and street fights, with the club's hooligan groups – the *Crvena Zvezda* fan group *Delije*, who were headed by the future Serbian war criminal and paramilitary leader Željko Ražnatović (better known as Arkan), and the *Dinamo* fan group *Bad Blue Boys* (*BBB*) – clashing. It resulted in the worst riots in Yugoslav sporting history. Journalists across the country described it as a Dantean 'circle of hell' where 'something wild awoke'.[25] According to Croatian accounts, the police – widely perceived as a mechanism of Serb domination – acted inadequately, intervening 'suspiciously' late, 'focusing' solely on the *BBB* and openly protecting the *Crvena Zvezda* supporters.[26] The Serbian press counter-narrative saw the events as a meticulously planned incident, orchestrated by Croatia's new government, which wanted to exploit the riots politically.[27] However, the riots should be understood as a 'condensed symptom' of an ongoing political radicalization in the Croatian and Serbian republics and a deductive 'consequence'[28] of these polarizing policies. Srđan Vrcan argues that:

> in fact, in the attitudes, behaviour and actions as well as the contents of mass chants and symbols used in Zagreb, Split and Belgrade [...] one could already see the unambiguous signals of a breakdown of the ruling socialist system and the appearance [...] of political strategies that would lead to the unavoidable conflicts [...] and consequently to a war.[29]

In the following weeks, the event served as a strong argument for one of HDZ's main political demands, the reduction of Belgrade-based governmental influence over police and state institutions in Croatia. By posing the question whether 'their police' could still be in charge of securing 'us', the government strategically underlined the 'urgent necessity'[30] for structural reforms.

Amidst the chaotic scenes of that day, one particular incident of great symbolic weight can be singled out. At one point, *Dinamo*'s team captain, Zvonimir Boban, entered the rioting crowd to help a *Dinamo* supporter who was being beaten by police. His – meanwhile – 'mythical'[31] kick against an officer strikingly captured the antagonisms of Yugoslavia's political situation and made him instantly 'immortal' not only for *Dinamo* fans, but also for many Croats. Boban's attack was perceived as a brave act of resistance against an alleged 'Serbian hegemony' within Yugoslav institutions, blatantly demonstrated by the unwillingness of the police to defend *Dinamo* supporters. Not even a month later, on 3 June 1990, the Yugoslav football association, in an attempt to regain the affection of Zagreb supporters, staged the last preparatory match ahead of the 1990 FIFA Football World Cup for the Yugoslav side against the Netherlands at *Maksimir* stadium. The officials had entirely misjudged the situation and the extent of fan politicization, which is why the game is mostly remembered for the spectators' behaviour; the predominantly Croat crowd of 20,000 shouted down the Yugoslav national anthem, insulted Yugoslav team players, cheered for the opposition and jeered national coach Ivica Osim, attacking him for allegedly disregarding Croatian players.[32]

By August 1990, the Yugoslav state crises had alarmingly deepened with the jibe rhetoric of the preceding months and the inability to resolve the 'constitutional crisis', leading to the so-called 'log revolution' (*balvan revolucija*). It saw the Serbian minority in the *Krajina* region revolting against Croatian governance by sealing off the region around the city of Knin, thus bringing the country to the brink of war. Over the next few weeks, the political situation remained tense with the Yugoslav People's Army backing the Serb rebels and preventing Croatian police forces from intervening to re-establish state power. This ongoing polarization was highly anticipated by Croatian 'fan tribes' and so on 26 September 1990, only 90 kilometres away from the uprising's epicentre, yet another football game caught Yugoslav-wide media attention. During a regular league game between *Hajduk Split* and *Partizan Beograd*, the home crowd made a far-reaching political statement when the organized section of *Hajduk* spectators – *Torcida* – invaded the pitch, set the Yugoslav flag on fire and hoisted the Croatian check-board flag while chanting 'Croatia – independent state'.[33] Hailed with 'salvoes of acclaim', the few hundred organized *Torcida* fans operated under the impressions of constant 'burn the flag' – chants coming from the spectators who remained in the stands.[34] Dražen Lalić attributes the game's significance to the fact that the aggression was not directed towards an opposing set of fans but directly against the Yugoslav state and its symbols. If the *Maksimir* riots are interpreted as the 'day the war started', then this game had to be termed as the 'day Yugoslavia stopped existing' (at least on sporting grounds) with the symbolic burning of the most meaningful national symbol which signalled a total lack of state legitimacy.[35]

Sport as an actor of international diplomacy

During the summer 1990, the HDZ government intensely pursued their political agenda by emphatically asserting nationalist standpoints and pushing towards independence. Wanting to create international support for the emerging nation- and state-building processes, Tudjman showed a remarkable awareness for the potentially influential role sport could have in affirming the government's political goals. An opportunity to capitalize politically from a sporting competition came at the peak of the *Krajina* crisis in late August 1990, when the coastal city of Split was to host the European Athletics Championships. Tudjman saw the games as a great chance to 'present Croatia to the world', to display his government's 'democratic maturity' and to underline Croatia's membership of 'old, good Europe's course of civilisation'.[36] Hence, the opening ceremony and its symbolic messages were consciously elaborated as a cultural performance promoting a particular 'narrative of nation'[37] which ostensibly represented the 'new values' of the host nation. Yugoslav's five-pointed star flags were outnumbered '1:1000' by Croatian flags including the historical coat of arms, and the attendees expressed a clear and distinctive sign of belonging by singing the Croatian national anthem in a state of 'emotional ecstasy',[38] while the president stressed in his opening speech that the event had more than a 'ceremonial, but a real and important meaning'[39] for the recognition of the political changes in the socialist federation.

As part of HDZ's efforts to galvanize popular support, numerous mass demonstrations and celebrations were organized all over the country throughout that summer and autumn. Most notably, on 16 October 1990, the Croatian government staged a 'grandiose celebration of mammoth proportions'[40] celebrating the re-installation of the *Ban Josip Jelačić* statue – a symbol for the Croatian resistance against the Ottoman forces removed during communist rule – in Zagreb's main square. An international football game between a selection of Croatian football players was also organized – advertised as the 'Croatian national team' – and the USA national football team. Although the Croatian branch of the Yugoslav Football Association had to use a legal loophole that allowed selections of republics to play against other international teams, the sheer fact that the game took place was seen as a huge diplomatic success. Regardless of what the game's outcome would be – the Croatian side won 2:1 – the game was perceived as an 'undeletable sign of international recognition of Croatia in the world of democracy'.[41] The spectacle glorified – as headlined by the daily *Večernji list* – the 'unsubmissive spirit of the Croatian people' with the crowd perpetually chanting traditional songs and political slogans such as 'Let's take Knin, we're not giving up Croatia!' or 'To battle, to battle, for your nation'.[42] Extensively using Croatian national symbols, particularly the checkerboard pattern, to juxtapose the present US symbols, the event also served to associate the proclaimed government's political affiliation with 'western values' and to suggest an informal recognition by the USA. The spectacle's dimensions, the 'vividness of the symbolism',[43] the charged atmosphere and belligerent rhetoric left no space for interpretation, but clearly signalled to the world's greatest power the irrevocable wish for independence.

Two months later, in December 1990, the Croatian parliament passed a new, ethno-nationalized constitution which had been first introduced to the public as a manifesto shortly after the *Maksimir* riots. Identifying Croatia henceforth as the homeland of Croats and thereby downgrading the Serb minority from a constitutional nation to the status of a minority, the already strained relations between the Croatian government and the *Krajina* Serbs subsequently worsened and led to a series of isolated armed incidents between Serbian paramilitaries and Croatian troops during the spring of 1991. At this point, the relationship between the Serbian and Croatian government, as they sought to restructure everyday life along ethnic lines, had worsened to such an extent that peaceful coexistence in one federative state seemed increasingly unfeasible. Soon after Croatia and Slovenia's declaration of independence on 25 June 1991, the military conflict escalated into a full-scale war.

Once the *Homeland War* broke out, many established athletes, in order to create pressure on the United Nations (UN) and the 'western world' – i.e. the footballer Davor Šuker, or Dražen Petrović, Dino Rađa and Toni Kukoč[44] who were among the first European basketball players to find success in the National Basketball Association – protested in various ways demanding help and immediate action from the international community. High-profile athletes refused to play for Yugoslavia, initiated the removal of Yugoslav flags at international tournaments, took part in international funding tours, demonstrated outside the UN headquarter or gave pathos-loaded interviews to international media, fighting 'their war' by peaceful means with the 'checker board on their forehead and the flag in their hands'.[45] 'Anyone can go and fight', tennis player Goran Prpić said, explaining why he had not taken up arms, 'because someone has to tell the world what's happening in Croatia'.[46] Tudjman affirmed athletes' outstanding significance saying that Croatian 'circumstances [sport had] a higher political dimension than elsewhere [because] when the world didn't want an independent Croatia our athletes contributed to the affirmation and recognition of our homeland, often more than some ambassadors',[47] especially because Croatia had no diplomatic missions abroad. During the first years of the war, another tennis player, Goran Ivanišević, proved to be one of the most notable 'patriotic defenders' of his country. His credo, 'my racket is my gun', was his way of 'fighting for the Croatian cause against the Serb propaganda' while 'his friends were dying in the war'.[48] When the international community recognized Croatia's independence in January 1992, the Croatian government asserted that this 'historical victory' was also partly achieved due to sports officials' and athletes' tireless endeavours taking over 'the responsible mission [to] interpret the incidents, inform about the atrocities of the war and spread the message of peace'[49] to the world. Although the intensity of the war decreased in the spring of 1992, athletes continued to be significant international promoters and advocates of the dominant national narrative on the *Homeland War*, securing its legitimacy and legacy.

Sport as a legitimator of politics

In the years following the signing of the Dayton Peace Accords in 1995, Croatia was still confronted by numerous challenges. The social and economic development was stagnating while thousands of displaced people and refugees awaited return to their homes. Many soldiers who had fought during the *Homeland War* returned to destroyed and deserted hometowns. In addition, Croatia's reputation suffered with the first indictments made by International Criminal Tribunal for the former Yugoslavia and international isolation. Bellamy argues that in the aftermath of the *Homeland War*, the HDZ purposefully mobilized athletes' international achievements in order to create a popular homogenizing sense of national pride, which could not be provided by other 'failed' social fields.[50] The political elites tried to transform the enthusiasm generated by sporting success into tangible political capital by using the national team's sporting superiority for the symbolic enhancement of the ruling political elite. These 'politics of *panem et circenses*' are best exemplified by the 1998 FIFA Football World Cup where the national team's success was portrayed as a sublimation of national character, culture, and collective will and strength.

Croatia finished third in the tournament and the success was ascribed to a unique feeling of togetherness, motivation and resilience uniting the national team with 'its people', drawing them mutually into a 'deep horizontal comradeship'.[51] Identified as a non-hierarchical community, every single victory was portrayed as a victory of the Croatian people, 'the result of the Croatian battle for freedom and independence'[52] and hence an evocative victory of the Croatian state and its political elites. The national team coach Miroslav 'Ćiro' Blažević repeatedly highlighted the president's 'invaluable role' declaring that 'without him all my young players would play for Yugoslavia and not for Croatia; [without] his bravery and his party we would not have experienced any of this'.[53] The team captain and 'national hero', Zvonimir Boban, added that the president had to be acknowledged for being the 'father of all things we Croats love, also the father of our national team'.[54] On return, Tudjman personally congratulated the players in front of a crowd of more than 100,000, insuring them that 'the entire Croatian people, numbering some eight million, from the homeland and abroad stood behind you'[55] attributing the success to the 'Croatian spirit' rather than actual skill. For a whole month, Croats 'across the homeland and from abroad were united' in a ritualistic performance of national unity 'around the common, holy interest – the national team's success'.[56] The ecstatic level of intensity with which the tournament was celebrated recalls Emile Durkheim's notion of 'collective effervescence'[57] to describe the essence of the ritualistic experience and its power to function as the nation's integrative cultural force. Tudjman elaborated that:

> sport is an integral part of the social and national life of a country [but] when you have equal physical conditions, not to mention material conditions, there is something above that. That is conscience, the will, and that is what our athletes have gained with the formation of Croatia.[58]

In his narrative the nation had returned to its essence, its 'initial phase of unity',[59] celebrating a spectacle of genuine patriotism.

Critical commentators, however, were quick to interpret the excessive exploitation and identification with the sporting achievement as a 'pathetic and desperate act' to divert the public's focus from the 'countless problems and political apathy' Croatia faced in the weeks and months prior to the tournament.[60] In 1997, Tudjman rejected the European Union's Regional Approach policy towards the 'Western Balkans' as being another attempt to force Croatia into a supranational entity with its neighbours, a re-establishment of a new Yugoslavia. It was particularly due to HDZ's unwillingness to cooperate in return of Serbian refugees who had fled the country after the military operations *Oluja* and *Blijesak*[61] in 1995, which left the country in 'unofficial isolation' with the European Union freezing Croatia's integration process.[62] Despite the criticism, Tudjman's isolationist politics indirectly gained legitimacy during the tournament when the international commentary addressed the level of nationalist euphoria and started scrutinizing Croatia's recent past. Some reports – although being rather scattered – portrayed Croatia as 'the most disgusting small nation in Europe' (*London Evening Standard*) saturated with 'fascist undertones' (*The Guardian*), causing outraged reactions. The attacks were shrugged off as 'remains of their genetically inserted colonial superiority'[63] and presented as evidence proving Europe's unchanged 'hypocritical' position 'against the formation of an independent Croatia'.[64]

Constructing identity against the 'other'

According to the presidential narrative, Croatia's formative years were defined as a time when the nation was denied a peaceful separation from socialist Yugoslavia to fulfil its democratic and historically legitimate right to independence. The Croatian people were subsequently forced into a bloody war triggered by nationalistic 'Greater-Serbian' aspirations towards 'holy' Croatian territory. This dominant binary of a 'peace and freedom loving Croatia' and an 'imperialistic and ferocious Serbia' prevailed during the war years and remained a potent marker of difference and 'othering' throughout the 1990s.[65] Since 'Croatianness' was defined in strict opposition to anything perceived as 'Yugoslav', the dichotomy between 'Croatia versus Yugoslavia' was determined as a significant element of national self-understanding. Thus whenever a Croatian team faced a Yugoslav team, sport transformed into a rallying point reasserting national identity in opposition to 'them', transferring war cleavages onto the sport field and constructing the games in question as a continuation of the *Homeland War* by other means.

Although Croatian sports officials called for calm whenever the national team faced a Yugoslav team – in order to demonstrate civilized behaviour and distance Croatian society from the 'wild and brutal Balkan'[66] fan culture – the games were emotionally and nationalistically charged. Hence, every defeat was titled a 'national tragedy' and every victory proclaimed a 'symbolic pay-back for all humiliation [. . .] we had to endure from the Great-Serbian aggressor'.[67] As much as fans and athletes, media commentators often expressed joy over 'historical' victories 'against those from the East' through the glorification of and comparison with the military operations *Oluja* and *Blijesak* as an additional way of humiliating their opponents and suggesting Croatian overall superiority.[68] These games were furthermore signified by a discourse of victimization and sacrifice in reference to the *Homeland War*. Particularly the city of Vukovar, a besieged and heavily bombarded Slavonian city during the war, was frequently mentioned as the sole motivator and driving force behind Croatian performances.[69] The fate of this completely destroyed city, which had been under UN transitional administration (UNITAES) until January 1998, is one of the constituting myths of post-socialist Croatia and still symbolizes a central moment of Croatian resistance, suffering and heroism during the *Homeland War*.[70] It was important to tell 'them the truth, [tell] them who suffered', the captain of the Croatian water polo team, Dubravko Šimenc, explained after a quarter-final encounter at the 1996 Olympic Games and dedicated the 'victory to Vukovar, to anyone who endured and suffered'.[71]

The biggest national spectacle, 'the game that wins the war',[72] took place in the autumn of 1999, when the two countries met in a qualification tie for the 2000 UEFA European Football Championships. Since football was considered the 'national sport' in both Croatia and Yugoslavia, the encounter was defined as the most prestigious and meaningful thus far. The game was additionally charged since the victor would go on to participate in the tournament. Only a year earlier, Tudjman confidently declared that his team would win this game because 'we have a team that knows that we are fighting for Croatia, against Yugoslavia, for one's homeland's reputation [while] the Yugoslav team will not be able to feature such homogeneity'.[73] The game was staged as a huge 'national spectacle', with patriotic musical acts being performed hours before the game had started. In the stadium, a huge, penalty-area-wide Croatian flag with a 'Vukovar '91' insignia was unfurled and wounded war veterans were 'presented' to the crowd as the heroes whose fight had made it possible for everyone to be there, 'reminding' the audience and the players of what was at stake. Although ending in a draw, the result meant that Yugoslavia progressed to the European Championships. The charged atmosphere, orchestrated and induced from above as to serve for electoral purposes at a time when HDZ's political dominance was already eroding, suggested that the game should have become an 'instantaneous myth' demonstrating an execution of ultimate superiority over the former enemy. However, it turned into a symbolic end for Tudjman with him and numerous members of his *nomenklatura* watching their downfall. 'If we lose, Tudjman will never be president again',[74] a young spectator said in an interview before the game and was to be proven correct. Two months later, in December 1999, Tudjman died from cancer only a few weeks before the scheduled presidential elections. In January 2000, a centre-left coalition government was elected and set out to change Croatia's political system by reducing presidential powers, introducing economic reforms to combat nepotism and corruption, and pursuing better cooperation with European institutions.

Politics of symbols and resistance

Croatian independence brought with it a fundamental revision of historical, political and social identities organized from above, with the state rigidly 'nationalizing'[75] public and symbolic space and eradicating previous Yugoslav symbols (flag, anthem, street names, monuments, etc.). As sport was ascribed the function of a powerful symbolic signifier, it was not spared these changes. While the removal of the Yugoslav's five-point star from their club's emblem by *Hajduk Split* players during the 1990 Australia summer tour was an entirely deliberate and proactive choice, echoed positively as a patriotic gesture, Tudjman's decision to rename *Dinamo Zagreb* sparked a heated protest accompanied by unexpected and unfavourable repercussions. The president had identified the club's name as not sufficiently 'national', handicapped by Yugoslav and socialist symbolic connotations and therefore could not be integrated in the newly established ethno-national narrative. A name change was propounded which saw the new club's name as a combination of two pre-WWII Zagreb clubs (*HAŠK* (*Hrvatski Akademski Sportski Klub*) and *Građanski*) signalling a return to pre-Communist culture and a clear break from Yugoslav sporting tradition. Two years later, the name was changed again, this time from *HAŠK Građanski* to *Croatia Zagreb*, tying the club unambiguously to the nation-building project.[76] Although underlining the invaluable role *Dinamo* had played throughout the communist rule in guarding the 'national essence' at a time when the expression of any patriotic feelings was punishable, club officials insisted that an alien and artificial name had been forced upon them. There is a 'Dinamo in Moscow, Kiev, Minsk, Tbilisi, Bucharest, Dresden, Tirana and Pančevo. But not in Zagreb',[77] Tudjman declared and made it clear that 'his' club cannot hold a name which stands for 'Stalinism, Bolshevism or repression'.[78]

However, the president failed to anticipate possible objections to a second politically motivated name change in two years and was quickly confronted with vehement opposition from the club's most influential fan group, the *BBB*. Formed in 1986, the group had constructed its fan identity on the basis of Croatian nationalism and anti-communism during the late 1980s eliminating any socialist or pro-Yugoslav connotation in the process.[79] BBB's fierce hostility towards the 'sport Frankenstein'[80] was exhibited through protest actions directly targeting Tudjman.[81] The president, not used to criticism, launched an acrimonious political campaign which included branding the *BBB* as 'foreign agents', 'anti-Croatian', 'alcoholics', 'drug-addicts' or 'Yugonostalgics',[82] demonizing their behaviour and blatant exposure to police harassment and persecution. With their 'Croatianness' questioned and denied, they felt betrayed – having been among the first to volunteer for the *Homeland War* and having openly expressed support[83] for the HDZ before it came to power – and not prepared to back off from their demands for the return of their *Dinamo*. Back in the early stages of the war, the Croatian army forces admitted a considerable number of volunteers who were recruited from the country's biggest football fan clubs (i.e. *BBB*, *Torcida* and *Armada*). In the aftermath of the war, some football clubs installed commemorative monuments in front of their stadia remembering 'their' dead and pledging their allegiance to the 'homeland'. In front of *Maksimir* stadium, the monument erected by the *BBB* in 1994 is dedicated 'to all Dinamo fans for whom the war started on 13 May 1990 and ended by laying their lives on the altar of the Croatian homeland'.[84] Formulated as a specific counter-narrative to authoritarian politics, the *BBB* protest eventually grew into a serious challenge to the dominant definition of 'Croatianness' propagated by the Tudjman regime and remained a troublesome spot until the president's death. After the general elections in 2000, the club was immediately renamed *Dinamo Zagreb* again.

Conclusion

Throughout the first decade of Croatian independence, athletes perpetually suggested that competing on the nation's behalf was 'more'[85] than 'just sport'. It was their 'duty' as 'Croatians' to fight a 'lofty battle for Croatia',[86] it was their way of fighting for independence and their way of participating in building national identity and promoting a certain image of Croatia, which would be free of stereotypes and fears of a repeating past. With the country's first president, Franjo Tudjman – often portrayed as a unique embodiment of 'statesman, historian, warrior, and sportsman'[87] – trying to conceptualize and foster a 'state-building sport' (*državotvorni sport*) which would support the dominant state narratives, sport adopted the function of a key symbol for creating a distinctive Croatian nationhood. It was the athletes' responsibility to represent a 'true manifestation and incorporation of almost all positive attributes attached to Croatians' and to be 'recognised by their original and true Croatianness'.[88]

Apart from the *Dinamo Zagreb* name dispute, symbolizing 'the total colonization of the social reality by the systemic ideological and symbolic contents'[89] and its failure to impose its own interpretation upon all parts of society, the Croatian sports field would remain a potent vehicle for expressing dominant conceptions of nationhood and inducing political homogeneity. The criminalizing feud against the *BBB* has to be seen as part of what Chip Gangnon called political 'strategies of demobilization'[90] which enabled the government to deprive ideological alternatives from challenging the state's symbolic space and power or to articulate truly challenging oppositional narratives. Ultimately sport-related narratives should pervasively assist the country's political elite in perpetuating a particular ideological goal: to meld and totalize the idea of the 'birth of Croatian statehood from the heroic and defensive *Homeland War*' with Tudjman's persona and the HDZ as his infrastructural apparatus. The construction of such a constitutive myth was of paramount importance to secure political legitimacy and to label any opposition as potentially devastating for Croatian national sovereignty. Recalling Rogers Brubaker's conception of nationalism as a product of 'political fields',[91] sport was used as a political communicator linking it to the symbolic power of the state and enabling political elites to exploit the social field as a powerful signifier of national identity.

Acknowledgements

I would like to thank Eric Gordy for his valuable comments and expert supervision. I am further indebted as ever to Thomas Jackson for his input.

Notes

1. Sack and Suster, 'Soccer and Croatian Nationalism', 307.
2. See Sack and Suster, 'Soccer and Croatian Nationalism'; Vrcan, *Nogomet, politika, nasilje*, 79–137; Dolić, 'Die Fußballnationalmannschaft als'; Bellamy, *Formation of Croatian National Identity*, 112–21; Džihić, 'Fußball am Balkan'; Biti, 'Vatreni – hrvatski nogometni proizvod'; Pezo, 'Sport i hrvatski identitet'.
3. Perica, 'United They Stood', 267; see also Nielsen, 'Goalposts of Transition', 88; Bartoluci, 'Sport, nacionalni identitet i nacionalizam', 86.
4. The 'Croatian War for Independence' was fought by forces loyal to the newly elected government of Croatia and the Yugoslav People's Army (JNA), operating with local Serb forces from the *Krajina* region and Eastern Slavonia, from 1991 and ended with the signing of the Dayton Peace Accords in the summer of 1995. The presidential 'Tudjmanist' narrative insisted on referring to the conflict as the Homeland War (*Domovinski rat*). Due to its ideological and political connotation, the term will be used in *italics*. For a detailed analysis of the conflict, see Magaš and Žanić, *War in Croatia*, 1–131.
5. Søberg, 'Croatia Since 1989', 31; see also Goldstein, *Croatia*, 257–63.
6. See Jović and Lamont, 'Introduction – Croatia after Tuđman'; Uzelak, 'Franjo Tudjman's Nationalist Ideology'; Winland, 'Ten Years Later'; Malešević, *Ideology, Legitimacy and the New State*, 223–72.
7. 'Tuđman se u sport upletao više nego Tito' [Tudjman interfered in sport more than Tito], *Slobodna Dalmacija*, October 14, 2007; 'Sport i Politika u Balkanskim Društvima' [Sport and Politics in Balkan Societies], *AIM Press*, October 7, 2001.
8. 'Od rupca do himne' [From rag to anthem], *Hrvatski Obzor*, April 24, 1995.
9. Anderson, *Imagined Communities*; see Billig, *Banal Nationalism*, 119–25; Edensor, *National Identity, Popular Culture*, 78–84; Fox and Miller-Idriss, 'Everyday Nationhood'.
10. MacClancy, *Sport, Identity and Ethnicity*, 4 (emphasis in original).
11. Fox, 'Consuming the Nation', 226.
12. Bellamy, *Formation of Croatian National Identity*, 113.
13. Hargreaves, 'Olympism and Nationalism', 128.
14. Hoberman, 'Sport and Ideology', 16.

15. Hoberman, 'Sport and Ideology'; Houlihan, *Sport and International Politics*; Bairner, *Sport, Nationalism and Globalization*; Cronin and Mayall, *Sporting Nationalisms*.
16. 'Jezik nogometa danas je jači od diplomatskog' [The language of football today is louder than the diplomatic one], *Vjesnik*, July 9, 1998.
17. Pezo, 'Sport i hrvatski identitet', 145.
18. 'Nitko nije bolji od Ćire' [Nobody is better than Ćiro], *Večernji list*, July 14, 1998.
19. See 'Predsjednik mi pomaže sastaviti momčad' [The president helps me to pick the team], *Globus*, May 7, 1993; 'Zabranio sam igračima da daju sedmi gol' [I forbade the players to score the seventh goal], *Nacional*, November 24, 1995.
20. 'Po naredbi Tuđmana tajna služba SZUP lažirala je završnicu nogometnog prvenstva Hrvatske' [Under the command of Tudjman the secret service SZUP faked the end of the Croatian football championship], *Nacional*, June 2, 1999.
21. Prnjak, *Bad Blue Boys*, 58.
22. Vrcan, *Sport i nasilje danas u nas i druge*, 22–3.
23. 'Ne nogometu mržnje i rata!' [No to football of hate and war!], *Sportske Novosti*, May 14, 1990.
24. 'Boban i BBB obranili Maksimir od Arkana i Delija' [Boban and BBB defended Maksimir against Arkan and Delije], *Jutarnji list*, May 13, 2010; 'Rat je počeo na Maksimiru' [The war started at Maksimir], *Kurir*, May 13, 2010.
25. 'Probudilo se nešto divlje' [Something wild awoke], *Nedjeljna Dalmacija*, May 20, 1990; 'Maksimirski krug pakla' [The Maksimir circle of hell], *Sport Magazine*, May 17, 1990; for a detailed description on the riots' course, see Mihailović, 'Rat je počeo 13. maja 1990'.
26. 'Zlo se trebalo spriječiti' [The evil had to be prevented], *Vjesnik*, May 15, 1990; 'Tko je odgovoran?' [Who is responsible?], *Sportske Novosti*, May 15, 1990.
27. 'Derbi mržnje' [Derby of hate], *Borba*, May 14, 1990; 'Masovna tuča na stadionu u Zagrebu' [Mass fight at the stadium in Zagreb], *Politika*, May 14, 1990.
28. 'Lopta u službi nacije' ['The ball in service of the nation'], *Vjesnik*, May 15, 1990.
29. Vrcan, *Nogomet, politika, nasilje*, 85. For other seminal work on the politization of (post-)Yugoslav football supporters in the late 1980s/early 1990s, see also Čolović, *Politics of Symbol in Serbia*, 259–87; Lalić, *Torcida*; Fanuko et al., *Zagrebački nogometni navijači*.
30. '"Nijhova I naša" milicija' ["Their and our" police], *Vjesnik*, May 15, 1990; 'Čija je to milicija bila?' [Whose police was that?], *Sport Magazine*, May 17, 1990.
31. See 'Zvonimir Boban – od nacionalnog mita do studenta povijesti' [Zvonimir Boban – from national myth to history student], *Globus*, November 19, 1999.
32. See 'Zar je Frank is Surinama draži od Dejana iz Titograda?' [Is Frank from Surinam really more likable than Dejan from Titograd?], *Sportske Novosti*, June 6, 1990.
33. 'Prekid na Poljudu' [Abort at Poljud], *Vjesnik*, September 27, 1990; 'Prebrzo zaboravljamo' [We forget too quickly], *Vjesnik*, September 28, 1990.
34. 'Stranka narančastih jakna' [The orange jacket party], *Nedjeljna Dalmacija*, September 20, 1990.
35. Lalić, 'Bad Blue Boys i Torcida', 51; see also Lalić, *Torcida*, 197–212.
36. 'Više od sporta' [More than sport], *Vjesnik*, August 27, 1990; see also '"Jugoslavenski" autogol' ["Yugoslav" own goal], *Večernji list*, August 12, 1990; on the political use of 'Balkanist' discourse in post-socialist Croatia, see Razsa and Lindstrom, 'Balkan is Beautiful'.
37. Hall, 'Question of Cultural Identity', 293.
38. 'Usamljeni kraci' [Lonely spikes], *Vjesnik*, August 29, 1990.
39. 'Otvoreno Evropsko prvenstvo u atletici' [European athletics championships are opened], *Vjesnik*, August 28, 1990.
40. Rihtman-Auguštin, 'Monument in the Main City Square', 188.
41. 'Znak međunarodnog priznanja' [A sign of international recognition], *Večernji list*, October 18, 1990.
42. 'Nepokoreni duh hrvatskog naroda' [The unsubmissive spirit of the Croatian people], *Večernji list*, October 17, 1990; 'Trijumf povijesnog pamćenja naroda' [A triumph of people's historical memory], *Vjesnik*, October 17, 1990.
43. Kertzer, *Ritual, Politics and Power*, 88–9.
44. See 'Srce u Zagrebu – noge u Sevilli' [Heart in Zagreb – legs in Sevilla], *Globus*, October 25, 1991; 'Volim Hrvatsku' [I love Croatia], *Večernji list*, August 30, 1991; 'Kukoč i Rađa ambasadori Hrvatske!' [Kukoč i Rađa ambassadors of Croatia], *Nedjeljna Dalmacija*, September 15, 1991.

45. Škaro, *Velikani hrvatskog sporta*, 65.
46. 'Prpić and Ivanišević Feel the Tug of War of Their Homeland', *New York Times*, November 1, 1991.
47. 'Smeš je moje oružje' [The smash is my weapon], *Sportske Novosti*, December 31, 1993 and January 1, 1994; see also 'I sportaši – hrvatski ambasadori' [Athletes are also Croatian ambassadors], *Večernji list*, September 16, 1991; Tudjman referred to the ambivalent position the international community had taken towards the recognition of Croatia (and Slovenia) as an independent state in the early stages of the conflict due to fears of a chain reaction in other republics.
48. 'Moj meč protiv srpske propagande' [My match against Serbian propaganda], *Globus*, February 28, 1992.
49. 'Pod hrvatskim barjakom na OI' [Beneath the Croatian flag to the OG], *Večernji list*, January 16, 1992.
50. Bellamy, *Formation of Croatian National Identity*, 113.
51. Anderson, *Imagined Communities*, 7.
52. 'Cijela je Hrvatska uz nogometaše' [All of Croatia is with the football players], *Večernji list*, July 5, 1998; 'Tuđman zaslužio Lyon i Paris' [Tudjman deserved Lyon and Paris], *Večernji list*, July 11, 1998; 'Veličanstvena hrvatska pobjeda' [Glorious Croatian victory], *Vjesnik*, July 12, 1998.
53. 'Za uspjeh hrvatskog nogometa najzaslužniji su predsjednik Franjo Tuđman i HDZ!' [President Franjo Tudjman and the HDZ are the most creditable for the success of Croatian football], *Globus*, February 5, 1999.
54. 'Ponosni smo na naš narod' [We are proud of our people], *Večernji list*, July 13, 1998.
55. 'Svijetu smo se nadmetnuli pobjedama' [We inflicted ourselves on the world with victories], *Večernji list*, July 13, 1998.
56. 'Hrvatska u slavlju!' [Croatia in celebration], *Jutarnji list*, July 2, 1998; see also 'Eksplozija radosti I veselja' [Explosion of joy and happiness], *Jutarnji list*, July 4, 1998.
57. Durkheim, *Elementary Forms of Religious Life*, 212; see also the notion of 'spontaneous communitas' in Turner, *The Ritual Process*, 132–6.
58. 'Svjetski licemjeri su u uspjehu hrvatskih nogometaša pridali tobožnji nacionalizam' [The world's hypocrites have attached a fictional nationalism to the Croatian footballer's success], *Vjesnik*, July 14, 1998.
59. 'Čemu moze poslužiti nogometno čudo?' [What can the football miracle be useful for?], *Vjesnik*, July 16, 1998.
60. 'Afrodizijak za politiku' [Aphrodisiac for politics], *Hrvatski Obzor*, July 18, 1998; 'Blaževićev nogometni lijek za Tuđmanovu vlast' [Blažević's football cure for Tudjman's authority], *Nacional*, July 8, 1998; 'Pustoš između rata i sporta' [The solitude between war and sport], *Jutarnji list*, July 13, 1998.
61. The operations 'Storm' (*Oluja*) and 'Flash' (*Blijesak*) were military actions carried out by the Croatian Army in the summer of 1995 with the goal to regain control over parts of Croatia claimed by the separatist Serb minority from 1991 onwards. Prior to, during and in the aftermath of the operations, a majority of the ethnic Serbs fled the country.
62. See Jović, 'Croatia and the European Union', 88–92.
63. 'Afrodizijak za politiku' [Aphrodisiac for politics], *Hrvatski Obzor*, July 18, 1998; 'Skandalozna podvala britanskoj javnosti' [Scandalous devilment to the British public], *Hrvatski Obzor*, July 11, 1998.
64. 'Svjetski licemjeri su u uspjehu hrvatskih nogometaša pridali tobožnji nacionalizam' [The world's hypocrites have attached a fictional nationalism to the Croatian footballer's success], *Vjesnik*, July 14, 1998.
65. See Uzelak, 'Franjo Tudjman's Nationalist Ideology'; Razsa and Lindstrom, 'Balkan is Beautiful'.
66. 'Dostojanstvo važnije od rezultata' [Dignity is more important than the result], *Večernji list*, July 3, 1997.
67. Škaro, *Velikani hrvatskog sporta*, 160; see also 'Hrvatska je bila Croatia' [Croatia was Croatia], *Vjesnik*, July 31, 1997.
68. 'Nakon "Bljeska" – "Oluja"!' [After "Flash" – "Storm"!], *Večernji list*, March 3, 1996; 'Vaterpolski Bljesak i rukometna Oluja' [Water polo flash and handball storm], *Hrvatski Obzor*, March 18, 1996; 'Plava oluja od pet bljesaka' [A blue storm of five flashes], *Večernji list*, July 31, 1997.

69. 'Plavi, plavi, vi ste dečki pravi' [Blues, Blues, you're real guys], *Večernji List*, July 21, 1997; 'Igrali i za Vukovar' [Also played for Vukovar], *Večernji List*, July 31, 1997.
70. See Kardov, 'Remember Vukovar', 81–2.
71. 'Sanjali i ostvariji pobjedu' [Dreamt and gained victory], *Večernji list*, July 28, 1996.
72. 'Utakmica kojom se dobiva rat' [The game that wins the war], *Vjesnik*, October 5, 1999.
73. 'Svjetski licemjeri su u uspjehu hrvatskih nogometaša pridali tobožnji nacionalizam' [The world's hypocrites have attached a fictional nationalism to the Croatian footballer's success], *Vjesnik*, July 14, 1998.
74. 'Navijači "ginuli" za karte' [Fans "died" for tickets], *Jutarnji list*, October 10, 1999.
75. Brubaker, *Nationalism Reframed*, 83–4.
76. 'Ne "bedastom imenu s istoka"!' [No to the "stupid name from the East"!], *Sport Magazine*, June 7, 1990; 'Skandal u Maksimiru' [Scandal at Maskimir], *Globus*, January 8, 1993; while the first name change had relative support from the public, the second name change in 1993 was implemented against the will of a majority of fans and the public in general who perceived the second name change in two years as a purely political interference without any relation to sporting matter.
77. 'Tuđmanova zdravica za najveću pobjedu Croatije' [Tudjman's toast for Croatia's biggest victory], *Vjesnik*, August 1, 1997.
78. 'Dinamo = HAŠK Građanski', *Vjesnik*, February 17, 1991.
79. See Fanuko et al., *Zagrebački nogometni navijači*; See Vrcan, 'Curious Drama of the President', 63–4.
80. 'Vratite nam Dinamo!' [Give us Dinamo back!], *Večernji list*, February 27, 1992.
81. Graffiti claiming that 'if there is freedom and democracy, it would be Dinamo and not Croatia' or chants demanding to 'change Dejan's name, not Dinamo's' ('Dejan' was Tudjman's grandson's name which is perceived as a 'Serbian name', while the 'Croatian' equivalent is 'Dean') and mocking the president: 'there is this weird man, Franjo Tudjman is his name, before every sleep, he changes Dinamo's name'.
82. 'Sretan ti 10. Rođendan!' [Happy 10. Birthday Dinamo!], *Slobodna Dalmacija*, February 14, 2010.
83. That is, through chants and banners expressing political support for Tudjman and his party: 'BBB for HDZ' or 'HDZ Hajduk Dinamo Zajedno' [HDZ Hajduk Dinamo Unified]; see Prnjak, *Bad Blue Boys*, 60.
84. See 'Ovjekovječiti uspomenu' [Eternalize the memory], *Večernji list*, September 9, 1994.
85. 'Više od sporta' [More than sport], *Vjesnik*, August 27, 1990; 'Više od igre' [More than a game], *Večernji list*, February 19, 1992; 'Hrvatske pobjede više od nogometa' [Croatian victories more than football], *Hrvatski Obzor*, July 11, 1998.
86. Šimleša, *Športske bitke za Hrvatsku* [Sport battles for Croatia], 4.
87. 'Smeš je moje oružje' ['The smash is my weapon'], *Sportske Novosti*, December 31, 1993 and January 1, 1994.
88. Vrcan, *Nogomet, politika, nasilje*, 20.
89. Vrcan, 'Curious Drama of the President', 63; see also Babić, *Etnonacionalizam i rat u Hrvatskoj*, 68–70.
90. Gagnon, *Myth of Ethnic War*, xv, 176–7.
91. Brubaker, *Nationalism Reframed*, 17.

References

Anderson, Benedict. *Imagined Communities: Reflections on the Origin and Spread of Nationalism*. London: Verso, [1983] 1991.
Babić, Dragutin. *Etnonacionalizam i rat u Hrvatskoj: Teorijski aspekti i istraživanje međunacionalnih odnosa u lokalnim zajdnicama* [Ethno-nationalism and war in Croatia: theoretical aspects and an investigation of inter-national relations in local communities]. Zagreb: Plejada, 2010.
Bairner, Alan. *Sport, Nationalism and Globalization: European and North American Perspectives*. Albany: SUNY Press, 2001.
Bartoluci, Sunčica. 'Sport, nacionalni identitet i nacionalizam u djelu Srđana Vrcana'. [Sport, national identity and nationalism in the work of Srđan Vrcan] In *Sociologija Srđana Vrcana: Između Utopije i Stvarnosti* [The sociology of Srđan Vrcan: in between utopia and reality],

edited by Malenica Zoran, Dražen Lalić, and Inga Tomić-Koludrović, 85–97. Split, Croatia: Pravni Fakultet, 2010.

Bellamy, Alex. *The Formation of Croatian National Identity: A Centuries-Old Dream?* Manchester: Manchester University Press, 2003.

Billig, Michael. *Banal Nationalism*. London: Sage, 1995.

Biti, Ozren. 'Vatreni – hrvatski nogometni proizvod'. [Vatreni – a Croatian football product] *libra libera* 11 (2002): 25–38.

Brubaker, Rogers. *Nationalism Reframed: Nationhood and the National Question in the New Europe*. Cambridge: Cambridge University Press, 1996.

Čolović, Ivan. *The Politics of Symbol in Serbia: Essays in Political Anthropology*. London: Hurst, 2002.

Cronin, Mike, and David Mayall. *Sporting Nationalisms: Identity, Ethnicity, Immigration and Assimilation*. London: Frank Cass, 1998.

Dolić, Dubravko. 'Die Fußballnationalmannschaft als "Trägerin nationaler Würde"? Zum Verhältnis von Fußball und nationaler Identität in Kroatien und Bosnien-Herzegowina'. In *Fußballwelten. Zum Verhältnis von Sport, Politik, Ökonomie und Gesellschaft*, edited by Zentrum für Europa- und Nordamerika-Studien, 155–74. Opladen: Jahrbuch für Europa- und Nordamerika-Studien, 2002.

Durkheim, Emile. *The Elementary Forms of Religious Life*. New York: The Free Press, [1912] 1995.

Džihić, Vedran. 'Fußball am Balkan – Erkundungen zwischen (nationalistischem) Wahn, heroischer Männlichkeit und der (Schein) Normalität einer Region im Umbruch'. In *Arena der Männlichkeit. Über das Verhältnis von Fußball und Geschlecht*, edited by Eva Kreisky and Georg Spitaler, 235–55. Berlin: Campus Verlag, 2006.

Edensor, Tim. *National Identity, Popular Culture and Everyday Life*. Oxford: Berg, 2002.

Fanuko, Nenad, Ivan Magdalenić, Furio Radin, and Zoran Žugić. *Zagrebački nogometni navijači: grupni portret s BBB u središtu* [Zagreb football fans: a group portrait with the BBB in focus]. Zagreb: Institut za društvena istraživanja, 1991.

Fox, Jon E. 'Consuming the Nation: Holidays, Sport and the Production of Collective Belonging'. *Ethnic and Racial Studies* 29, no. 2 (2006): 217–36.

Fox, Jon E., and Cynthia Miller-Idriss. 'Everyday Nationhood'. *Ethnicities* 8, no. 4 (2008): 536–63.

Gagnon, Valère Philip. *The Myth of Ethnic War: Serbia and Croatia in the 1990s*. Ithaca, NY: Cornell University Press, 2004.

Goldstein, Ivo. *Croatia: A History*. London: Hurst, 1999.

Hall, Stuart. 'The Question of Cultural Identity'. In *Modernity and Its Futures*, edited by Stuart Hall, David Held, and Tony McGrew, 273–326. Cambridge: Polity Press, 1992.

Hargreaves, John. 'Olympism and Nationalism: Some Preliminary Consideration'. *International Review for the Sociology of Sport* 27, no. 1 (1992): 119–35.

Hoberman, John. 'Sport and Ideology in the Post-Communist Age'. In *The Changing Politics of Sport*, edited by Allison Lincoln, 15–36. Manchester: Manchester University Press, 1993.

Houlihan, Barrie. *Sport and International Politics*. Hemel Hempstead: Harvester Wheatsheaf, 1994.

Jović, Dejan. 'Croatia and the European Union: A Long Delayed Journey'. *Journal of Southern Europe and the Balkans* 8, no. 1 (2006): 85–103.

Jović, Dejan, and Chrisoph Lamont. 'Introduction – Croatia after Tuđman: Encounters with the Consequences of Conflict and Authoritarianism'. *Europe-Asia Studies* 62, no. 10 (2010): 1609–20.

Kardov, Kruno. 'Remember Vukovar: Memory, Sense of Place, and the National Tradition in Croatia'. In *Democratic Transition in Croatia: Value Transformation, Education and Media*, edited by Sabrina Ramet and Davorka Matić, 63–88. College Station: Texas A&M University Press, 2007.

Kertzer, David. *Ritual, Politics and Power*. New Haven, CT: Yale University Press, 1988.

Lalić, Dražen. 'Bad Blue Boys i Torcida'. *Erasmus* 10 (1995): 51–5.

Lalić, Dražen. *Torcida*. Zagreb: AGM, 1993.

MacClancy, Jeremy, ed. *Sport, Identity and Ethnicity*. Oxford: Berg, 1996.

Magaš, Branka and Žanić, Ivo, eds. *The War in Croatia and Bosnia-Herzegovina*. London: Frank Cass, 2001.

Malešević, Siniša. *Ideology, Legitimacy and the New State: Yugoslavia, Serbia and Croatia*. London: Frank Cass, 2002.

Mihailović, Srećko. 'Rat je počeo 13. maja 1990'. [The war started on 12 May 1990] In *Rat je počeo na Maksimiru: govor mržnje u medijima: analiza pisanja "Politike" i "Borbe" 1987–1991* [The war started at Maksimir: hate speech in the media: content analyses of Politika and Borba newspapers, 1987–1991], edited by Svetlana Slapšak, 77–125. Beograd: Medija centar, 1997.

Nielsen, Christian Axboe. 'The Goalposts of Transition: Football as a Metaphor for Serbia's Long Journey to the Rule of Law'. *Nationalities Papers* 38, no. 1 (2010): 87–103.

Perica, Vjekoslav. 'United They Stood, Divided They Fell: Nationalism and the Yugoslav School of Basketball, 1968–2000'. *Nationalities Papers* 29, no. 2 (2001): 267–91.

Pezo, Vladimir. 'Sport i hrvatski identitet'. [Sport and Croatian identity] In *Hrvatski nacionalni identitet u globalizirajućem svijetu* [Croatian national identity in a globalising world], edited by Neven Budak and Vjeran Katunarić, 135–57. Zagreb: Centar za demokraciju i pravo Miko Tripalo, 2010.

Prnjak, Hrvoje. *Bad Blue Boys – prvih deset godina* [Bad Blue Boys – first ten years]. Zagreb: Marjan Express, 1997.

Razsa, Maple, and Nicole Lindstrom. 'Balkan is Beautiful: Balkanism in the Political Discourse of Tuđman's Croatia'. *East European Politics and Societies* 18, no. 4 (2004): 628–50.

Rihtman-Auguštin, Dunja. 'The Monument in the Main City Square: Constructing and Erasing Memory in Contemporary Croatia'. In *Balkan Identities: Nation and Memory*, edited by Maria Todorova, 180–97. New York: New York University Press, 2004.

Sack, Allen L., and Zeljan Suster. 'Soccer and Croatian Nationalism: A Prelude to War'. *Journal of Sport and Social Issues* 24, no. 3 (2000): 305–20.

Šimleša, Božo. *Sportske bitke za Hrvatsku* [Sport battles for Croatia]. Zagreb: Meditor, 1995.

Škaro, Damir. *Velikani hrvatskog sporta – sport u promociji Hrvatske* [The greats of Croatian sport – sport in the promotion of Croatia]. Zagreb: Golden Marketing, 2001.

Søberg, Marcus. 'Croatia Since 1989: The HDZ and the Politics of Transition'. In *Democratic Transition in Croatia: Value Transformation, Education and Media*, edited by Sabrina Ramet and Davorka Matić, 31–63. College Station: Texas A&M University Press, 2007.

Turner, Victor. *The Ritual Process*. Chicago, IL: Aldine, 1969.

Uzelak [sic!], Gordana. 'Franjo Tudjman's Nationalist Ideology'. *East European Quarterly* 31, no. 4 (1998): 449–72.

Vrcan, Srđan. 'The Curious Drama of the President of a Republic Versus a Football Fan Tribe: A Symptomatic Case in the Post-Communist Transition in Croatia'. *International Review for the Sociology of Sport* 37, no. 1 (2002): 59–77.

Vrcan, Srđan. *Nogomet, politika, nasilje: Ogledi iz sociologije nogometa* [Football, politics, violence: views from football sociology]. Zagreb: Jesenski i Turk, 2003.

Vrcan, Srđan. *Sport i nasilje danas u nas i druge studije iz sociologije sporta* [Sport and violence today in our country and other studies from the sociology of sport]. Zagreb: Naprijed, 1990.

Winland, Daphne. 'Ten Years Later: The Changing Nature of Transnational Ties in Post-Independence Croatia'. *Ethnopolitics* 5, no. 3 (2006): 295–307.

'A Croatian champion with a Croatian name': national identity and uses of history in Croatian football culture – the case of Dinamo Zagreb

Tea Sindbæk

Department of Cross-Cultural and Regional Studies, University of Copenhagen, Copenhagen, Denmark

This article investigates the role of Croatia's leading football club, Dinamo Zagreb, in the negotiation of history as a crucial element of national and other identities in Croatia in the 1990s and early twenty-first century. During this turbulent period, Croatia abandoned communism, seceded from Yugoslavia, survived a war of independence, and rebuilt and redefined itself as an independent and democratic national republic. Historical interpretations needed to adapt to these changes, both on the levels of state and institutions and within popular culture. Emphasizing Dinamo's role as a national and political symbol, the article analyses how history and identities were being represented and used in Dinamo's club magazine and in tabloid comments. The article points out how football club discourse interacted with and challenged national narratives, and highlights the struggle between politics and football culture, particularly with regards to the creation of national histories and the establishing of national and other identities.

Introduction

From 1990 to 2000, Zagreb's main football club, Dinamo, changed its name three times, which in itself testifies to a certain crisis of identity. This was the turbulent decade when Croatia abandoned communism, seceded from the Yugoslav federation, lived through a four-year war of independence, and rebuilt and redefined itself as an independent republic. New state-bearing ideologies were introduced in the form of nationalism and (at least formal) multiparty democracy, and history needed to adapt to these changes. From 1990 onwards, history and historical identities were fundamentally revised in the independent Croatian republic.

The different names carried by Dinamo in these years illustrate these revisions: its first new name, 'Hašk-Građanski', adopted in June 1991, signalled a return to a pre-communist Croatian football culture. Its second name, 'Croatia', the Latin name for the country, was used from February 1993 onwards. This name made the club, in the words of Croatia's President Franjo Tuđman, 'a Croatian champion with a Croatian name' and tied it to a new nation-building project.[1] And, finally, the return in February 2000 to 'Dinamo', the club's name during the communist period 1945–1990, signified a reconnection to the club as most supporters knew and revered it.

These changes in Dinamo's name were deeply disputed, reflecting diverging opinions about which parts of history – and consequently which version of Croatian national identity – the team was to be associated with. In essence, what unfolded around Dinamo and the name dispute was a struggle over history and identities, especially national identity.

The aim of this article is to investigate the role of Croatia's leading football club, Dinamo Zagreb, in the negotiation of historical and national identities in Croatia in the 1990s and early twenty-first century. By analysing how history was being represented and used in the club magazine of Dinamo Zagreb, and in descriptions and comments in tabloids, the article points out how football club history interacted with grand national histories, how history was being used and for which purposes, and how this contributed to the establishment of new identities, based on new historical interpretations, in Croatian society.

The case of Dinamo Zagreb is particularly interesting for this kind of analysis, because the club throughout the 1990s was ascribed special importance as a symbol of Croatian national identity. The Dinamo case also highlights the role of politics and the struggle between political power and popular football culture over which historical identity was to define Zagreb's main football club. The article thus contributes to a closer understanding of the roles played by history in football culture, particularly with regards to the creation of national histories and the establishing of national and other identities.

Use of history and football culture

History plays many and important roles in society; it is constantly being used in numerous ways for countless purposes.[2] Whereas the use of history on the level of state politics, e.g. to legitimize national or political ideologies, is probably dominant, the most widespread use of history takes place at individual levels and in smaller communities, when we use history as a source of orientation in time and space, and when we define ourselves through our past and connect it to the wider national and international history.[3]

Popular culture is one field where the relations between individual historical identities and the official institutionalized national or stately ones are constructed and negotiated. Popular culture may be a particularly important field, because it is, by definition, widely liked and has as its specific aim to be popular.[4] Being more accessible than much historical writing, popular culture may reach different audiences at different times than much conventional history communication does.

Both in Croatia and elsewhere, popular culture is known to contribute decisively to political and ideological mobilization such as constructions of national identity.[5] Within Croatian popular culture, football occupies a special position as the most popular sport with a long and strong tradition. Football clubs often constitute local subcultures, a special type of communities characterized by shared passions and ideas of strong loyalties. As such, a football club is an obvious source of identity. Though clubs are tied to specific groups and places, club football still appeals widely across cities, regions and in international contexts, and also nationally.

On all these levels, as club community and as a symbol both for Zagreb and Croatia, Dinamo's use of history played a role. Compared to other football clubs, Dinamo Zagreb seems exceptionally preoccupied with history. Dinamo's club magazine is stuffed with features or feuilletons on football history, and repeatedly through the 1990s, Dinamo club representatives pointed out the need to educate the youth about the history of the club.[6]

By far the most prominent use of history in Dinamo's club magazine is the inward-looking use of internal club history. The Dinamo magazine contains long and detailed descriptions of the club's own history, thus constructing a historical identity founded in a well-documented past. Articles make frequent references to the club's glorious past, most often in the form of purely sports-related references to fantastic results made by the team and its individual players. This serves not only to celebrate the club as a community, but also to mobilize for further attainment in order to live up to the glorious heritage. The prime mythical figures of football club history are famous old players and 'golden generations' that gained great results. Thus, the club and its members themselves, their titles and other attainments, and their football playing are the core of these internal histories.

Nevertheless, Dinamo Zagreb's use of history is deeply influenced by widespread turns and themes in the historical culture of Croatian society in general. At times, the grand political narratives serve as frameworks according to which ongoing events are interpreted or the club's historical identity can be constituted. Elements of national and political history are selected and incorporated as signature parts of the club's own history, while other bits are discarded. Thus, both subcultural and grand histories are negotiated.

What generally characterizes the uses of history in the club magazine of the Dinamo Zagreb football club since 1990 are the following elements: first, a prolonged negotiation about which 'past', and consequently which historical identity, is relevant for the club. This issue was clearly crystallized in relation to the struggle that continued throughout the 1990s about the name of the football club. The second element refers to a certain narrative of Croatia's recent history (that of victimization under Yugoslav communism) and the third element points to the selection and foregrounding of specific elements of history with the aim to construct what we may call a 'usable history' for the club.

I will discuss each of these elements below. But first, the special position that Dinamo occupied in Croatian society in the 1990s will be discussed in the following section.

The importance of Dinamo

Dinamo Zagreb was one of the four clubs that dominated the football league in socialist Yugoslavia. The other three were Partizan and Crvena zvezda (Red Star), both from Belgrade, and Hajduk from Split. Since the late 1980s, as national rivalry frustrated Yugoslav politics, football support and fan culture were increasingly associated with radical nationalism.[7] During the 1990s, Dinamo Zagreb representatives repeatedly claimed that the football club played a special role as a symbol of Croatian national identity. According to an editorial of the club's magazine in September 1990, it was widely argued that Dinamo, along with the Catholic Church, had played a large, invaluable role in guarding the national essence and strengthening patriotic feelings during communism.[8] And in January 1998, Zlatko Canjug, the club President, emphasized how in the communist period Dinamo's football had instigated open national passion among the Croatian people. Thus, Canjug said, the club had been an enthusiastic contributing factor to the creation of the independent republic of Croatia.[9]

The symbolic importance of the Dinamo football club for Croatian society in the 1990s is clear from the visible ties to the political elite. Franjo Tuđman, Croatia's President from 1990 to 1999, very regularly made public appearances in connection to Dinamo (see Figure 1). Tuđman would be present at important matches, he would participate in events and celebrations and he would personally congratulate players with important results. Furthermore, Tuđman gave interviews to the club's magazine and contributed to discussions.[10] Allegedly, the club was also connected to Croatia's governing party, the right-wing HDZ, and President Tuđman via the President's friendship with Miroslav Blažević, Dinamo's coach in the early 1990s and later coach for Croatia's national team.[11] The football club itself revered the connection to the President and often celebrated his presence. In April 1997, the club magazine stated:

> The President of our republic, Dr Franjo Tuđman, is a great fan of football...This is also proven by his regular presence at matches, whenever obligations of state affairs allow it. Apart

Figure 1. Croatian President Franjo Tuđman reading the magazine of the Croatia (Dinamo) football club, for which he was made honorary president. *Source:* From the club magazine, December 1998.

from the fact that he loves football, the president is also a true football expert . . . even though as president of the state he loves all Croatian teams equally, it is no secret that the blue colours of our team Croatia [Dinamo's official name in those years] is dearest to his heart.[12]

In the spring of 1998, Tuđman was made 'honorary president' of the club.[13]

The importance of Dinamo as a national symbol was established most clearly at the famous incident on 13 May 1990, when a match that should have been the game of the year, against Belgrade's Crvena zvezda at Dinamo's stadium Maximir, was cancelled due to fan disorder. It was a frustrating moment for the Dinamo club. The team's spring season had been dreadful; after leading the Yugoslav tournament midway through, the Championship was lost to Zvezda. Both Dinamo supporters and Zvezda's notorious fan group 'Delije' had arrived early, and in the hours before the match the stadium became the stage of looting, vandalism and provocation. The fences separating the fan groups were broken, and violence erupted. With the match delayed and the players waiting in the field, riot police attacked the fans, and Dinamo's young captain and star player, Zvonimir Boban, jumped up and kicked a policeman, allegedly in order to stop him from beating a Dinamo supporter.[14] In the end, the match was cancelled, and Dinamo had to accept an administrative defeat and heavy fines.

The Croatian and Yugoslav football organizations condemned the incident and fan violence in general, and Boban was initially excluded from the Yugoslav football league for years to come. Yet, the Dinamo magazine suggested that the club was treated unfairly and that the fault was mainly Delije's, but the police acted only against Dinamo's supporters and not against Zvezda's.[15] The Dinamo magazine also stood behind Boban and rejected the public condemnation of him, suggesting that he was attacked because of his declared support for HDZ, Tuđman's nationalist Party.[16] In any case, the incident made Boban a national hero in Croatia, as well as in Dinamo's own history. In a book celebrating the 60th anniversary of Dinamo in 2005, the author, Fredi Kramer, who was also the editor of Dinamo's club magazine for several decades, stated:

In that jump was a lot of symbolism. It was resistance against violence, injustice and savagery. Therefore that date of the match that was never played will remain forever written into the history of our club, but also of the united political life of Croatia.[17]

Dinamo's role as a national symbol remained throughout the 1990s and was, not surprisingly, especially outspoken when the team faced one of the strong Serbian clubs. Following the dirty war in Croatia from 1991 to 1995, when Croatian armed forces fought the Serbian-dominated Yugoslav army supporting rioting Croatian Serbs, and war crimes were committed both by Serb and to a lesser extent also by Croat paramilitaries, tensions between the two countries ran high, and Serbia constituted the most significant 'Other' for Croatia. When in July 1997, Dinamo, under the name NK Croatia, met Partizan from Belgrade in Champions' League, the two matches were invested with enormous interest from the public. The Croatian tabloid *Večernji list* suggested that even the international media present at the matches were aware that this was about 'more than football and sports'.[18]

The Zagreb team lost the first leg in Belgrade 1-0. The return match in Zagreb was awaited with even more anxiety and excitement. Zagreb team's most experienced player, Goran Jurić, said to *Večernji list*: 'I have played more than a thousand matches, I have been professional for 16 years, but this is the most important match for me'.[19] Partizan's coach reckoned that the match had reached a level of importance in Croatia approaching that of a matter of national interest.[20]

The tension before the match was also visible because of increased security concerns. Before the match in Zagreb, the head of the city police said to *Večernji list*: 'This match has strong emotional impact and it is more risky than ordinary high risk matches'.[21] The question of security at the match became another issue of national importance. Since the match in Belgrade was completed without incidents, parts of Croatian football culture apparently considered it a question of national honour to display even neater organization. The match, according to one commentator, constituted a chance to demonstrate the civilized level of Croatian society and distance it from what was considered Balkan connotations of wildness and brutality.[22]

The match was so important that it enabled a short-lived unity of purpose between usually uncompromising archrival fan groups. Even Torcida, the ill-famed fan club of Split's Hajduk and Zagreb team's main rival in the Croatian league, expressed their support: 'In connection to the football match Croatia–Partizan, which is in its significance much more than a match', they said:

> we fully support the players and organisation of NK Croatia in that they with all heart and knowledge defeat the opponents 'from the other side of Drina'. On that day we will all be Croatia [Hrvatska, the name of the country, not the club] as we also were when it was most important.[23]

The last part is obviously a reference to the war in the first half of the 1990s, when many hard-core football fans volunteered for the Croatian forces. Torcida thus offered another instance of national unity in the face of a Serbian threat from the other side of Drina.

Dinamo (or NK Croatia) defeated Partizan 5-0, causing widespread euphoria in Zagreb. One tabloid journalist declared that for this night, the team was not just 'heroes of the streets' but 'heroes of Croatia'.[24] Also the players were touched: after the victory, Silvio Marić, Dinamo's striker and one of the stars of the match, said to journalists: 'let this victory be for Croatia [Hrvatska, the name of the country] and let the tears flow. Look, mine flow as well, from the heart'.[25]

Dinamo's symbolic importance in Croatian society gave the struggles over historical interpretations within the football club a wider and more acute relevance. Most arguments took place within the club magazine, but much spilled over and involved different fan groups and wider society as well. The negotiation of history was most clearly visible in relation to the long debate about the name of the team.

The name disputes

The question of changing the name of the club that had since June 1945 been known as Dinamo Zagreb was first raised in the club magazine in July 1990, in connection to the club's 45-year anniversary. The editorial introduction to that issue emphasized how Dinamo's greatness was really founded on three traditional Zagreb clubs, Građanski, HAŠK and Concordija, which were all annihilated through government intervention in 1945, when Dinamo was created. Describing the glorious feats of those clubs, the editorial underlined how their abolishment showed no respect for the great tradition of Zagreb football. Furthermore, according to the editorial, the club was named after Dinamo of Moscow, the club of the dreaded Soviet secret police.[26] Elsewhere, the Dinamo magazine drew attention to the continuity between the Zagreb clubs of the early twentieth century and the Dinamo club established in 1945. It was emphasized how Dinamo had taken over 'the blue colours of Građanski and of the city of Zagreb', as well as the players and supporters of Građanski, HAŠK and Concordija. 'So', continued the article, 'it is not strange that Dinamo is considered the real heir to the old good "Burgers"'.[27] Burgers, or 'Purgeri', was a nickname for the members of the Građanski club, emphasizing its ties to a German-Austrian bourgeois city culture.

The debate about the name reflected a wish among some of the members of the Dinamo football club to distance the club from its communist identity and rather emphasize the glorious interwar period of Zagreb football. Kramer, editor of the club magazine, reminded 'those, who for sentimental reasons oppose a change of the club's name' that Dinamo was really a continuation of the tradition from Građanski, the most popular Zagreb club before the Second World War. Moreover, Građanski was the 'most Croatian Club', claimed Kramer, as it was characterized by culture and rationality and was closely connected to the Croatian Peasant Party, which was the most influential Croatian party in interwar Yugoslavia and the main opponent to the Serbian-dominated centralism that characterized the country in that period.[28] The magazine also printed a photograph of the leader of the Croatian Peasant Party, Stjepan Radić, at the opening of Građanski's stadium in 1924. The text below the photograph stated that Građanski was so popular, because it was the only Croatian club that never forgot or neglected its duty to its city and fatherland.[29] Obviously, this type of associations, connecting the team emotionally and morally with the city of Zagreb, the Croatian nation and the struggle against Yugoslav centralism, was what groups within Dinamo's organization wanted to attach to the club.

Kramer and his like-minded were really aiming at tying Dinamo's identity to Croatian nationality as opposed to communism and Yugoslavism, by connecting it to pre-communist Croatian history. Kramer aligned this with the general 'return to Croatian national history' that characterized the early 1990s.[30] The change of the name was seen as another contribution to the removal of symbols of communism and the introduction of democracy in Croatia.[31]

For Kramer, it was essential to underline that Dinamo was never close to the communist regime, that the club was always 'a black sheep' and that Dinamo was the only one of the great Yugoslav clubs that was never honoured or decorated by the communist leadership. According to Kramer, employees of Dinamo had even been persecuted because of their Croatian identity.[32] There was a general juxtaposing of Croatian nationality on one side and communism and Yugoslavism on the other, the latter often including Belgrade centralism and Serbian domination.

The proposed new names for the club focused on three possibilities: Građanski, HAŠK and Croatia. As both HAŠK and Građanski were names of interwar clubs, these proposals were aimed at reviving the memory of pre-communist Croatian and Zagreb football cultures. Several articles in the Dinamo magazine in 1990 and 1991 exposed and praised the history of Građanski and HAŠK.[33] Građanski was especially hailed: one article claimed that Građanski was popular throughout Yugoslavia and that the club spreads both football culture and Croatian culture.[34] Zvonimir Magdić, football journalist and historian, wrote an article in strong support of changing the name into Građanski drawing heavily both on internal football history, citing Građanski's excellent results, and on the history of Građanski's symbolic role in the interwar period as the main opponent of 'Great Serbian hegemony'.[35] In a review of Građanski's history, it was also emphasized that Građanski's full name, Prvi Hrvatski Građanski Športski klub (the First Croatian Citizens Sports Club), was a symbol of Croat resistance to the forced Magyarization of Croatian society before the First World War, thus underlining again Građanski's role as a historical guardian of Croatian nationality.[36]

When on 25 June – the day that Croatia became independent – it was decided to change Dinamo's name into HAŠK-Građanski, the Dinamo magazine commented that this combined the great tradition of the two interwar clubs and disposed of the last bits of the old socialist system.[37] But, the magazine continued, Dinamo was not wiped away: 'only the name, which wasn't ours, Croatian, bourgeois, is changed. It was a Bolshevik fabrication'.[38] However, the change of name was not a success. After less than a year, the club magazine started to criticize the choice, calling HAŠK-Građanski an unlucky mixture and a 'bastard name', because the two clubs combined in it were actually rivals.[39] In February 1993, the name was changed again, this time into the Latin and internationally widely used name of the country, Croatia.[40] This name was already in play, allegedly because some of Dinamo's 'friends' wanted it.[41] In later volumes of the Dinamo magazine, President Tuđman confirmed that he had been among the supporters of the name Croatia.[42] The name changes obviously challenged the club's claims to historical continuity, which forced the club magazine to emphasize connections to earlier names (see Figure 2).

The name changes display an interesting collusion of dates: the name Dinamo was first abandoned on the day when Croatia became independent. And the club returned to Dinamo in February 2000, a few months after Tuđman's death.[43] Since Tuđman's presence was indeed very prominent in the club, and since he repeatedly stated an intense dislike of the name Dinamo, while he promoted Croatia, it seems obvious that the dates were if not dictated by Tuđman then certainly chosen with him in consideration.

Yet, the second new name, Croatia, was no more popular than Hašk-Građanski, and Tuđman continuously felt the need to defend it. For Tuđman, Dinamo was unacceptable, because it was a 'Bolshevik name'. Croatia, he claimed, signalled connections to the rich interwar football tradition before the club became Dinamo.[44] Needless to say, the name Croatia certainly emphasized the national adherence of the club. Tuđman argued that most young football fans would soon realize 'what and how much it means to us when a Croatian champion enters Europe with a Croatian name'.[45] Thus, Tuđman saw in naming the club Croatia a way of binding pre-communist national tradition to the present, while at the same time using the club and the publicity it created to brand the new nation-state internationally and support the internal nation-building project. Tuđman obviously

Figure 2.   Front page of the club magazine, October 1996. The club was then called Croatia, but to emphasize continuity, the club shield included the shields of Dinamo (with the d) and the interwar clubs: Hašk (with the Š) and Građanski (with G, k and s). Moreover, star players from all of these clubs are pictured.

wanted the club to function as a second national team. The President argued that those cheering against the club's new name belonged to groups of politically misguided persons, who did not support the democratic changes and who were paid by outsiders.[46] In effect, he suggested that groups such as Dinamo's fan club, the Bad Blue Boys (BBB), who were among the main protesters, were disloyal to Croatia by being loyal to the Dinamo name. This message was not received well by the fans.[47]

In changing the club's name to remove any traces of socialist history, emphasizing instead Croatian national traditions, the club management was clearly following the dominant political line. Yet, other groups connected to the team challenged the club's role as a political mouthpiece.

The opposition: Bad Blue Boys and others

Whereas contributors to the Dinamo magazine generally agreed on the desirability of changing the club's name, both the first and the second time, it is clear from comments and discussions that the changes met considerable opposition from elsewhere. Especially Dinamo's fan club, the BBB, was vehemently opposed to changing the name.[48]

In the 1980s, the BBB fought with other Yugoslav football club hooligans and established an identity based on Croatian nationalism and anti-communism.[49] The phenomenon of hooliganism hit Yugoslavia hard in the late 1980s, and like the fan organizations of most other Yugoslav football clubs, the BBB repeatedly caused serious trouble for the club it claimed to support. BBB significantly damaged Dinamo's stadium at Maksimir and their behaviour resulted in expensive fines for the club. In an interview with the Dinamo magazine in January 1990, Dinamo's President strongly criticized the dangerous activities of some supporters.[50]

Yet, during the spring of 1990, a new amity developed between BBB and the club, and the club magazine increasingly supported the BBB arguing that Dinamo's fans were unfairly blamed for the acts of other fan groups.[51] After the infamous incident at Maksimir stadium on 13 May 1990, Dinamo stood behind the BBB and claimed that Delije was responsible for most provocation and aggression, and that the police attacked members of the BBB only.[52] The good relationship between the Dinamo club and the fan organization was further improved in spring 1991, when BBB were allowed to move to a more attractive stand at Maksimir stadium.[53]

In the early 1990s, members of the BBB volunteered to fight with the Croatian forces, and many were killed.[54] In 1994, BBB's Zagreb organization erected a monument dedicated to 'all the supporters of Dinamo for whom the war began on 13 May 1990 at the Maksimir Stadium and ended with the laying down of their lives at the altar of the Croatian homeland' (Figure 3).

Figure 3.   Monument dedicated to members of the BBB fan club who volunteered for the Croatian forces in the Yugoslav wars and were killed in the battle. The inscription reads: 'To all the supporters of Dinamo, for whom the war began on the 13 May 1990 and ended with the laying down of their lives at the altar of the Croatian homeland'. The event of 13 May 1990 was the match between Dinamo and Crvena zvezda that was cancelled due to excessive fan violence.

However, in spite of their obvious patriotism and anti-communism, the BBB was absolutely unwilling to accept the change of Dinamo's name. In the spring of 1992, according to the club's magazine, till then called 'HAŠK-Građanski', the BBB ran a campaign for returning the club's name to Dinamo, and they were supported by other youths and parts of the opposition.[55] Even voices within the club, such as coach Ćiro Blažević, suggested that it might be sensible to return to Dinamo.[56] Throughout the 1990s, the BBB continued to oppose the new names of the club and chanted instead for Dinamo, to the utter dismay of editor and authors of the club magazine.[57]

Partly, this must be explained as a generational conflict. To members of the older generation like Kramer, Magdić, Tuđman and the veteran players from Građanski and HAŠK, who also participated at the meetings where the name was discussed, the continuity between the interwar clubs and Dinamo was obvious, and they regarded the opposition by the youth as pure ignorance.[58] Most members of the BBB, however, were younger people who had followed Dinamo in the 1980s and earlier, and to whom the interwar clubs would probably seem too distant to bolster any sort of emotional attachment.

But the BBB also rejected the second change of the club's name into Croatia. What they refused to accept was not simply the change to the interwar club names, but the change of name at all. For the radical and violent parts of BBB, Dinamo was also the symbol of their own experience and glorious past of combating other fan clubs. As such, it was the symbol not only of their beloved club, but also of their own particular identity and history. While for Tuđman and others, the communist past implicated by the name Dinamo was undesirable and unworthy of commemoration, for BBB it was a period of brave exploits made both by themselves and the club, despite regime opposition, and certainly worth remembering.[59] The BBB's view on the club and its name was shared by a large part of Zagreb's youth for whom the name Dinamo had nothing to do with support for Yugoslavia or socialism, but rather with the club as a symbol for Zagreb and Croatian football.[60]

Yet, the protests were perhaps also directed against the style of leadership. According to some researchers, the BBB rejected the top-down decision-making on behalf of their club and saw it as authoritarian abuse of power.[61] The BBB protests were joined by others, some of which were also directed against the Tuđman administration and its autocratic politics of symbols. In 1996, while officials of the Dinamo club struggled to convince sceptic fans to support the name Croatia, Zagreb's city council, apparently in an act of defiance, decided to rename Maksimir stadium, where Dinamo and before them Građanski played their home matches, into 'Dinamo's Stadium' (Dinamov Stadion). This clearly provoked the football club officials, who had to accept the absurdity that the team called Croatia was playing its home matches at Dinamo's Stadium.[62]

The struggle continued until February 2000, shortly after Tuđman's death, when the club surrendered and reinstalled the name Dinamo. Even Kramer eventually decided that the change of the club's name was a mistake. In a book titled *The Sacred Name of Dinamo*, he called the change of name unfortunate, because the club and its name were important symbols for the people, invested with great emotional charge.[63] By 2011, the Dinamo club opted for a compromise. Calling the club 'GNK (or 'Građanski Nogometni Klub') Dinamo Zagreb' and tracing the club's history back to the founding of Građanski in 1911, the club kept the name of the communist era, preferred by most fans, while also promoting its share in the glorious football tradition of the interwar period.[64]

Thus, during these disputes, groups of Dinamo supporters succeeded in opposing the political elite's line on the very symbolic issue of the club's name. By insisting on the 'Bolshevik' name, the supporters quite spectacularly challenged the very one-sided national and political use of history made by both Croatia's and the club's leaderships.

Dinamo and Yugoslav communism

Other types of use of history in connection to the football club were much less contested. Dinamo Zagreb's version of Yugoslav history largely echoed the one promoted more generally in Croatian society, which was one that thematized Croatian national suffering under centralist repression.

Dinamo Zagreb's history in the period of communist Yugoslavia was presented in the club magazine in two main narratives. The first glorified the club, emphasized its golden achievements and underlined that the club competed in the very top of the Yugoslav league on an equal level with the Belgrade clubs, Crvena zvezda and Partizan, as well as with Hajduk from Split. The second suggested that Dinamo generally suffered under Yugoslav communism; that the club was being cheated and treated unfairly and at times, both club and players were pressured and even persecuted by Belgrade authorities. This perspective on Yugoslav history sometimes served to explain unsatisfying results or to suggest that Dinamo were deprived of its rightful triumphs and thus deserved more glorification and support than results seemed to justify. And, naturally, this narrative helped to mobilize a grudge among Dinamo's supporters against the central Yugoslav football authorities in Belgrade and the privileged Belgrade clubs, represented in the 1990s by Serbian football.

This narrative was clearly presented in the club magazine following the events on 13 May 1990 and Dinamo's subsequent administrative defeat. The editorial comment of the club magazine concluded that Dinamo's misfortunes were not at all accidental. Rather, they should be interpreted in the light of history:

> It is just a continuation of everything our club has experienced right from its establishment. Already in the first championship match in 1946 we were cheated in Titograd. After we had defeated Budućnost 3-2, the day after we realised, namely, in Belgrade that the registered result was 2-2. They said that Blažo Jovanović [Montegrin top communist] wanted it like that. Unfortunately it didn't stop at that, so in its 45 years of existence our club has experienced a row of different injustices, which among others also explain why Dinamo has so far been Yugoslav champion only four times.[65]

This story about the stolen victory in 1946 is repeated numerous times in the club magazine throughout the decade, often accompanied with claims that Dinamo lost several championships under suspicious circumstances, that the referees were always disposed against Dinamo, or that Belgrade teams conspired against the Zagreb club.[66]

These stories of unfair treatment of Dinamo were also revived in the face of a match between Dinamo and Crvena zvezda in May 1991, then obviously serving as a way of warming up, mobilizing enthusiasm and a taste for some kind of revenge for the injustice of the past. Included herein were also the events on 13 May the year before and what the writers of Dinamo magazine perceived as an 'alliance' between Crvena zvezda's fans and the (non-Croat) security forces, and also the punishments that Dinamo received in that connection.[67]

Another unfairness said to hit Dinamo under Yugoslav communism was the transferring of young talents from Zagreb to Partizan in Belgrade. According to the Dinamo magazine of July 1990, players hardly had a choice, but were threatened with unpleasantness if they objected.[68] Again in August 1997, after the celebrated victory over Partizan on 30 July, the club magazine found it relevant to remind its readers how Zagreb was drained of great football players after the Second World War in order to create a strong Partizan team, and this was again tied to the alleged unfairness and the fixed results that deprived Dinamo of the Yugoslav championship after the Second World War.[69]

That the club magazine's use of the narrative of victimization in communist Yugoslavia was interconnected with those of the regime was perhaps most clearly demonstrated by President Tuđman when he participated in the football club's Christmas celebration in 1997. According to the magazine, Tuđman, having congratulated the team and players on their fantastic results, recalled a certain victory in Titograd that had been annulled by the time the team returned to Zagreb. Tuđman suggested that such were the conditions under Yugoslav communism. The President associated the establishment of the new Croatian state with great results both within football and in society in general. Such successes were deliberately obstructed, according to both Tuđman and the Dinamo Zagreb magazine, when Croatia was a part of communist Yugoslavia.[70] Though their points of focus were different, the national and the football uses of the victim narrative of communist history ran parallel, enforced each other and supplied mutual glorification.

Useful selections of history

One probably should not be surprised that a football club's use of history is highly selective. Sport in public culture is about pleasure and sense of community and the elements of history that are being used are selected to support such experiences. On the other hand, certain parts of history are simply not referred to.

In Dinamo's official publications, one such obviously absent topic is the Second World War. Croatia's Second World War history as an extremely violent Nazi puppet state, run by the Croatian fascist Ustasha movement had hardly anything positive to add to a Croatian football club's perspective on history. Moreover, the Ustasha persecuted and murdered tens of thousands of civilian Serbs as well as Jews and Roma, which made this history a particularly emotional issue in relation to Serbia. On the other hand, Second World War history and terminology were used widely by Belgrade clubs in the 1990s, both in the critique of Croatian nationalist hooliganism, usually somehow more condemning than the critique of similar groups in Serbia, and for producing enemy images and stigmatizing Croatian nationalism in general.[71] Reflecting this, the Dinamo magazine printed offended reactions to use of Second World War history by Belgrade clubs and tabloids.[72]

For Dinamo, one useful element of history was the interwar period. The reference to Stjepan Radić and the repeated features in the Dinamo magazine on the glorious football culture of interwar Zagreb demonstrates that the connection to bourgeois pre-communist Croatia was indeed seen as attractive by the club's spokesmen.

Another type of history frequently used in the Dinamo magazine during the second half of the 1990s is that of the recent Yugoslav wars and Croatia's military victories. Thus, when Dinamo on 30 July 1997 defeated Partizan with 5-0 on the way to Champions' League, the victory was compared to the victories of the Croatian army at the end of the Yugoslav Wars, the so-called operations 'Flash' (Bljesak), which conquered Slavonia from the Yugoslav Army in May 1995, and 'Storm' (Oluja), which in August same year conquered Krajina. Storm also made most of the area's Serbian population flee to Serbia and led to several Croatian generals being indicted for war crimes at the International Criminal Tribunal for the Former Yugoslavia. The source for the Flash and Storm metaphor was apparently the President of the Zagreb football club, Canjug, who after the match told the journalists: 'You have the occasion to declare Flash and Storm and that at the same time'. The article in the Dinamo magazine consequentially proclaimed the match 'The Flash and Storm of football'.[73] Following a similar line, the front page of a tabloid covering the match was titled 'The blue storm of five lightnings' (Figure 4).[74] The Flash and Storm metaphor was also used by the Dinamo club magazine to describe the triumphs of the Croatian national football team in the 1998 World Cup.[75] At a celebration of the club's victories in the autumn of 1998, even Tuđman made a connection between the

Figure 4. 'The blue storm of five lightnings'. Front page of the tabloid *Večernji list*, 31 July 1997, marking the Zagreb team's 5-0 victory over Partizan from Belgrade by referring to Croatia's military victories in the Yugoslav wars. The pictures show the players celebrating on the field and jubilant supporters bathing in a fountain in the centre of Zagreb.

football club's battles in sport and the Croatian war for an independent republic: 'We have fought for our independence in spite of numerous enemies. Likewise, you have fought for Champions' League in spite of strong rivals...'.[76]

The sacrifices and victims of the war in the 1990s were also drawn upon in Croatian football culture. According to tabloid descriptions, when Partizan was defeated at Maksimir stadium in July 1997, the fans and audience chanted 'Vukovar, Vukovar', thus commemorating the sieged and bombarded city that symbolized Croatian suffering and heroism more than any, and perhaps also suggesting that some sort of revenge was being taken.[77] Also the football team seemed to link Dinamo's experiences with Croatia's recent history. Marić, one of the heroes of the match, said: 'That victory we gave to all of Croatia. Especially to the lads who were killed for its freedom'.[78]

Such selective uses of history are really cases of picking historical examples that fit the purpose. Comparing hard-won national triumphs on the football field with celebrated victories in battle underlines the importance of the former and suggests a position along major events in national memory.

Conclusion

In the 1990s, the Dinamo Zagreb football club, along with the wider Croatian society, participated in a general rethinking of Croatian national history and identity. Dinamo's negotiation of history and historical identities was particularly visible in the case of the struggle over the club's name. According to Dinamo officials and the club magazine, the team should be distanced from its communist history and identity, symbolized by the very name Dinamo. By changing the name, the club was attached first to what was considered a more national Croatian football culture of the interwar years, and later literally to Croatian national identity as such. The name changes were met with enthusiastic protests, which testifies to divisions both within the football community and in Croatian society: it became clear that different parts of history carried different meaning for the club's official representatives and the Tuđman regime, on one hand, and for the fan groups, on the other. In the end, the official agenda was abandoned, and the Dinamo club was re-attached to its history under communism, but with due recognition also of its origins in Zagreb's football culture of the interwar period.

The story of Dinamo demonstrates the function of the football club as a midfield in a struggle for history and identity that was fought between official political uses of history and more intimate personal ones. The Dinamo football club was a part of both: in the 1990s, it was first conquered by official stately views on Croatian history and identity and then, after a decade of opposition, recovered by the more intimate, personal and unofficial uses that were channelled through less public and far-reaching media, but which were so much more present in everyday life. While in the 1990s, it had been a part of a national project of rethinking Croatian history and identity, by the 2000s the Dinamo team was again primarily a part of the identities and histories of individual football fans and the football club community – though its past as a symbol of Croatian national identity remains with it as well.

Notes

1. Anonymous, 'Hrvatski prvak s hrvatskim imenom u Europi', *NK Croatia*, August 1997, 10–11.
2. On various types of uses of history, including that of the everyday, see for example Nielsen, *Historiens forvandlinger*; Aronsson, *Historiebruk – at använda det förflutna*.
3. Rosenzweig and Thelen, *Presence of the Past*, 15–36, 115–46.
4. Harrington and Bielby, 'Constructing the Popular', 2.
5. For example, Edensor, *National Identity, Popular Culture*. Specifically, on the case of pop music culture in Croatia, see Baker, *Sounds of the Borderland*.
6. Anonymous, 'Mladu publiku treba odgajati', *NK Croatia*, August 1997, 22; Anonymous, 'Građanski klub puka', *Dinamo*, March 1991, 22–3. On the ways in which Serbia's two dominant clubs relate to history, see Sindbaek, 'Football Commentators as Historians'.
7. Čolović, *Politics of Symbol*, 259–86; Lalić, *Torcida*.
8. Fredi Kramer, 'Građanski, HAŠK ili Croatia?' *Dinamo*, September 1990, 3.
9. Zlatko Canjug, 'Ime Croatia obvezuje', *NK Croatia*, January 1998, 9.
10. Also according to coach Ćiro Blažević, see Anonymous, 'Imamo i motiv i – momčad!' *HAŠK-Građanski*, October 1992, 4–5.
11. On Tuđman and Blažević, see Bellamy, *Formation of Croatian National Identity*, 118–23.
12. Anonymous, 'Predsednik republike Dr. Franjo Tuđman na našem stadionu', *NK Croatia*, April 1997, 11.
13. Anonymous, 'Dr. Franjo Tuđman počasni presednik NK Croatia', *NK Croatia*, May 1998, 3.
14. Abramović, 'Bojne polje u Maksimiru', *Vjesnik*, May 14, 1990, 1; D.D., 'Igrali su delije', *Večernji list*, May 14, 1990, 16–17.

15. Anonymous, 'Smiriti loptu', *Dinamo*, June 1990, 3.
16. Anonymous, 'Nekom se, očito, jako žuriti', *Dinamo*, June 1990, 22.
17. Kramer, *Sveto ime Dinamo*, 112–13.
18. Anonymous, 'Od Hilandarskog ulja do bioritma', *Večernji list*, July 23, 1997, 45.
19. Anonymous, 'Pobjeda i u posljednjoj minuti', *Večernji list*, July 30, 1997, 44.
20. Anonymous, 'Flaster za Prosinečkog', *Večernji list*, July 29, 1997, 28.
21. Anonymous, 'Sigurnost, red i mir', *Večernji list*, July 26, 1997, 45.
22. R. Junaci, 'Dostojanstvo važnije od rezultata', *Večernji list*, July 30, 1997, 44.
23. Anonymous, 'Torcidini potpora Croatiji', *Večernji list*, July 29, 1997, 28.
24. Flak, 'I u noć sa njima', *Večernji list*, July 31, 1997, 34.
25. Ibid.
26. Anonymous, 'Dvojbe novog imena', *Dinamo*, July 1990, 3. See also Fredi Kramer, 'Oni su stvarali Dinamo', *Dinamo*, October 1990, 26.
27. Anonymous, '45 godina plavog kontinuiteta', *Dinamo*, July 1990, 5.
28. Fredi Kramer, 'Kakvo ime Dinamo', *Dinamo*, August 1990, 7.
29. D.N. Kasapinović, 'Stjepan Radić na otvorenju igrališta Građanskog', *Dinamo*, October 1990, 17.
30. Fredi Kramer, 'Kakvo ime Dinamo', *Dinamo*, August 1990, 7.
31. Anonymous, 'Novo ime kluba', *Dinamo*, November 1990, 3.
32. Fredi Kramer, 'Građanski, HAŠK ili Croatia?' *Dinamo*, September 1990, 3.
33. Fredi Kramer, 'Građanski ili HAŠK', *Dinamo*, September 1990, 8–9.
34. D.N. Kasapinović, 'Stjepan Radić na otvorenju igrališta Građanskog', *Dinamo*, October 1990, 7.
35. Zvonimir Magdić, 'Građanski 36 x zašto', *Dinamo*, October 1990, 22–3.
36. Anonymous, '80 godina od postanka Građanskog', *Dinamo*, April 1991, 6.
37. Anonymous, 'Novo ime – stare ambicije', *Dinamo*, July 1991, 3.
38. Anonymous, 'HAŠK-Građanski', *Dinamo*, July 1991, 8–13.
39. Anonymous, 'Uskoro novo staro ime?' *HAŠK-Građanski*, April 1992, 7; Fredi Kramer, 'Još o imenu', *HAŠK-Građanski*, April 1992, 13.
40. The Latin version of the name also had fitted widespread efforts to underline Croatia's Latin and thus Western European historical identity. I am grateful to Bojan Bilić and Ana Ljubojević for pointing this out to me.
41. Fredi Kramer, 'Građanski, HAŠK ili Croatia?' *Dinamo*, September 1990, 3.
42. Anonymous, 'Dr. Franjo Tuđman počasni presednik NK Croatia', *NK Croatia*, May 1998, 3; Anonymous, 'Razgovor s presjednikom republike, Dr Franjom Tuđmanom', *NK Croatia*, October 1997, See also Zlatko Vitez, 'Croatia već 1990, ali . . . ', *NK Croatia*, December 1996, 4–5; Anonymous, 'Imamo i motiv i – momčad!' *HAŠK-Građanski*, October 1992, 4–5.
43. For the dates, also see Dinamo's web page: http://www.gnkdinamo.hr/povijest#anchor (accessed November 26, 2011).
44. Anonymous, 'Razgovor s presjednikom republike, Dr Franjom Tuđmanom', *NK Croatia*, October 1997, 25.
45. Anonymous, 'Hrvatski prvak s hrvatskim imenom u Europi', *NK Croatia*, August 1997, 11.
46. Ibid.
47. Bellamy, *Formation of Croatian National Identity*, 118–21.
48. Anonymous, 'BBB sele na "jug"!' *Dinamo*, March 1991, 19; Anonymous, 'HAŠK-Građanski', *Dinamo*, July 1991, 10.
49. Vrcan, 'Curious Drama of the President', 63–4. For an insight account of similar developments within Hajduk's fan club Torcida, see Lalić, *Torcida*.
50. Fredi Kramer, 'Obavili smo pola posla (interview with Zdenko Mahmen), *Dinamo*, January 1990, 4–5.
51. Anonymous, 'Zašto su dinamovi navijači uvijek na meti?' *Dinamo*, March 1990, 22–3. See also Anonymous, 'Ostajemo plavi', *Dinamo*, March 1991, 16–17.
52. Anonymous, 'Smiriti loptu', *Dinamo*, June 1990, 3.
53. Anonymous, 'BBB sele na "jug"!' *Dinamo*, March 1991, 19; Anonymous, 'Bad blue boysi proslavi rođendan', *Dinamo*, April 1991, 41.
54. Vrcan and Lalic, 'From Ends to Trenches'.
55. Anonymous, 'Uskoro novo staro ime?' *HAŠK-Građanski*, April 1992, 7.
56. Anonymous, 'Imamo i motiv i – momčad!' *HAŠK-Građanski*, October 1992, 4–5.
57. Anonymous, 'Mladu publiku treba odgajati', *NK Croatia*, August 1997, 22; Anonymous, 'Plavi, Plavi . . . ', *NK Croatia*, November 1997, 3.

58. Anonymous, 'Građanski klub puka', *Dinamo*, March 1991, 22–3.
59. Vrcan, 'Curious Drama of the President', 63–4.
60. Vujević, 'Semantički profil imena NK'.
61. Vrcan, 'Curious Drama of the President', 65–9; Bellamy, *Formation of Croatian National Identity*, 118–23.
62. Anonymous, 'Wembley, Heysel, Waldstadion, Prater', *NK Croatia*, October 1996, 19.
63. Kramer, *Sveto ime Dinamo*, 114–15.
64. See the club web page: http://www.gnkdinamo.hr/povijest#anchor (accessed November 26, 2011).
65. Anonymous, 'Smiriti loptu', *Dinamo*, June 1990, 3.
66. Anonymous, '45 godina plavog kontinuiteta', *Dinamo*, July 1990; Fredi Kramer, 'Nepravde', *Dinamo*, August 1990, 12–13.
67. Anonymous, 'Dolazi zvezda', *Dinamo*, May 1991, 18–19. See also Anonymous, '13 Svibanj 1990', *NK Croatia*, May 1997, 10–11.
68. Fredi Kramer, 'Umjesto u Dinamo u Partzan', *Dinamo*, July 1990, 26–8.
69. Anonymous, 'I naši igrači stvarali povijest Partizana', *NK Dinamo*, August 1997, 38–9.
70. Anonymous, 'Za jaku Croatiju i svjetsku Hrvatsku', *NK Croatia*, January 1998, 4–5.
71. Sindbaek, 'Football Commentators as Historians'; Čolović, *Politics of Symbol*, 259–86.
72. Anonymous, 'Nekom se, očito, jako žuriti', *Dinamo*, June 1990, 22; Anonymous, 'Dolazi zvezda', *Dinamo*, May 1991, 18–19.
73. Anonymous, 'Nogometni Bljesak i Oluja', *NK Croatia*, August 1997, 4–5.
74. Anonymous, 'Plava oluja od pet bljesaka', *Večernji list*, July 31, 1997, 1.
75. Anonymous, 'Bronca zlatnog sjaja', *NK Dinamo*, July 1998, 29.
76. Anonymous, 'Dr. Tuđman: Nemojte se opustiti!' *NK Croatia*, September 1998, 9.
77. R. Junaci, 'Plavi, plavi, vi ste dečki pravi', *Večernji list*, July 31, 1997, 31; Anonymous, 'Igrali i za Vukovar', *Večernji list*, July 31, 1997, 32.
78. Anonymous, 'Usrećio sam ljude', *NK Croatia*, August 1997, 18–19.

References

Aronsson, Peter. *Historiebruk – at använda det förflutna*. Lund: Studentlitteratur, 2004.
Baker, Catherine. *Sounds of the Borderland: Popular Music, War and Nationalism in Croatia since 1991*. London: Ashgate, 2010.
Bellamy, Alex. *The Formation of Croatian National Identity: A Centuries Old Dream?* Manchester: Manchester University Press, 2003.
Čolović, Ivan. *The Politics of Symbol in Serbia*. London: Hurst, 2002.
Edensor, Tim. *National Identity, Popular Culture and Everyday Life*. Oxford: Berg, 2002.
Harrington, C. Lee, and Denise D. Bielby, eds. 'Constructing the Popular: Cultural Production and Consumption'. In *Popular Culture: Production and Consumption*, 1–14. Oxford: Blackwell, 2001.
Kramer, Fredi. *Sveto ime Dinamo*. Zagreb: Topical, 2006.
Lalić, Dražen. *Torcida: Pogled iznutra*. Zagreb: AGM, 1993.
Nielsen, Niels Kayser. *Historiens forvandlinger: Historiebrug fra monumenter til oplevelsesøkonomi*. Aarhus: Aarhus Universitetsforlag, 2010.
Rosenzweig, Roy, and David Thelen. *The Presence of the Past: Popular Uses of History in American Life*. New York: Columbia University Press, 1998.
Sindbaek, Tea. 'Football Commentators as Historians: Uses of History and Serbian Club Football, 1990–2005'. *Kultura polis* (Novi Sad) 7, no. 13–14 (2010): 535–547. http://kpolisa.com/KP13-14/Pdf/kp13-14-VII-2-TeaSindbaek.pdf
Vrcan, Srđjan. 'The Curious Drama of the President of a Republic versus a Football Fan Tribe'. *International Review for the Sociology of Sport* 37, no. 1 (2002): 59–77.
Vrcan, Srđjan, and Drazen Lalic. 'From Ends to Trenches: Yugoslavia'. In *Football Cultures and Identities*, ed. Gary Armstrong and Richard Giulianotti, 176–85. London: Macmillan, 1999.
Vujević, Miroslav. 'Semantički profil imena NK 'Dinamo' i NK 'Croatia'. *Politička misao* 37, no. 1 (2000): 141–47.

Football matches or power struggles? The Albanian case within historical conflicts and contemporary tensions

Falma Fshazi

École des Hautes Études en Sciences Sociales (EHESS) Paris, France

Disputes over results of football matches, violent conflicts and claims of political intervention are evident in both the contemporary and the early beginning of the national football championships in 1930s Albania. The article questions the 'reappearance' of contested winners and violent confrontations in football matches through continuity and change in the relationship between state and sport. The relationship is examined socio-historically through the struggle for power between *centre* and *localities*. The article claims that the radical changes in social conditions and the transitions from one form of society to the other have not radically changed the form of interactions of power struggles with football and have not immunized public institutions from being used in the profit of groups in power. The tensions in football demonstrate the unsuccessfulness of central attempts in disempowering and subordinating localities. However, on the other hand they show the continuation of such attempts. Finally, the article underlines the possibilities of empowering communities through sport, in this case, football.

Indeed, the history of sport hitherto is not that of a 'hidden hand' modelling sport behind our backs, neither is it only the story of a powerful elite, of great men and a few great women shaping sport in their own image and likeness. It is rather an ongoing narrative of struggle that blends individual and collective action or agency with political, economic and cultural flows and forces.[1]

Introduction

Power could be basically defined as 'the capacity of an individual or group to command or influence the behaviour of others', following Grant Jarvie.[2] More broadly, it would include the capacity to shape politics and determine policies. Yet, power, defined as the capacity to influence/command/shape/dominate does not either include or exclude the power struggle inferring a relationship, which I would briefly explain using Hargreaves' definition of power: '... a relationship between agents, the outcome of which is determined by agents' access to relevant resources and their use of appropriate strategies in specific conditions of struggle with other agents'. These two complementary approaches to power are invoked in this study, through football the central and local agents' tensioned relationship emerging from the Albanian central governments' understanding of the capacity to control the country – as the ability to command and influence all local actors is disclosed.

This article proposes a consideration of the conflicts in football matches by a closer analysis of the disputes between football clubs and the national football federation, regarded as local and central actors, respectively. I maintain that these disputes emanate from the power struggle between centre and locality in the country. Moreover, I regard the power struggle occurring between these two main axes as having been determinant in the institutional development of the Albanian state recognized as such by the international community in 1913. Since the broad political accord on a national government in 1920, groups in control of government have been applying centralizing politics, which reached its peak during the years of the 'communist' dictatorship (1945–1991).[3] The centralizing attitude of groups in power in 1920–1939 and 1945–1991, and political parties in government since 1992 have been characterized by the attempt to influence local agents and institutions according to the interest of groups in government. In spite of the changing socio-historical conditions, the effort to subordinate multiple interests and instead prioritize the political agendas and economic profits of groups in power has been persistent. And, football has continuously been part of strategies to achieve such subordination.

The centre, in this case, refers to the central institutions controlling the sport organization in the country and the groups in government that exercise control on these institutions. Locality refers not only to local actors such as football clubs but also to the municipalities. In the 1930s the newly independent state had a period of stability during the interwar years when central authorities engaged in the developing of sports in the country. I call this engagement and the network of interactions in which it was immersed 'The making of national sport'.[4] 'The making of the national sport' has been completed during the communist period.[5] Duly, I would broadly call the following period, mid-1950s[6]–1992, the 'Managing of national sport'. Since the early 1990s, society has been adapting to radically changing social conditions. In this sense the dynamics between the centre and locality, and actors related to each, as well as many individual and communal values, have been redefined; the relation of state and sport is still being reshaped. To label this third and contemporary period of development of sports in Albania, I would propose 'Structuring of the national sport'.[7]

The article develops a comparative analysis of power tensions lying behind conflicts in particular football matches between 1930 and 1937 (the making of national sport) and football matches in 2000s (the structuring of national sport). At these moments of multiple social redefinitions continuities and changes are examined in the relation state–sport and the interaction of football clubs with the Albanian Football Federation (AFF). The article is structured in four parts. The introduction is followed by an account of the beginning of the national championships in Albania and the institutional framework endorsing such organization. The second part focuses on the tensions between the sport federation and some particular clubs in the 1930s. The third reviews present day football institutionalization in Albanian and it is followed by an analysis of conflicts in the 2011 national football championship.

Making of the national sport

Although the first football teams are reported to have been founded since 1910–1913[8] the first Albanian national football championship was organized in 1930. The first five championships were managed by the National Entity the Albanian Youth (Enti Kombëtar Djelmënia Shqiptare – Enti),[9] a public institution founded with Italian support that operated due to Italian technical assistance. The first Albanian Sport Federation (Federata Sportive Shqiptare [ASF]) was part of this organization and was defined in its founding statute of 6 July 1930.[10] The ASF, directed for four years by Izedin Beshiri, was under the patronage of Princess Myzejen the sister of King Zog.[11] Enti, which in terms of activities, responsibilities and field of action can be regarded as a preliminary form of a Ministry of Culture, Youth and Sports and was an inter-ministerial institution declared under the auspices of the King.

All decisions related to Enti should have the approval of the King to whom young people had to swear loyalty.[12] Through Enti the state claimed total control over sports and arts in the country with the (declared) aim of developing the moral, physical, patriotic, artistic and sportive education of the Albanian youth.[13] The transformation of the Enti to the department for 'The Albanian Youth' in the Ministry of Education in 1934 did not change this claim. The department was given particular duties over the physical and moral education of the students, while in 1935 the Federation of Cultural and Sportive Association 'The Albanian Brotherhood'/(Federata e Shoqnive Kulturore e Sportive 'Vllaznia Shqiptare' – the Federation) was formed, to which all the sportive and artistic associations in the country were to enrol. The head of the Federation was the Minister of Education, and the vice head was the chief of the department the Albanian Youth in the Ministry of Education.[14] The sixth (1936) and seventh (1937) Albanian National Football championships were organized by the Federation that in international events and correspondence was presented also as the sportive federation.

Sports and arts in the country remained under the patronage of the King and his sisters. Between 1935 and 1939 all local sportive and artistic associations had to be founded or reshaped following the sample statute provided by the Federation. Their direction had to be approved by the Federation and sportsmen had to have federal identity cards in order to participate in matches. Sportive Clubs had to have the consent of the Federation before engaging in any local, national or international activity. Even the maintenance staff of the associations was approved by the Federation, which was also in charge of the main financing of the associations. The head of the associations were members of the Federation's assembly whose duties did not go beyond the approval of the yearly sportive calendar. The only elective capability of the assembly was the election of the central council of the Federation. However, the council could be summoned when required by the Minister of Education for consultation.[15]

Institutionally, the possibility of associations' directors, and particularly players to shape the sportive life of the country was almost non-existent. Their influence was effective locally. The intervention of the state with the local associations, which culminated in 1935 with the attempt to collect all existing associations in a locality in one approved association, was intended to diminish this effect.[16] This enterprise was part of multiple interacting processes among which the most distinctive were the nation-construction and the struggle of power in the new nation-state. Accordingly, the conflicts amongst teams, arbiters, fans, clubs and organizers reflected and symbolized the tensions in the emerging structure and geography of power. This was the reason why centre–locality confrontation was particularly evident in the largest northern city Shkodra[17] and the largest southern city Korça. The following part analyses these confrontations through the most debated matches of the period: Sport Klub Tirana–Skënderbeu of Korça, 1930/1934 and Sport Klub Tirana–Vllaznia of Shkodra 1937.

Football matches or power struggles?

A festive dinner was organized and sponsored by the merchants of Tirana in honour of Sport Klub Tirana,[18] the winner of the first national championship of football (1930) and of six titles in a total of seven national championships organized in the interwar years. In his salutary speech one of the founders of the club, Stefan Shundi,[19] criticized the team Skënderbeu of Korça for defamation of the *Tirana team*. He maintained that the players and directors of the *Korça club* were victims of malevolent individuals that considered the national football championship as a war on localism. He considered it 'shameful', that the *Korça's team* failed to arrive at the match leaving the Tirana Club players waiting in the field to be confronted with the dirty language of *Korça's fans*.[20] The dispute between Sport Klub Tirana and Skënderbeu of Korça had started with the match of 22 June 1930 played in Tirana, where the Korça's team pretended that the referee had favoured Sport Klub Tirana denying two penalties and a goal to Korça.[21]

Immediately after the match the directors of Skënderbeu team presented their objections to the representatives of the ASF, which proposed a play-off in their own city. According to the journal *Arbënia*, which in this dispute favoured the Sport Klub Tirana, this proposal was accepted by Skënderbeu of Korça. Yet, the *Journal of Korça*[22] that defended the position of Skënderbeu team claimed that the play-off was not accepted as a remedy for the unjust result of the match in Tirana. While the journal *Arbënia* claimed that it was impossible to change a match result without written opposition officially submitted to the ASF, the *Journal of Korça* insisted that the ASF had accepted the verbal opposition submitted immediately after the match. On the one hand, *Arbënia* regarded the boycott of the play-off by Skënderbeu as an offence to Sport Klub Tirana. On the other hand, the *Journal of Korça* regarded it as the continuation of favouritism to Tirana Klub that would serve to do nothing, but repeat the referee's injustice to Korça.[23]

The dispute between Sport Klub Tirana and Skënderbeu would not lose its momentum through the years. In 1934, the journal *Besa* wrote that the football match between Sport Club Tirana and Skënderbeu of Korça resembled a violent match of rugby with a lot of punching and kicking.[24] The article underlined the importance of sport as a promoter of national brotherhood, and the regret that regional fans and teams came to matches with such animosities.[25] A few years later, the tension between the team of Shkodra, Vllaznia, developed very similarly including analogous counter-accusations. Towards the end of seventh national football championship (1937) a decisive match took place between Sport Klub Tirana and Vllaznija of Shkodra, the two main rivals for the title. The match ended with a score 1–2 in favour of Vllaznija.[26]

Yet, after the match the referee applied to the Technical Committee (TC)[27] to change the result of the match maintaining that the penalty in favour of Vllaznija was given under the pressure of players and fans of Shkodra.[28] Such claim was met with bitterness in Shkodra's sportive association. In a telegram sent to the Federation, the head of Shkodra's sportive association Cin Serreqi explained that Vllaznia of Shkodra had won this match due to its efforts and ability. He demanded the recognition of the result and underlined that the verdict of the TC was crucial for the existence of this association and the development of sport and youth in Shkodra.[29] Confronted with the complaint of the referee and the accusation of favouritism by the Shkodra's association, the Federation asked by secret order the prefect of Shkodra to give a detailed report on the match. The report of the prefect[30] backed the claims of *Shkodra team* implying that a change of result would not be correct towards *Shkodra*.[31]

Because of the risk of a harsh reaction towards an eventual change of result the vice head of the Federation Col. Aqif Permeti tried to conciliate the parties asking the *team of Shkodër* to come for negotiations in Tirana. In a secret report, the Shkodra's inspector of education Kol Margjini explained that the reunion of Aqif Permeti with the Vllaznija footballers was 'a total failure and there was no way for reconciliation'.[32] After four months of debates over the match the Federation decided that the match should be repeated in Shkodra on 23 January (1937). As pre-announced, the Vllaznija team did not present for the match.[33] This time, not only the team had boycotted the match but also Shkodra's sportive association had sent its resignation to the Federation. The motivation put forward was 'failure to defend the righteous position of the team, which was affronted with an unjust referee'.[34] The resignation telegram of 27 January 1938 regarded the whole situation as a violation of the association and attack to the youth of Shkodra.[35]

In both the cases, and as usual during the period, all the parts in conflict perceived the team of the locality as the locality itself. Even, Oakley Hill, the British officer who was member of the TC and refereed many matches in interwar Albania, in his memoirs while referring to teams uses the localities name more than the name of the team.[36] Actually, before the foundation of the Enti, cities such as Shkodra and Korça had several football teams. Moreover, both of these cities were more developed than Tirana when it was declared capital in 1920. Nevertheless, the new state's centre of power was delineated at a distance from such socioculturally dynamic areas such as Shkodra and Korça. Particularly since 1928 the government promoted the existence of the state and the continuation of the regime and leadership of the King Zog. The success of the state, the regime and the King was also the success of the capital over these previously more developed cities that could produce eventual alternative actors to power.

The inexistence of political parties under the authoritarian regime of the 1930s not only gained a particular meaning within football in terms of possible areas of reaction to power but also converged the struggle of power in two main axes, *centre* versus *locality*. The centralizing efforts of the government, obviously, had not succeeded in controlling the attitude of local associations towards decisions of the AST, then the Federation.[37] Yet, they had assembled diverse and contradictory groups in localities around a local solidarity/localism. Matches among schools or teams of Shkodra during the period reflected tensions between various cultural (religious, intellectual) groups and their associations in the city. The effort of the government to assemble all the clubs under one local association, as was the case of Vllaznija of Shkodër, the head of which was a Catholic from Shkoder Cin Serreqi and the vice a Muslim Faik Ulqinaku, had somehow succeeded in gathering different local actors in one organization shaped by the government.[38] Yet, in this way they damaged the local multiplicity without much gain for what was called national solidarity or brotherhood. The centralizing attitude had fostered localism, while the imposition of central decisions and non-participatory institutions had disempowered localities.

Structuring the national sport: contemporary football

The contemporary sport institutionalization in Albania is rooted in the 1930s, although it had passed through six years of sport activity under occupation, Italian/German period (1939–1943/1943–1944) and then the *communist* period (1945–1991). The sociocultural history of sport under occupation and then during the communist period in Albania has been barely studied.[39] From the point of view of this work the power struggles during these periods were radically different, in this sense they require separate analysis. On the other hand, after the total centralization and invasion by the state of every aspect of sociocultural life of the citizens during the *communist period,* the state's intervention in the sportive life of the country has been redefined and repositioned during the 1990s. The repositioning has evolved as a process that included the struggles of groups to control the government and its institutions. This resurrected clashes between localities, local and central actors. Such struggle very much resembled those in the 1930s.

Obviously, the post-communist institutionalization, in sports as well as in many other areas, was based in a legacy of excessive centralization, meaning total control of local associations by the government. Contemporary institutionalizations still hold the marks of such control. The central financing of sports federations and the appointment of the

National Council of Sport by the government represent the most distinctive benchmarks in this sense. The country's sportive clubs are recently privatized following FIFA conditions. Nevertheless, according to the Law for Sport, sportive federations to which these clubs must adhere, although regarded as private juridical entities, obtain the most important part of their financing from the state.[40] The federations profit from the state budget, the National Fund for the Development of Sport and the state grants that are given following various sports federations' demands. These demands are considered by the Ministry of Culture, Youth and Sport (the Ministry), which gives the final decision about the distribution of the grants.[41]

The government's way of applying its financial means remains a tool to shape the decisions of the sportive federations, as obviously federations' general assemblies would not be eager to elect a directorship that cannot obtain grants and funding from the state. On the other hand, the government had been accused for favouring some candidates for heads of federations. Such favouritism would establish a network of supporting actors, which profit from the means of the state while providing political support in localities through sport clubs. Duly, sportive federations directorship elections have been submerged in tensions and debates.[42] The tensions were reflected also in the elections of the head of the Albanian Olympic Committee in 2009.[43] Because of irregularities giving way to an eventual repudiation by the International Olympic Committee, the election was repeated in three months.[44]

The National Sport Council, which is defined as a consulting organ participating in the formation of sports politics in the country is structured by the Councils of Ministers. The Ministry approves its regulation and appoints its members.[45] Although local authorities are meant to have a say in the politics of sport and the Olympic Committee and federations are in charge of the organization of the sportive life in the country, the Law for Sport leaves the politics of sports to the government without determining an institutional input from sportive federations, sportive associations or clubs. This constitutes a crucial similarity with the 1930s. Consequently, radical changes in social conditions since the 1930s have not radically altered the logic of operation of public sportive institutions in the country, and there have been uneven developments due to which institutions are re-affronted with structures disempowering some actors to empower others, particularly those in government and government supporting networks.

Contemporary tensions

The 2011 football championship that coincided with the local elections was the best demonstration of the effect the contemporary struggle for power has on sports' practice in Albania. During and after the championship press analyses, as well as declarations of involved actors, were dominated by insinuations and in many cases by open accusations about what was termed *political intervention* in football. In one of these articles the champion Skënderbeu of Korça was defined as the 'the team of power'. After analysing the events and the teams' play during the championship the article concluded with a last section titled 'Stain'(Njolla):

> The winner is not judged, maintains an Italian saying, but the fact is that Skënderbeu also this year has had some 'favours' assured by the condition of being a powerful club. The accusations for the Korça team culminated with the matches against Dinamo, all of the three doubtful. The ex-champions of the country had openly tolerated, a situation that created antipathy in the other cities. The Football Federation started an inquiry for one of the matches, but as always in Albania, that one also ended with no result.[46]

The tension between Skënderbeu of Korça and other teams, particularly Flamurtari of Vlora that came second with four point of difference, dominated the analysis on 2011 national football championship. Another article characterizing as 'strange' the events in matches, explained that the wish of all was for this championship to hopefully end soon and be forgotten.[47] The championship 'to be forgotten' was criticized amongst other things, also for the way of awarding the cup to the winner. One of the analyses considered the decision of the AFF to organize the awarding ceremony in the city of Korça one day after the match as 'without precedents'. In this article it was explained that the AFF may have decided to award the winners due the to harsh reaction to alleged favouritism. Yet, whatever the reason, announced the article, this championship will be remembered for a winner awarded one day after and a football federation applying double standards.[48]

The doubts over the championship put forward in the written press had been fully articulated when the opposition candidate for the municipality elections in Vlora accused, while on one of the most prestigious TV shows in the country, the Minister of Finances of stealing the championship in order to win the municipality elections in the city of Korça. He openly blamed the Federation for taking sides and politicizing the football championship.[49] The conflict between the second placer Flamurtari of Vlora, the champion Skënderbeu of Korçë and the AFF hastened towards the end of the championship with the match between Flamurtari and the team of Laçi. Flamurtari representatives demanded that a victory be recorded in the table due to the fact that Laçi's fans' had violently attacked Flamurtari's goalkeeper.[50] The AFF decided to fine the team of Laçi without according a victory to Flamurtari. This decision was regarded as favouritism by Flamurtari's direction. The club declared that they would apply to The Court of Arbitration for Sport in Lausanne and even protest by blocking a bridge entering their city.[51]

Nevertheless, the process of transforming the club associations to limited (Ltd) companies highlighted already existing political conflicts. This process was intensified immediately after the municipal elections, as the municipalities became the main shareholders in the sportive limited companies. Accusations of political interventions came from Shkodra when during the process of transformation of the Club Vllaznija to a limited company the president noted that politics was intervening.[52] Later, accusations of political intervention came during the transformation to a limited company of the Sport Club Tirana. The process lasted longer than in other cases[53] and one of the directors of the club claimed that directors and players were under political pressure. He maintained that the new direction was trying to do a cleaning up in terms of political adversaries, meaning supporters of the opposition.[54] Similarly, political tensions were insinuated during the process of transforming the Sport Club Flamurtari of Vlorë to a limited company. The club was henceforth administered by the municipality of Vlora, which had been won by the Socialist Party in opposition following the 2011 elections, but it risked failing the UEFA deadlines while waiting for the final approval for its Ltd status from the prefecture of Vlorë.[55]

In the 2011 championship, the focus of favouritism accusations was inverted. This time not Sport Klub Tirana, but Skënderbeu of Korça was claimed the *team of power*. Yet, the striking similarity between the tension in the 1930s and those in 2011 resides in the main actor behind the eventual favouritism. The groups controlling the government and accordingly the central football institutions have been in both cases accused of favouring a team in order to control the locality it represents and support groups in power to advance their domination in the country. In the 1930s authoritarian regime, the reasons of favouring could not be put bluntly. However, obviously local associations, and local newspapers regarded such favouritism as an attack to the whole local community. And, obviously, in the present day local representatives have been regarding such favouritism as the strategy of using a team to control a locality, while concomitantly disfavouring localities where influence of groups in government remained limited, particularly in terms of controlling the municipality.

Conclusion: football and the power struggles

The centralizing attitude in the organization of sports of the interwar Albanian regime was not unique, but part of an international trend, and in the Albanian case it was mainly inspired by the Italian example. Similarly, the contemporary situation of sports' institutionalization in the country cannot be understood detached from the process of transformation of post-communist societies. Moreover, in an article about football in contemporary Turkey, Bora underlines an increasing identification with local teams at the expense of support to the national team.[56] In this sense, trends in Albanian football are not detached from the transnational trend of the growing importance of local versus national in the conditions of globalization. Nevertheless, evident in the Albanian case is the continuity in politics that make sports, in this case football, a means of immediate political gain. The concerns for political gains of groups in government have hampered the development of institutions that still do not function based on larger participation and the feedback of clubs and players, but stand as agents imposing some groups' interests to the rest.

The centralizing politics since late 1920s have succeeded in reducing the football organization of the country in one locality one team in the majority of the cases. Yet, this has not contributed in creating stronger local teams, but in homogenizing localities and strengthening localism, which became a strategy of resistance to central domination. The attitude of groups in power towards football reveals persisting in spite of changes in social conditions. There are persisting aspects also in the way of operation of favouritism. The most evident is the ability and possibility of groups in government to manipulate public institutions favouring their continuation in power. And, repeatedly such attempts have been provoking tensions among localities. In the 1930s, Sport Klub Tirana, denoted as Tirana, confronted Vllaznija regarded as Shkodra, and Skënderbeu perceived as the city Korça in a conflict that obviously went beyond players and teams, but resided in the symbolic of power. Contemporarily, the team of Skënderbeu of Korça has been confronted with other teams in conflicts that were not to be resolved in the field. In this sense, in both cases, confrontations of fans, teams and players were exacerbated, even induced by power confrontations.

The repertory of action in terms of resistance to alleged favouritism has changed over time. In the 1930s both the *Shkodra* and *Korça* teams applied to boycott, while contemporary local teams have threatened to block important national road access and to have recourse to international institutions. Since the 1920s it is evident that the media, except for the totalitarian years (1945–1991), and less during the authoritarian period (1925–1939), have been playing an important role in strengthening the position of local clubs by voicing their claims. In both the interwar and the contemporary cases, the importance of football is evident for groups in power and for local communities that through football have reacted to and resisted what they regard as injustice and an attack on their communal achievements.

Contemporary increase in violence in football matches in Albania could be analysed from various perspectives.[57] Yet, this article shows how conflicts in football matches and disputes over them are also and particularly rooted in the struggle of power centre – locality, and as a production of this, in the tension locality versus locality. This characteristic of the power struggle in Albania is transverse to its other aspects such as the class struggle, or tensions between various social groups. It is this specificity that contemporarily as well as in the beginning of sports institutionalization in the country has been sharpening and multiplying conflicts in football.[58] While this sport in both the periods has constituted a sphere of affirmation and emergence of multiple actors and their resistance.[59] Duly, in spite of changing social conditions, football in Albania remains an area involving spaces and possibilities of empowering local actors.

Notes

1. Hargreaves, 'Theory and Method', 8, cited in Sugden and Tomlison, *Power Games*.
2. Jarvie, *Sport, Culture and Society*, 66.
3. It is common to note the period of the totalitarian regime in Albania as 1945–1991. However, in terms of accessibility to local and national sources we could have full-fledged scholarly research on the period only since early 1990s. In this sense, I think, we need further studies on the epoch after World War II to 1992 in order to avoid oversimplifying sociopolitical dynamics of the period by generalizations through dates or labels of regimes.
4. I develop a socio-historical analysis of sportive and cultural activities through the lenses of public youth organizations in interwar Albanian in my PhD diss., see Fshazi, 'Morality, Loyalty and Citizenship'.
5. Since the collapse of the *communist dictatorship* the history of Albania is being revised in the light of new sources. For a distinctive study within a socio-historical perspective on the development of Albanian nationalism see Clayer, *Aux origines du nationalisme albanias*. For a political history of the interwar years in Albania see Fischer, *King Zog and the Struggle*. For a general overview of Albanian history see Vickers, *The Albanians*.
6. Membership to FIFA, 1932. Membership to UEFA, 1954.
7. Although football studies have particularly advanced since the late 1980s the socio-historical and cultural analysis of football in Albania remains still almost unexplored. Separate studies should be conducted as far as it concerns football and cultural tensions, nationalism, religion, ethnic identification or social tensions as class struggle, control of individual body, etc. For a basic guide to sport studies see Coakley and Dunning, *Handbook of Sportive Studies*. See also Horne, Jary, and Tomlison, *Sport, Leisure and Social Relations*. Particularly interesting would be the advancement of a study in terms of football, politics, power and international relations in the Albanian case. For an example of such work see Beck, 'Relevance of the "Irrelevant"'.
8. For a very brief overview of the main developments in Albanian football see http://www.uefa.com/memberassociations/association=alb/profile/index.html (accessed October 10, 2011). For a history of the Albanian national football championships see Dizdari, *Historia e Kampionateve të Shqipërisë*, Dizdari, *Historia e Kampionateve të Shqipërisë 2* and Dizdari, *Historia e Kampionateve në Shqipëri*. In Cungu, *Shkodra, the Sounding Values*, 144, it is maintained that the first football team in Shkodra, "Leka i Madh", was founded in 1905.
9. In my PhD diss., I focus on the foundation, development, operation and institutional structure of the National Entity the Albanian Youth – Enti, see Fshazi, 'Morality, Loyalty and Citizenship'.
10. Mbretnija Shqiptare, *Dekret-Ligje*, 9.
11. Albania was declared a Kingdom and Ahmet Zogu King of Albanians on 1 September 1928.
12. The act of declaring loyalty to the King was done after public ceremonies when students and young boys enrolled in paramilitary troops marched through the city or made gymnastic performances. Such episodes can be found in the press of the period since 1928. See 'Një festim i madhnueshëm gjimnastikuer me rastin e marrjes së flamujve prej Entit Kombëtar'. *Gazeta e Re*, June 13, 1929; and 'Enti Kombëtar dhe Komandanti i Përgjithshëm në Vlorë'. *Gazeta e Re*, July 13, 1929. See also AQSH, Fondi Ministria e Arsimit, 1936. For an analysis of public ceremonies organised by the government since 1928 see Fshazi, 'Morality, Loyalty and Citizenship'.
13. Mbretnija Shqiptare, *Dekret-Ligje*, 1.
14. For foundation and structure of the Federation see the statute: Mbretnija Shqiptare, *Statuti i Federatës*, 1935. For the foundation of the department "Djelmënia Shqiptare" in the Ministry of Education see the Gazeta Zyrtare (Official Journal), 1934, 1.
15. Mbretnija Shqiptare, *Statuti i Federatës*, 1935.
16. The law founding the Federation sanctioned the existence of cultural and sportive association with membership in the Federation. However, it did not prohibit the existence of more than one

association in a locality. Nevertheless, the authorities pressured various associations in a locality to assemble in one association. This was particularly evident in the case of Shkodra. The attempts of the government are disclosed in internal correspondence between institutions. For examples of such correspondence see AQSH, Fondi Ministria e Arsimit, 1935–1936. For an analysis of these tensions between 1934 and 1939, see Fshazi, 'Morality, Loyalty and Citizenship'.

17. In Albanian the name of the cities Shkodra, Korça, etc., according to their position in the phrase can be used also as Shkodër or Korçë. In this article I have used only the version Shkodra, Korça, etc.

18. For Stefan Shundi as one of the promoters of the nationalist intellectual current known as neo-Albanianism (neo-Shqiptarizma) in the 1930s Albania see Fshazi, 'Morality, Loyalty and Citizenship', chap. 2. For an example of his articles see Shundi, 'Lëvizja e Djalëris'.

19. Dizdari, *Historia e Kampionateve të Shqipërisë*, 143.

20. *Arbënia*, 1930, 1.

21. Ibid., 4.

22. *Gazeta e Korçës*, July 1–15, 1930.

23. *Arbënia*, 1930, 1–4. *Gazeta e Korçës*, 1930.

24. *Besa*, 1934, 1.

25. Ibid.

26. Dizdari, *Historia e Kampionateve të Shqipërisë*, 145

27. Komiteti Teknik Arbitral Shqiptar – Albanian Technical Referee Committee found in 1930 as part of the Sport Federation.

28. Dizdari, *Historia e Kampionateve të Shqipërisë*, 146 and for this conflict see 145–8.

29. AQSH, Fondi Ministria e Arsimit, 1937. Date on telegram, October 31, 1937. From, Cin Serreqi, Head of Vllaznija Association. To, The Federation 'The Albanian Brotherhood'.

30. The Prefecture is a main administrative unit, which is headed by the prefect who is appointed by the government. A prefecture includes rural areas and several cities, among which the largest becomes the centre of the prefecture. The prefecture is mentioned by the name of its largest city.

31. AQSH, Fondi Ministria e Arsimit, 1937.

32. Ibid. The coded message was sent from the Inspectorate of Education in Shkodër to the Ministry of Education in Tirana. Date and number on telegraph: 'Nr. 21/2, 23.XI.1937'.

33. AQSH. Fondi Ministria e Arsimit, 1938. Date and place on document: Shkodër, January 23, 1938.

34. Ibid.

35. Ibid. The association Vllaznia of Shkodra had been complaining even previously for favouritism underlining that efforts were spent to impede the victory of the team. The head of the association in 1936, Tush Kakarriqi, explained that such situation was demoralizing the youth of the city, while leaving no enthusiasm in the championship. See AQSH, Fondi Ministria e Arsimit, 1936. Letter sent on April 30, 1936, from the head of the Vllaznia association to the Sports Federation after the match Besa of Kavaja – Vllaznija of Shkodra. According to Kakarriqi there were many incidents during the match and the Sports Federation was not inquiring these incidents.

36. 'In the course of the game there was a crowd of players in the Tirana goal area, and in the general scrimmage an arm in the Tirana colours was thrust out and it stopped a shot by a Shkodër player. I had no doubt about it and awarded a penalty. The entire Tirana team clustered around me, protesting and arguing. I stuck to my decision and explained it . . . Of course I made my report to the governing committee and the match was awarded to Shkodër . . . My reputation at Shkodër, naturally enough, had gone up and the next time I refereed there the Shkodër team accepted a decision of penalty against them with only a little grumbling'. Hill, *An Englishman in Albania*, 49.

37. For centralizing politics through football see Clignet and Stark, 'Modernisation and Football in Cameroon'.

38. These claims were put forward by representatives of the associations as well as the press supporting them, see AQSH, Fondi Ministria e Arsimit, 1937. Date on telegram October 31, 1937. From: Cin Serreqi. To: The Federation 'The Albanian Brotherhood'. See also *Gazeta e Korçës*, July 1–17 Korrik, 1930 [in English].

39. For a general overview of Football in Eastern Europe see Duke and Crolley, *Football Nationality and the State*, 86–99. An interesting work on football in the Nazi era is done about the Viennese football, see Marschik, 'Between Manipulation and Resistance'.

40. See *Ligji për Sportin* (Law for Sport), 2005, art. 16. This article also referred to other sources of financing without precisely indicating what they could be. Yet, this law's 11th section is titled 'Financial Sources'. In two articles, (art. 36–37), it is explained that sport in the country is financed by central and local government sources, incomes of sportive organizations, the National Found for the Development of Sport (Fondi Kombëtar i Zhvillimit të Sportit), financing from international sportive organizations and other legal sources. This found is based in the Ministry of Culture, Youth and Sport and its income derives from the sportive lotteries. Its use is subject to the Minister's order and is applied according to the regulation issued by him in accordance with the law. Consequently, not only grants given to the federations are distributed by the Ministry but also the use of National Fund for the Development of Sport is left to the initiative and decision of the Minister.

41. *Ligji për Sportin*.

42. The elections for the head of the Weightlifting Federation in February 2009 were immerged in a scandal of accusations for favouritism of the government to certain candidates. The election process degenerated in violent clashes among participants. See 'Esat Ademi konfirmohet te peshëngritja. Gjergj Ruli, rikthehet tek atletika' [Esat Ademi confirmed in peshëngritja. Gjergj Ruli returning in athletics federation], *Gazeta Shqip*, http://forum.albaniasite.net/index.php?topic =4875.0 (accessed October 1, 2011).

43. 'Esat Ademi zgjidhet në krye të KOSH. Pritet njohja nga Komiteti Olimpik Ndërkombëtar' [Esat Ademi elected head of the Albanian Olympic Committee. waiting the approval of the International Olympic Committee], http://index.fieri.com/sports/1038-esat-ademi-zgjidhet-president-i-koksh-pritet-njohja-nga-komiteti-olimpik-nderkombetar.html (accessed October 1, 2011).

44. The present president of the Albanian Olympic Committee is Agim Fagu elected on 14 July 2011. See http://www.nocalbania.org.al (accessed October 2011). This election was approximately three months after the disputed one.

45. *Ligji për Sportin*, art. 9.

46. See 'E gjithë Korça në festë Skënderbeu është kampion' [Korça celebrates Skënderbeu is a champion], http://www.balkanweb.com/sport/2692/e-gjithe-korca-ne-feste-skenderbeu-eshte-kampion-61476.html (accessed May 4, 2011).

47. 'Skënderbeu is Albanian champion for the second time since 78 years when it won the first title in the forth Albanian National Championship. This victory is for the moment held with a difference of four points from Flamurtari, only one match before the end of this championship, which is eagerly waited to end and hopefully be forgotten for all what happened until these last matches'. http://top-channel.tv/artikull.php?id=210358&ref = fp (accessed May 5, 2011).

48. Peçi, 'Flamurtari - Skënderbeu'.

49. 'Në studion e Top Story, Shqipëria Vendos 2011, kryetari i Bashkisë së Vlorës, Shpëtim Gjika akuzoi Federatën Shqiptare të Futbollit se është bërë palë me politikën duke vjedhur futbollin' [In the studio of Top-Story, Albania Decides 2011, the mayor of Vlora, Shpëtim Gjika accused the Albanian Football Federation of taking sides in politics by stealing football], http://top-channel.tv/artikull.php?id=210281&ref = fp (accessed May 4, 2011). Parts were immerged in a series of conflicts on matches where the Club Flamurtari accused the Albanian Football Federation for politicizing the championship and acting against Flamurtari, while the Football Federation, accused the club of putting blame on it for its own defeats. See 'Përplasja FSHF-Flamurtari, Gjika anulon Francën' [The clash Flamurtari-Albanian Football Federation, Gjika cancels the match with France], http://www.shekulli.com.al/2011/03/16/perplasja-fshf-flamurtari-gjika-anulon-francen.html (accessed March 16, 2011).

50. About the situation of Flamurtari's goalkeeper see: 'Moçka në spital, policia: Faji i tij' [Moçka in hospital, the Police: It was his fault], http://top-channel.tv/artikull.php?id=209766&ref = fp (accessed May 3, 2011).

51. 'Disiplina refuzon kërkesën e Flamurtarit' [Discipline refuses the demand of Flamurtari], http://top-channel.tv/artikull.php?id=210236&ref = fp (accessed May 3, 2011). During this conflict the candidate of the Democrat Party in government was accused for favouring the team of Korça as a strategy of his campaign for mayor in the ongoing municipal elections. See http://www.balkanweb.com/sport/2692/penallti-per-vllaznine-flamurtari-braktis-ndeshjen-61466.html (accessed May 3, 2011).

52. 'Fushaj le Vllazninë' [Fushaj leaves Vllaznija], http://top-channel.tv/artikull.php?id=217162& ref = fp (accessed August 19, 2011). 'Vllaznia do administrohet nga Bashkia Shkodër'

[The Municipality of Shkodër will administer Vllaznija], http://top-channel.tv/artikull.php?i
d=217197&ref = fp (accessed October 19, 2011). Kodheli, 'Fushaj dorëhiqet nga Vllaznija'.
Kodheli, "Fushaj: Bashkia më largoi'.

53. ''Emërohet Tafaj, pritet privatizimi i klubit' [Tafaj appointed, the privatization to follow], http://
www.gazeta-shqip.com/#/sport/e3b22d1dc5ed8e17fb3c7fc04e920ac8.html (accessed August
23, 2011).

54. 'Vazhdon odiseja e pushtimit të SK Tiranës nga militantët' [Continues the Odyssey of Sport
ClubTirana's invasion from militants.], http://www.gazeta-shqip.com/#/sport/
b0e7816b2af9275f548d6d9ee942f33c.html (accessed November 17, 2011).

55. Marsi, 'Flamurtari, Prefekti i Vlorës nuk';'Privatization, Waiting for the Signature of Prefect
Veçani. Then, Tirana Remains the Unique Non-Private Club', http://www.gazeta-shqip.com/#/s
port/1c2ec2c25cf40a4cedb566049e7ae9e8.html (accessed July 6, 2011).

56. Bora and Özgehan, 'Nationalism, Europeanization and Football'. A different perspective we
find in Hare, *Football in France*. The book emphasises the increasing importance of football in
the creation of national identity in contemporary France.

57. One of the first aspects to inquiry on violence in matches would be hooliganism. A broad
perspective to such studies is given in Dunning, Murphy, Williams, 'Spectator Violence at Football
Matches'.

58. The analysis of football and various identifications (regional, national, individual and
communal), football and culture (popular, political, etc.), football and spaces (urban, rural,
public, etc.) represents very interesting and unexplored paths in the historical and contemporary
analysis of Albanian football. On the other hand, these have been explored through particular
case studies and theoretical approaches to football. See Tomlison, *Sport and Leisure Cultures*.
See also Tomlison and Young, *German Football History*.

59. Clashes between localities through football in the case of Real Madrid and Barcelona during the
Franco regime are analysed in Duke and Crolley, *Football Nationality and the State*, 1–8, and
24–49.

References

AQSH. Fondi Gazetë Zyrtare, D.16, V.1934.
AQSH. Fondi Ministria e Arsimit, Nr. 195, V.1935.
AQSH. Fondi Ministria e Arsimit, Nr. 195, D.335, V.1936.
AQSH. Fondi Ministria e Arsimit, Nr. 195, D.329/1, F.296/371, V.1936.
AQSH. Fondi Ministria e Arsimit, Nr. 195, D.352/2, F.96-97, 196, 204, V.1937.
AQSH. Fondi Ministria e Arsimit. Nr. 195, D.271, F.7, V.1938.
AQSH. Fondi Ministria e Arsimit. Nr. 195, D.271, F.16, V.1938.
Arbënia. 'Fletore e perditeshme Neo-shqiptare'. July 12, 1930, 1.
Arbënia. 'Fletore e perditeshme Neo-shqiptare, Nr. 35'. July 8, 1930, 4.
Arbënia. 'Fletore e Perditeshme Neo-shqiptare'. July 17, 1930, 1–4.
Beck, Peter J. 'The Relevance of the "Irrelevant": Football as a Missing Dimension in the Study of
British Relations with Germany'. *International Affairs* 79, no. 2 (March 2003): 389–411.
Besa. 'Gazete Politike e Përditëshme. Tiranë'. July 5, 1935.
Bora, Tanıl, and Özgehan Şenyuva. 'Nationalism, Europeanization and Football: Turkish Fandom
Transformed?' in *Football, Europé et Régulations*, ed. Guillaume Robin (France: Presses
Universitaires du Septentrion, 2011), 35–52..
Ceremonia e dhënies së kupës së kampionatit do të zhvillohet nesër në Korçë'[Flamurtari -
Skënderbeu, stone and seats thrown to those from Korça. The title award will take place tomorrow
in Korça]. http://www.shekulli.com.al/2011/05/16/fshf-bojkoton-vloren-kupa-do-te-jepet-ne-korce.
html (accessed May 16, 2011).
Clayer, Nathalie. *Aux origines du nationalisme albanias. La naissance d'une nation
majoritarirement muslumane en Europe*. Paris: Éditions Karthala, 2007.
Clignet, Remy, and Maureen Stark. 'Modernisation and Football in Cameroon'. *Journal of Modern
African Studies* 12, no. 3 (September 1974): 409–21.
Coakley, J. and Dunning, E., eds. *Handbook of Sportive Studies*. London: Sage, 2002.
Cungu, Maxhid. ed. *Shkodra, the Sounding Values*. Shkodër: Botimet Camaj, 2007.
Dizdari, Besnik. *Historia e Kampionateve të Shqipërisë*. Vitet 30'të Tiranë: Albin, 1999.
Dizdari, Besnik. *Historia e Kampionateve të Shqipërisë 2*. Vitet 40' Tiranë: Albin, 2000.

Dizdari, Besnik. *Historia e Kampionateve në Shqipëri vitet 1939–42*. Tiranë: OMBRA GVG, 2004.

Duke, Vic, and Liz Crolley. *Football Nationality and the State*. New York, London: Longman, 1996.

Dunning, Eric, P. Murphy, and J. Williams. 'Spectator Violence at Football Matches: Towards a Sociological Explanation'. *The British Journal of Sociology* 37, no. 2 (June 1986): 221–44.

Fischer, Bernd. *King Zog and the Struggle for Stability in Albania*. New York: East European Monographs, 1984.

Fshazi, Falma. 'Morality, Loyalty and Citizenship: The Organization of Youth in Interwar Albania'. PhD Diss., EHESS and Bogaziçi University 2012.

Gazeta e Korçës, July 1–15, 1930.

Hare, Geoff. *Football in France: A Cultural History*. Oxford/New York: Berg, 2003.

Hill, Oakley. *An Englishman in Albania. Memoirs of a British Officer 1929–1955*. London: The Centre for Albanian Studies, 2002.

Horne, John, Jary, D., and Tomlison, A., eds. *Sport, Leisure and Social Relations*. London/New York: Routledge & Kenan Paul, 1987.

Jarvie, Grant. *Sport, Culture and Society*. London: Routledge, 2006.

Kodheli, Erald. 'Fushaj: Bashkia më largoi nga Vllaznija'. [Fushaj: The municipality made me leave Vllaznija]. http://www.gazeta-shqip.com/#/sport/e760063a6c539fc47a320dfb32a6631a.html (accessed August 23, 2011).

Kodheli, Erald. 'Fushaj dorëhiqet nga Vllaznija: Edhe "senatorët" drejt largimit'. [Fushaj, resigns from Vllaznija: the senators are also leaving]. http://www.gazeta-shqip.com/#/sport/f91315fdb2c3ba51da839976911196b7.html (accessed August 19, 2011).

Ligji për Sportin [Law of sport], Nr. 9376, April 21, 2005.

Marschik, Matthias. 'Between Manipulation and Resistance: Viennese Football in the Nazi Era'. *Journal of Contemporary History* 34, no. 2 (April 1999): 215–29.

Marsi, Mikel. 'Flamurtari, Prefekti i Vlorës nuk miraton kthimin në "sh.a"'. [Flamurtari, the Prefect of Vlora does not approve the transformation into "LTD"]. http://www.gazeta-shqip.com/#/sport/70c026e2ba13a6b0a477e366a88a7d3e.html (accessed July 6, 2011).

Mbretnija Shqiptare. *Dekret-Ligje per Themelimin e Entit Kombtar "Djelmënia Shqiptare."* Tiranë: Shtypshkronjet "Mbrothësia" Kristo P. Luarasi, 1930.

Mbretnija Shqiptare. Ministria e Arsimit. *Statuti i Federatës së Shoqnivet Sportive e Artistike "Vllaznija Shqiptare"*. Tiranë: Shtypshkronja e Ministris s'Arsimit, 1935.

Peçi, Anila. 'Flamurtari - Skënderbeu, gurë e stola kundër korçarëve nga tifozët'. http://www.shekulli.com.al/2011/05/16/fshf-bojkoton-vloren-kupa-do-te-jepet-ne-korce.html (accessed May 16, 2011).

Shundi, Stefan. 'Lëvizja e Djalëris'. *Arbënia Fletore e Përditëshme Neo-Shqiptare* (August 12, 1930).

Sugden, John and Tomlison, Alan, eds. *Power Games: A Critical Sociology of Sport*. London: Routledge, 2006.

Tomlison, Alan. *Sport and Leisure Cultures*. Minneapolis, MN/London: University of Minnesota Press, 2005.

Tomlison, Alan, and Christopher Young. eds, *German Football: History, Culture, Society*. London: Routledge, 2006.

Vickers, Miranda. *The Albanians: A Modern History*. New York: St. Martin's Press, 1997.

Stronger than the state? Football hooliganism, political extremism and the Gay Pride Parades in Serbia

Christian Axboe Nielsen

Department of Culture and Society, Aarhus University, Aarhus, Denmark

Football and politics have been linked inextricably in Serbia since the collapse of Yugoslavia in 1991. This article examines the Serbian state's reluctant struggle with football-related violence and political extremism in the period from 2009 until 2011. The analysis rotates around the Gay Pride Parades in Serbia, which have become an annual contested event pitting progressive and pro-European forces against a 'patriotic' coalition of extreme nationalist organizations, associations of football hooligans and the Serbian Orthodox Church. Despite Serbia's ostensibly reformist path and its professed desire to advance rapidly towards membership in the European Union, the state's reaction to threats and acts of violence against proponents of Gay Pride has to date been hesitant, ambiguous and inconclusive.

Two developments in 2011 symbolize the particularly inextricable link that exists between football and politics in Serbia. On 11 October 2011, Serbia suffered a 1–0 defeat to another former Yugoslav republic, Slovenia, a loss that ended Serbia's hopes of qualifying for the 2012 European football championship. The following day, the European Union Commission recommended that Serbia finally receive the status of formal candidate for European Union (EU) membership. Perhaps partly due to the massive outpouring of discontent provoked by the defeat on the football pitch, the Commission's decision provoked no euphoria, but instead found Serbia in a foul mood additionally aggravated by consternation about Kosovo and a stagnant economy. The fatalistic sentiment was amply illustrated by the most popular reader comment on an article on the *B92* news portal about Serbia's prospects for EU membership: 'Yes, well we were candidates for the European Championship as well …'

Building on my earlier research exploring the link between political reforms and football in Serbia, this article examines the ongoing struggle in Serbia to reduce the incidence of violent acts related to a toxic combination of political extremism inherited from the 1990s and football hooliganism.[1] Both in Serbia and abroad, recurring violent incidents related to Serbian football have fostered the perception that the state continues to be unwilling or unable to confront amalgamations of hooligans and ultra-nationalists. Such incidents have caused FIFA to threaten Serbia repeatedly with suspensions from international competitions. In principle, more robust prosecution of the most violent perpetrators, combined with the adoption of new laws on sport, criminal procedure and organized crime, augurs well for an endgame that will put Serbia and Serbian football solidly on course towards Europe. Unfortunately, however, many indications remain that substantive change remains elusive, with state authorities and political leaders unwilling to break decisively with the 'culture of violence' that has plagued Serbia for much of the past two decades.

Before embarking upon the description and analysis of extremism and football hooliganism in Serbia, it is necessary to emphasize that this combustible mixture is by no means unique to Serbia or other former Yugoslav republics. The link between football hooliganism and right-wing extremism is well documented in Europe, if sometimes exaggerated, and the threat posed by this nexus is arguably once again on the rise in EU members such as the UK.[2] Many countries are attempting to cope with the new challenges presented by, among other things, the ability of fans to mobilize and organize online. In Serbia, the authorities confront similar problems, but Serbia's status as a candidate for EU membership means that its efforts in this field are subject to extraordinary scrutiny and may negatively affect membership prospects.

In this article, extremism is treated as a political orientation that refuses to accept the democratically established constitutional order, and threatens or acts violently to challenge this order.[3] While agreeing with Ramón Spaaij's definition of football hooliganism as 'the competitive violence of socially organized fan groups in football, principally directed against opposing fan groups', this article treats the product of this phenomenon's intersection with political extremism.[4] Hooliganism is primarily linked to violence in football stadiums, but is by no means restricted to this location, as anyone who has witnessed the streets of Belgrade on the day of a Red Star–Partisan derby can easily attest. Hence, this article uses 'hooligan' in a broader sense, including in the term those who practice, condone or advocate the use of violence and threats of violence, and who use fandom as a pretext for extremist political organization.

While informed by the literature on the connections between sports, hooliganism and violence, the present article does not attempt to further investigate the causes of this phenomenon. Rather, the article attempts to provide a summary of recent developments on the ground in Serbia. Nevertheless, an examination of the ongoing phenomenon of violent hooliganism and right-wing extremism must observe at least three factors that combine to explain the situation. First, there continues to be a sizeable contingent of the young male population that revels in the sense of belonging and group identity that football fan groups offer. This is unlikely to change, as a similar phenomenon can be observed throughout the world. Second, the remnants of the 'culture of violence', dominant in Serbia in the 1990s, remain visible and active, and this militates against public condemnation and censure of violent acts, particularly when these are committed against minorities. For a substantial part of the population, a division of society into 'us and them' or 'patriots and enemies or traitors' continues to be acceptable. Third, the organs of the state, and particularly the judiciary, remain unwilling to prosecute hooligan violence in a robust and consistent manner. In summary, given the linkage between society as a whole and violence in sport, 'it is not possible to change relations in sport... without changing the social relations which reproduce sport'.[5]

The recent history of football in Serbia is inextricably linked to the violent history of the collapse of Yugoslavia and can in many ways be read as a metaphor for the country's overall development. This linkage has been acknowledged by the pro-European coalition that won the May 2008 elections, and it has manifested itself on several occasions since then, most dramatically on the occasion of the annual Gay Pride Parade held in October. For this reason, this article is structured around three milestones: the Gay Pride Parades in 2009, 2010 and 2011, of which only the 2010 Parade was actually held. Pairing each of these events with violent, football-related incidents, this article assesses these as tests of the political will of the authorities in Serbia to confront extremism and of the Serbian judicial system's willingness and ability to enforce relevant legislation.

Gay Pride 2009 and the Brice Taton case

In the summer of 2009, Serbian lesbian, gay, bisexual and transgender (LGBT) organizers announced their intention to hold a Gay Pride Parade in September.[6] Such an event had last been held in 2001, when marchers were brutally beaten while the police watched. A planned parade in the spring of 2004 had been cancelled because of violence against Serbs in Kosovo. Hence, in 2009, the initiative was widely perceived both in Serbia and in the EU as a test of the maturity of post-Milošević Serbia, and in particular as a test of the new law on discrimination, which the Serbian parliament had adopted after a protracted and acrimonious debate in March that year. The announcement of the parade was welcomed by EU, UN and OSCE [Organization for Security and Co-operation in Europe] representatives and was greeted cautiously by the authorities, even as conservative and right-wing extremist opponents mobilized against the event in the weeks leading up to it. An interlinked coalition of football hooligans and right-wing extremists covered Belgrade with graffiti tags reading 'death to faggots' and 'blood will flow across Belgrade, the parade will not take place'.[7] Despite state assurances that the parade would receive the necessary police protection, the authorities in the end *de facto* banned the parade by proposing that it be held at an isolated location removed from the city centre.

On 17 September 2009, in the midst of the controversy surrounding the Gay Pride Parade, a group of hooligans attacked a French football fan named Brice Taton who had come to Belgrade to watch a football match between Partisan Belgrade and Toulouse.[8] The brutality of the attack was so intense that Taton shortly thereafter died from his wounds. After a long period in which football hooligans had enjoyed impunity in Serbia, such a tragedy with international dimensions created the opportunity for a test case of the Serbian state's declarations of decisive action against violence. Jean-François Terral, France's ambassador to Serbia, noted that 'such events, especially the lynching of Brice Taton, cast a shadow on Serbia's image in the world', and he deplored 'a certain [complacency] towards this phenomenon, especially the statements that deny the need to break up these groups, which in the end leads to them being able to act freely'.[9]

The ambassador's comments impressed upon Serbian authorities the need to act decisively to investigate and prosecute the killing. And, indeed, some domestic commentators argued plausibly that the authorities would have shrugged off the incident had the victim not been a foreigner. As it was, Serbian president Boris Tadić stated that 'Serbia will react with the greatest possible gravity . . . to all groups that have been promoting violence in recent days'.[10] Whereas earlier attacks had seen prosecutors reluctant to use the more robust end of the criminal code, Taton's death led to charges of premeditated murder against 10 suspects, meaning that they could face up to 40 years in prison. In January 2010, the state prosecutor filed an indictment against 15 individuals for their role in the attack.[11] The accused in the case went on trial in April 2010. The two main suspects in the case were tried in absentia and sentenced to over 30 years in prison each, but have still not been apprehended.[12]

As a direct result of the Taton incident and another attack against an Australian in Belgrade, the Ministry of Justice began to consider legal bans against 'patriotic organizations' such as *Obraz* (Dignity), *Dveri srpske* (Serbian Doorway), 1389 and *Naši* (Ours), a number of whose leaders were arrested. Experts on security issues in Serbia argued that the examples of other countries showed that extremism could only be dealt with successfully in the context of a broad strategy incorporating numerous sectors and both preventive and oppressive measures.[13] The state prosecutor, Slobodan Radovanović, began considering bans on right-wing organizations in accordance with the 2009 laws on discrimination and on the banning of the display of fascist symbols.[14]

The controversy surrounding the 2009 Gay Pride Parade and the Taton incident combined to produce an explicit recognition on the part of the authorities of the linkage between political extremism and football hooliganism. Hence, Radovanović initially called for banning all the fan clubs associated with some of Serbia's largest football clubs: the *Grobari* (Partisan), *Delije* (Red Star) and United Force (Rad). 'A whole bunch of groups and groupings exist which commit criminal acts under the veil of cheering. These are not fans, but instead criminals, as emerges from evidence that the police is collecting and which we will use in [our] demand for the banning of these groups.'[15] Radovanović promised concerted action by all relevant state authorities in an effort to end hooliganism, noting that the aforementioned fan groups were also linked to broader forms of organized criminal activity such as narcotics trading.[16] By early November 2009, the list of forbidden organizations had been narrowed down to the more extreme fan factions of the aforementioned groups – with names such as 'Ultra Boys', 'Brain Damage' and 'Alcatraz'.[17] Radovanović's colleague, Slobodan Homen, state secretary in the Ministry of Justice, announced amendments to several existing parts of the criminal code and a streamlining of judicial proceedings, all designed to make legal punishments for hooliganism swifter and more severe.[18] This notwithstanding, the autumn Partisan–Red Star derby featured unusually high levels of disorder and destruction of material property in the stadium.

Behind the tough talk, some observers also detected bluster covering a lack of political will and procrastination, such as when a spokesperson for the state prosecutor at the end of November stated that '1 January is the date when the real settling of accounts begins between the state and the hooligans. Either we or they will win, there is no third option'.[19] Similarly, Defence Minister Dragan Šutanovac called for 2010 to be the year of combatting hooliganism.[20] Yet the noted Belgrade defence attorney Tomo Fila disparaged the government for busying itself with writing new laws which, he argued, they lacked the resources or will to implement.[21] Adding a note of comedy to matters, President Tadić found himself apologizing to the Serbian public after being photographed consuming champagne at Red Star's Marakana stadium, even while state officials were deploring the link between alcohol and hooliganism.[22]

Nor did the government's announced policies meet with universal political support. The investigations into right-wing organizations were derided by opposition parties as politically motivated. Dragan Šormaz, a parliamentary deputy for the Democratic Party of Serbia, while disputing the links between his party and Obraz and 1389, simultaneously opposed any ban. In his view, 'this is only an attempt to turn the story away from the main topic in Serbia: how is it that the state and the citizens are living ever worse?'[23] Thoughts about cracking down on football violence also seemed to be somewhat overwhelmed by the positive news that the Serbian national team had qualified for the 2010 World Cup in South Africa.

A group of intrepid journalists affiliated with the media outlet *B92* kept the pressure on the state authorities by launching a new expose of the state's approach to the challenge of violent hooliganism. Rather than treating the problem as one confined to the excesses of isolated groups of sociopathic young men, the three-part documentary titled 'The (Non-)Power of the State' laid bare a troubling combination of factors that contributed to chronic violence and a general atmosphere of impunity for perpetrators. This included the complicity of prosecutors, judges and law enforcement officials – often appointees from the Milošević era – as well as the managements of top football clubs. The series quickly garnered the attention not only of state officials but also of extremists who threatened the programme's host, Brankica Stanković, with violent assault.[24] These threats were sent through social media and uttered as chants at football matches, where a plastic effigy of Stanković was tossed about and abused by hooligans. Although a number of persons were arrested and prosecuted for these threats, the penalties meted out in these and other cases related to threats and attacks on journalists were lax.[25] The only severe hooligan-related sentence issued by the end of 2009 was a 30-year prison sentence against a supporter of Rad, Bojan Hrvatin, for the 2006 killing of Bojan Majić, a supporter of the Voždovac football club.[26]

At the end of 2009, the Minister of Internal Affairs and Deputy Prime Minister, Ivica Dačić, emphasized that organized crime was another important aspect of the problems facing football in Serbia. He claimed that he had cancelled an important meeting with the leadership of Serbia's football clubs when he saw the list of attendees. 'Half of them are in the [government] white book of organized crime'.[27] Yet despite brief earlier promising signs, state authorities continued to drag their heels in the prosecution of prominent persons such as Svetlana 'Ceca' Ražnatović, the widow of the notorious paramilitary leader Željko Ražnatović 'Arkan'. Ceca had inherited Arkan's football assets after his assassination and, as such, she was suspected of being intertwined in organized criminal activity linked to sport.[28] Only in 2011 did the Serbian courts finally sentence her to house arrest and to restitution of a portion of the funds that she was alleged to have embezzled. This sentence was widely perceived as being very lax.

Despite the numerous proclamations and promises made by politicians in the last months of 2009, the first half of 2010 witnessed little substantial change. In April 2010, a mass brawl and shooting incident *during* a semi-final match between Red Star and OFK Belgrade in the Serbian Cup football tournament amply illustrated that violent hooliganism remained a problem. The incident prompted a Serb journalist to write that 'images of violence at football matches come not only from Serbia, but are also found in the most developed countries of the European Union. But probably only here is it possible that a hooligan in spite of a large number of police officers brings a pistol into a stadium and then wounds someone'.[29] After this incident, Dačić repeated his earlier calls for a strict enforcement of all provisions of the law on preventing violence at sporting events.[30] Again, however, these tough signals quickly became mixed when a judge threw out the case in which six 'fans' of Partisan were accused of threatening Stanković.[31] The judge in the case even claimed that there had been no reason to detain the six in the first place, as they allegedly only insulted rather than threatened Stanković. This development highlighted the discrepancy between the government's policies and the recalcitrant attitude of the judiciary, whose members are almost impossible to remove in Serbia.[32] The decision was also widely criticized by journalists' associations, which pointed to the continued threatening environment in Serbia for investigative journalists and argued that they should enjoy special protection under the law comparable to that held by police officers on duty.[33] Stanković, who had in the meantime been put under police protection, noted that while she appreciated that the state was taking the threats seriously, the combination of lacking prosecution and police protection meant that she was effectively unable to continue with her investigative journalism. Interviewed in May 2010, she said that essentially nothing had changed, not even after the death of Taton.[34]

Gay Pride 2010: a reluctant state permits a 'European' parade

By the late summer, preparations began to get underway for the holding of Gay Pride 2010 in Belgrade.[35] In an ominous echo of the murder of Taton in September 2009, the police in August 2010 arrested a young Serb in Belgrade on charges of stabbing two young

Germans whom the former had suspected of being gay.[36] Combined with rapidly increasing pressure from the EU, this highlighted for the authorities the need to prepare for the upcoming parade. Symbolically, on 17 September, the mayor of Belgrade, Dragan Đilas, accompanied the French ambassador in unveiling a memorial to Taton. On that occasion, Đilas stated that the city would always act to protect the rights of all citizens to live and walk freely in the city, regardless of religious, national, sexual or other affiliation.[37]

At the same time, however, the combustible mixture of hooligan clubs and right-wing organizations such as Obraz, 1389 and Dveri srpske were mobilizing their forces to oppose the parade. The slogan 'we are waiting for you' (*čekamo vas*) was spray-painted all over Belgrade, a message generally regarded as threatening violence against participants in the parade. An important part of the strategy of the opponents of the parade was to identify the opposition to the parade as a 'patriotic act' and hence as linked to support for the Serbian stance on Kosovo, opposition to NATO and the EU, etc. Therefore, the LGBT community organizing the parade was labelled as 'anti-Serbian' or 'traitorous'. Yet some observers also argued that the parade organizers were complicit in the politicization of the parade by making support for it into a broader issue about the direction that Serbia should take as a society.[38] Left generally unheard were broad sections of the population who arguably supported neither the 'patriotic' front nor the LGBT movement and who therefore viewed the whole parade as an event that merited battening down the hatches and keeping one's head low.

The 2010 Gay Pride Parade was held on 10 October, almost 10 years after the demonstrations that had brought about the collapse of the Milošević regime.[39] On 5 October, the EU's ambassador to Serbia announced that he wanted to participate in the march.[40] Combined with an impending visit to Serbia by US Secretary of State Hillary Clinton, this essentially gave reluctant Serbian officials no choice but to issue a green light to the event. 'At the Parade itself, Vincent Degert, Head of the Delegation of the EU to Serbia, held the first speech; also speaking were Head of Council of Europe Delegation to Serbia, Head of OSCE Mission to Serbia and a Dutch member of the European Parliament'.[41] The Ministry of Internal Affairs mobilized thousands of police officers to protect the much smaller group of participants. On the day of the parade, roving and well-organized bands of young men, unable to get at the well-protected parade, instead attacked numerous buildings, the headquarters of the governing parties, private vehicles, a mobile mammography unit and media outlets throughout Belgrade. More than 100 people, including many police officers, were treated for injuries sustained in street clashes.[42] More than 200 people, including the leader of Obraz, were arrested.[43] While state officials including President Tadić immediately condemned the violence and rioting, some opposition representatives again reacted by predicting that the state would use the incidents as a pretence to crack down on the political opposition. As for foreign observers, both the EU and the USA chose publicly to focus on the fact that the event had been held.[44]

Despite the contrast with 2009, when the event had effectively been cancelled, celebration seemed premature. Everyone in Serbia knew that right-wing forces aligned with football hooligans intended to oppose the parade. These groups had spent months organizing their networks online throughout Serbia so successfully that the police later reported that a majority of the rioters stemmed from areas outside Belgrade.[45] In other words, the police and the civilian intelligence agency arguably had plenty of advance warning and could have acted pre-emptively to stop the rioting.[46] As with earlier incidents of violence, the signals sent by government officials after Gay Pride 2010 were mixed. While thanking his police officers for their efforts and also promising robust punishments of the rioters, Minister of Internal Affairs Ivica Dačić lashed out at the EU for forcing the event to be held.[47] The EU replied that it had not insisted on the holding of the parade, but that it expected Serbia to uphold European standards, which included respecting the Serbian state's own law against discrimination.[48]

Only days after the rioting in Belgrade, another incident in Italy emphasized the scope of the problem. At a Euro 2012 qualifying match between Serbia and Italy in Genoa, Serb hooligans nearly lynched their own goalkeeper and then interrupted the match while causing substantial damage to the stadium.[49] It subsequently emerged that Ivan Bogdanov, one of the main architects of this incident, was well known to the police in Serbia and had been involved in the February 2008 attack on the US Embassy in Belgrade. Moreover, the hooligans had announced their intent to provoke disorder on online forums in advance.[50] While the Serbian ambassador to Italy issued an official apology, both Dačić and the Football Federation of Serbia accused the Italian authorities of not having been sufficiently vigilant to prevent the problems in Genoa.[51] In the meantime, alarming questions were asked about the funders of hooligan groups and their travels abroad.[52]

The combination of the violence in Belgrade and Genoa sent alarm bells ringing among Serbian commentators. Retired football star Savo Milošević – one of the rare voices in Serbian football to speak out against hooliganism – called Genoa 'one of the darkest days in the history of Serbian football'.[53] According to Milošević:

> These are matters which the state should have controlled. Unfortunately the state has for the past 20 years stood on the sidelines regarding sport. The state institutions that are responsible for our sport have their responsibility, because no one can tell me that these people cannot be controlled or held under observation. There were also indications that something could happen in Italy. All this was known by certain persons. Why the state does not react, why such things must happen before anyone reacts, I really do not know. I know that sports has been left for last in this kind of reorganization in our state.... Once again we will pay a high price because of our inertia, our disinterest, our lack of will to grab the problems by the root.[54]

Precisely as a year earlier, the events of Gay Pride 2010 and the debacle in Italy rekindled a debate on the causes of football-related violence. Once again, calls were made to confront the combination of political indifference and extremism that formed the backdrop to hooliganism.[55] Perhaps the best example of this was an op-ed written by Bruno Vekarić, Serbia's deputy war crimes prosecutor. Vekarić cited assassinated Prime Minister Zoran Ðinđić's statement that 'there are weeds in every state, only in Serbia the weeds are watered'.[56] Retracing the riots of recent years against homosexuals, the independence of Kosovo and the arrest of Radovan Karadžić, Vekarić argued that these matters were only nominal excuses for hooligans and their institutional supporters. In unusually direct terms, he specifically criticized former prime minister Vojislav Koštunica's Democratic Party of Serbia and ultra-conservative members of the Serbian Orthodox clergy for fanning the flames of hatred. Vekarić concluded by stating that the unrest in Serbia 'showed that our society is seriously ill', and arguing that the country's prosecutorial organs and judiciary now had to treat this problem, and hence to pass a test that they had failed for years. Along with other leading government officials, Vekarić issued calls for bans against extremist organizations.[57] The leader of the opposition Liberal Democratic Party, Čedomir Jovanović, also argued that this was the last chance for decisive action against hooligans and their political sponsors.[58] However, in the light of the preceding year's stasis, these pronouncements seemed to appear ritualistic rather than decisive.

Notwithstanding the holding of the parade, pro-European commentators felt quite unsure that Serbia had decisively answered the question of whether it was, in fact, stronger than the hooligans.[59] The renowned anthropologist Ivan Čolović, whose research often treated hooliganism, observed links between the recent violent acts and threats of violence on the one hand, and right-wing extremist organizations, conservative political parties and the Serbian Orthodox Church on the other hand. In his words, the violence 'was not chaos, it was not blind, it was not crazy, but terror with so to say patriotic and revolutionary motives, to beat and kill in the name of Serbian tsars and the glorious Serb tradition'.[60] Čolović rejected the argument that the hooligans were traumatized or misunderstood youths. He further observed that the hooligans such as the ones arrested in Genoa claimed political status and seemed to regard their own acts as part of a campaign aimed at keeping Serbia out of the EU and opposing the independence of Kosovo. In that sense, members of these groups regarded all legal moves aimed against them and their violent acts as political in nature and themselves as 'victims of democratic terror in Serbia'. Čolović spoke of the long-term consequences of a successful 'hooligan revolution' in the 1990s and deplored how little had changed since he had been interviewed about the same matter in October 2009.[61] He noted that he still differed from President Tadić in believing that 'fascism leads to violence', not the other way around.

After the Gay Pride Parade, the Red Star–Partisan derby was the next challenge. The Serbian parliament restricted the law on criminal proceedings on the eve of the derby, permitting those suspected of illegal activities to be detained for 30 days instead of the previous 8 and to face accelerated criminal proceedings.[62] This was also in part designed to rectify a situation in which *only 2.4% of criminal complaints against hooligans resulted in final convictions*.[63] However, the proposal was criticized by lawyers who pointed out that the Ministry of Justice was rushing to action in a way that could have a 'boomerang effect' on Serbia's prospects for EU membership.[64] In the event, the derby was held with more than 5000 uniformed police officers on duty, police special forces on alert and several thousand undercover officers. No incidents were recorded.[65] Yet Zoran Dragišić, a professor of security studies in Belgrade, saw this more as the product of a short-term ceasefire between hooligan groups and the state than as a victory for law and order. 'After the derby, the authorities have bought time and now do not need to work hurriedly as earlier. However, I fear that after the 'peaceful derby' public pressure to solve this problem will fall'.[66] This view was supported by sociologist Dragan Koković.

Gay Pride 2011: the state capitulates

Events of the first half of 2011 showed limited developments towards addressing the issue of football hooliganism and political extremism in Serbia. When the president of UEFA, Michel Platini, visited Serbia in February 2011 and spoke with both President Tadić and the director of the Serbian civilian intelligence agency, it was emphasized that Serbia would not be able to participate in international club matches or tournaments if events such as those in Genoa were to recur.[67] However, in March, the Constitutional Court rejected the demand of the Public Prosecutor's Office to outlaw selected hooligan groups, which had been pending since October 2009. According to the Court, there were 'no existing constitutional or legal premises for the proceedings before the Constitutional Court and for a decision on this request'.[68] This raised the question of whether the legal provisions for banning extremist organizations were robust enough. The only organization successfully banned in Serbia to date had been the neo-Nazi organization *Nacionalni stroj* (National Formation).[69] And mixed signals continued to emerge from the judiciary in the most important cases on violence linked to hooliganism and to the protests against Gay Pride. In April, the leader of Obraz, Mlađen Obradović, was sentenced to two years in prison.[70] However, almost simultaneously, the Court of Appeals reduced the sentence of Uroš Mišić for his notorious attack on an undercover policeman during a football game in December 2007 from 10 to 5 years in prison.[71] This meant that Mišić could be paroled later in 2011. The First Basic Court in Belgrade also issued a very mild sentence to those who had physically attacked a journalist in 2008, prompting the prosecutor to file an appeal.[72] The Serbian media noted that this confirmed a troubling trend of virtual impunity for violence against journalists.[73] Summarizing the prevailing atmosphere, sociologist Jovo Bakić wrote that:

> ... he who best insults, who is most adroit in a fight, who has the closest connections with neo-Nazis, who most aggressively and least mercifully attacks the opposing fan or police tribe, he is worth the most respect – a real man and a role model. If the representatives of the state dare to detain him and accuse him, we will defend him publicly, we will pay for shameless lawyers, and we know what to do with the judges. The parents will, it is understood, tell how the child is wonderful and always law-abiding.[74]

With Serb politicians thinking increasingly of the parliamentary elections scheduled for the first half of 2012, the support for the Gay Pride Parade – never more than reluctant and lukewarm even at its peak in September 2010 – quickly ebbed away. Ivica Dačić stated that the police had better things to do than to protect the parade and would be happier if it were not to be held.[75] Further positioning himself as the voice of Serbs who viewed the parade as an alien event imposed by the EU, Dačić proposed that the Europeans provide the police with the necessary equipment if they continued to insist on the staging of the parade.[76] This again created the impression that the organization of the parade, rather than the threats of violence against participants, was the real threat to security. Nor was Dačić alone in his scepticism of the parade. His comments were reinforced by the mayor of Belgrade, Dragan Đilas, who stated that Serbia had much more pressing issues to take care of than holding another Gay Pride Parade. While claiming to support minority rights, Đilas insisted that 'I will never support any manifestation which carries with it a danger of threatening the security of Belgrade and its citizens'.[77] An admission that the real threat came from opponents of the parade could be found in a statement of the otherwise equally reluctant police union, which alluded to the threat of coordinated destructive actions in the capital under the title 'Belgrade in Flames'.[78] Meanwhile, Obraz announced that it would hold a 'Prayer Walk for a Healthy Family', as a counterdemonstration on the same day as the Gay Pride Parade.

In the end, Serbian authorities, citing the risk of widespread physical and material damage, decided to ban all public demonstrations and gatherings in the first weekend of October, when the Gay Pride Parade had been scheduled.[79] Referring to the persistent disagreement between the EU and Serbia on Kosovo, Dačić also stated that Serbia and the police had had to show that they, and not the EU, were at least in charge of making the decision on the parade. 'Unfortunately, we have become too submissive to pressure, so now they think that they can blackmail us for everything that occurs to them. Everyone needs to understand that parades and various prayer marches are an internal problem of Serbia ... I am the minister of internal affairs of Serbia, not the commissioner for internal affairs of the EU. Probably I know better than them what are the security risks for my state.'[80] Even more provocatively, Dačić stated that 'perhaps yesterday was, as Amnesty International states, a black day for human rights, but it was a wonderful day for citizens of Belgrade. No one here banned the Parade of Pride, but rather all gatherings were banned because security was threatened, and I believe that that decision was supported by the majority of the population'.[81] This claim was belied, however, by declarations of victory by Obraz, Dveri srpske and similar organizations, which also used the opportunity to call their supporters to exhibit similar levels of energy with respect to Kosovo.[82]

Liberals and social media in Serbia widely criticized the decision to ban the 2011 Gay Pride Parade, and ironically agreed with their right-wing opponents in assessing the decision as a victory for hooliganism and extremism.[83] Belgrade University professor Ljubiša Rajić pointed out that the state had violated the constitutional right to assembly and the law on discrimination.[84] And independent police and security experts argued that if the state had gathered as much intelligence about the identities and intentions of extremists prepared to undertake violent acts, then the state should have acted decisively and pre-emptively to disable these groups.[85] In an article with the deliberately provocative title 'Who Is the Faggot Now?' (*Ko je ispao peder*), Filip Švarm pointed out the numerous logical gaps and contradictions that characterized the rhetoric surrounding the decision to ban the parade.[86] Perhaps most convincingly, Švarm began his article by simply repeating the tough quotes of state officials from October 2010 after the violent riots that had accompanied Gay Pride 2010. A year later, the same officials insisted that their decision was not a defeat or a capitulation of the state in the face of extremism.[87] Yet not coincidentally, the term 'capitulation' had been used two years earlier in the wake of the series of violent incidents that included the attack on Taton.[88]

Conclusion

To understand why it apparently has been so difficult for the Serbian state to crack down on violent forms of hooliganism, it is essential to consider the links that exist between these organizations and the political party system in Serbia. As Svetislav Basara pithily put it, 'the state truly is stronger, but it would be thousands of times stronger if it in the past had not cooperated with hooligans and extremists'.[89] From the early 1990s, when the Serbian state used football fan organizations as recruiting grounds for paramilitary groups, there have been links to political parties. The toppling of the regime of Slobodan Milošević in October 2000 featured active participation by football fans who helped to coordinate street demonstrations and attacks on key state institutions.[90] As the anti-Milošević coalition rapidly splintered into bitterly opposed political blocs, politicians realized the utility of maintaining and nurturing their contacts to these fan organizations, which could be used as a potential source of pressure on political opponents and as bodyguards for politicians. In the case of the conservative bloc led by Vojislav Koštunica, there was a natural affinity for the more right-wing 'patriotic' organizations such as Obraz and 1389. Well aware of this, reformist coalitions proved reluctant to act against the nexus of right-wing extremism and football hooliganism. Even after the reformists' convincing electoral victory in 2008, moves aimed at strengthening the rule of law and cracking down on violence in sport and society brought forth allegations by the conservatives and their extremist allies of the establishment of a 'democratic dictatorship'.

Prominent politicians also served on the executive boards of football clubs such as Red Star and Partisan even as these clubs continued to tolerate hooliganism. In 2009, the executive boards of these two clubs included prominent politicians from the two main governing parties, the Democratic Party and the Socialist Party of Serbia, as well as one of the main opposition parties, the Democratic Party of Serbia.[91] Far from discouraging hooliganism, the management of major football clubs in Serbia often seemed to support it, not least from a fear of potential personal repercussions if they were to provoke the ire of the most powerful fan 'firms'. Dragan Koković observes that the most extreme football fan clubs in Serbia place themselves above the club and frequently engage in confrontations with the management of the very clubs that they ostensibly worship.[92] In this manner, fan clubs insist that they know better than the professional management of the club what is best for the club. If this power relationship is not adjusted so that the club management is in a dominant position, it will be very difficult to change the behaviour of the fans. It was an open secret in Serbia that football clubs paid for the travel expenses of fans to international matches, supported the visa applications of fans and attempted to smooth over incidents involving fans both at home and abroad.[93] The membership of key judges and law enforcement officials in the executive boards ensured that the right strings could be pulled to protect 'fans' accused of legal infractions. As of mid-2010, for example, the head of the Serbian Ministry of Internal Affairs' Service for the Struggle against Organized Crime was still Svetislav 'Bata' Đurović, who had earlier served as security commissioner for the Football Federation of Serbia (*Fudbalski savez Srbije* [FSS]). At that time, the head of the FSS was Zvezdan Terzić, who was later accused of extensive corruption. And until October 2010, Marko Vučković, the leader of the Red Star 'Ultra Boys' hooligan faction, remained on the board of the club despite numerous pending criminal charges against him.[94] Meanwhile, the management of football clubs and the state authorities keep insisting that the responsibility for violence in football stadiums is the responsibility of the other side.

In summary, the political utilization of hooligan groups that characterized the 1990s and 2000s in Serbia acted as an open invitation for these groups to enter the political arena and to act as political agents. As Serbia has normalized its relationship with the outside world, moved towards EU membership and attempted to introduce the rule of law internally, the nexus of violent hooligan groups and political opponents of this path have repeatedly challenged the state's monopoly on power. These groups conform to a significant extent to Spaaij's concept of societal fault lines, with Serbian hooligans staking out their position as 'patriots' defending the nation and traditional values against a European and homosexual onslaught.[95] During periods such as the lead-up to the Gay Pride Parade, 'patriots' unite to challenge the state and their perceived opponents. At such times, the club affiliations and antagonisms that divide them become less important and even briefly disappear altogether. Yet the political aspect of football-related violence should not blind us to the (perhaps even more disturbing) reality in which 'ethnic nationalism is merely used as a flag of convenience by young fans who wish to engage in collective violence'.[96]

This hints at a probable reason for the reluctance of politicians in Serbia to condemn hooliganism. Their 'patriotic' outbursts, while posing a threat to public security, are to some extent welcomed by a Serbian political community that seeks to convince the EU and other international actors that Serbia must receive more benevolent treatment on issues such as Kosovo. By pointing to the ostensible 'anger of the street', moderate Serb politicians such as those of the Democratic Party seek a reprieve from the taking and implementation of unpalatable decisions. This was demonstrated repeatedly in successive Serbian governments' policy on the issue of the arrest of fugitives wanted by the United Nations' International Criminal Tribunal for the Former Yugoslavia. The message from Belgrade was that too much pressure on the government would lead to mass protests, imperilling the stability of the government, and leading perhaps to an extreme nationalist government. Even after the 2008 elections and the splintering of the fervently nationalist Serb Radical Party into a much smaller party and a larger, pro-EU Serb Progressive Party, this bugbear was not put aside.

Moving beyond the political sphere, coming to terms with extremism and hooliganism in Serbia also necessitates a direct confrontation with the support that such behaviour receives from prominent members of the Serbian Orthodox Church. While formally and repeatedly distancing itself from the use of violence, the Church has not distanced itself from extremist organizations that openly cloak themselves in the robe of religious identity and patriotism.[97] On the contrary, the statements of top clergy such as the metropolitan Amfilohije Radović about homosexuals can easily be read as veiled incitements to violence. In 2009, for example, Radović spoke of 'Sodom and Gomorrah' and used the aphorism 'the tree that does not bear fruit must be cut and thrown into the fire'.[98] And Miša Vacić of the right-wing organization 1389 stated that the LGBT organizers 'themselves incite violence by bringing out their satanic rituals on the streets of the capital'.[99] In 2010, Radović called the parade a 'parade of shame' and argued that the organizers of the parade were primarily responsible for the violence. From his point of view, the march itself was an act of 'violence against the majority of people who live here'.[100] Radović's words were echoed by Vladan Glišić of the right-wing organization Dveri srpske, who claimed that his organization rejected violent homophobia but carried out a struggle 'against the aggressive propaganda of homosexuality which is being carried out today through official institutions and the media'.[101] For Glišić, homosexuality is an ideology with totalitarian tendencies.[102] Hence, in the eyes of both the Serbian Orthodox Church and Glišić, the LGBT population and its 'extreme' claims, not 'patriotic' organizations, pose the real threat to law and order and to Serbian society as a whole. And, as has been pointed out elsewhere, a considerable portion of Serbs perceived it as a foreign and elitist event foisted upon Serbia.[103]

A final chronic aspect of the state's attitude towards hooliganism in Serbia has been an unwillingness to label violent hooliganism as such. Dragan Popadić, a social psychologist, observed in 2009 that the state seemed to condone violence against 'others', and that the authorities often spoke of 'fans' even when the violent acts of these people had little or no connection to sport.[104] As a result, violence by 'fans' is either downplayed or explicitly supported by broad sections of the political spectrum, the media and the public as manifestations of 'patriotism'. According to security expert Zoran Dragišić:

> ...the professional apparatus of state repression has the power to put an end to [extremists]...but the problem is with the politicians who do not have enough courage to enter into that clash because they believe that they will lose the support of one part of their constituency.[105]

The main lesson drawn by many top officials in Serbia seems be that violence on the scale seen on the occasion of the 2010 Gay Pride Parade is unacceptable. Among liberals and EU observers, the presumed consequence of this conclusion was that the state would act proactively and decisively to thwart those hooligans and extremists who wished to prevent the 2011 Gay Pride Parade. Instead, the state officials, facing an election in 2012, seemed to decide that the real threats to security were the LGBT activists. Apart from demonstrating a fundamentally flawed understanding of minority rights and violating the Serbian constitution, such a view will continue to ensure that no robust action will be taken against instigators and perpetrators of violence in football and society. Unless the Serbian state clearly identifies the threat to the rule of law and acts consistently to prevent violent incidents and prosecute those responsible for them, Serbia is at real risk of continuing to score own goals even as it attempts to enter the EU.

Epilogue

This article was completed in the spring of 2012 and hence does not take into account the 2012 Gay Pride Parade. Unfortunately, the Serbian state's behaviour towards violent hooliganism and political extremism throughout 2012 confirmed the pessimism that informs the conclusions of this article. In the summer of 2012, Serbia elected a new president, Tomislav Nikolić, and a new government was formed, headed by Prime

Minister Ivica Dačić. This gave the reins of power to a coalition of ostensibly reformed former ultra-nationalists (Nikolić's Serb Progressive Party) and Dačić's Socialist Party of Serbia. In October 2012, the government again capitulated to pressure from a coalition of right-wing organizations, hooligans and the Serbian Orthodox Church.[106] The government refused to grant permission for the holding of the parade, again siding with those threatening violence instead of with the minority threatened by the violence. At the same time, President Nikolić and the government promulgated an amnesty law that quickly resulted in early release for some of the perpetrators of the most notorious and violent attacks in recent memory. Uroš Mišić and Miladin Kovačević were among the first to be released pursuant to the new law. Nebojša Trajković, the police officer who had been brutally attacked by Mišić, speaking for the victims of these crimes, stated: 'Now the state is rewarding [Mišić], and I am dragging myself around to doctors. One message is being sent to my colleagues, and another to young perpetrators – that they can get away without punishment'.[107]

Notes

1. Nielsen, 'The Goalposts of Transition', 87–103.
2. Garland and Treadwell, '"No Surrender to the Taliban": Football Hooliganism, Islamophobia and the Rise of the English Defence League'. As the title of the article indicates, there has to some extent been a shift in British hooliganism from traditional racist forms of extremism to (allegedly) interracial extremism focused 'defensively' against the 'Islamic threat'.
3. This is, in fact, a close approximation of the legal definition of extremism in the republics of the former Yugoslavia and also of Germany.
4. For a comparative overview of definitions of football hooliganism and approaches to the study of this phenomenon, see Spaaij, *Understanding Football Hooliganism*, 9–53.
5. Koković, *Doba nasilja i sport*, 70.
6. The background and circumstances of Gay Pride 2009 are detailed in Jovana Gligorijević, 'Hronologija događaja koji se nije desio', *Vreme*, September 24, 2009.
7. Marija Vidić, 'Anatomija jednog rizika', *Vreme*, September 24, 2009.
8. Miloš Vasić, 'Pravda za Brisa Tatona', *Vreme*, October 1, 2009.
9. *BBC*, 'French fan dies after Serb attack', September 29, 2009.
10. *B92*, 'Taton killers facing aggravated murder', September 30, 2009.
11. Danijela Vukosavljević, 'Optuženi navijači za ubistvo Tatona', *Politika*, January 21, 2010.
12. S.G., 'Oštre kazne na prvom stepenu', *Vreme*, January 27, 2011; Tatjana Tagirov, 'Dirigovana navigacija smrti i pravde', *Vreme*, January 27, 2011.
13. *Blic*, 'Tužilac hoće zabranu Obraza i 1389', September 22, 2009; S. Georijev, 'Oživljavanje mrtvog slova', *Vreme*, October 8, 2009.
14. Tatjana Tagirov, 'Ustavna kozmetika', *Vreme*, October 8, 2009.
15. Slobodan Radovanović quoted in *Blic*, 'Državni vrh traži strožije kazne za huligane', October 2, 2009; see also interview with Radovanović in *NIN*, October 1, 2009.
16. Gordana Raković, 'Zabrana', *Kurir*, October 2, 2009.
17. Vuk Z. Cvijić, 'Stigli dokazi protiv navijačkih grupa', *Blic*, November 5, 2009.
18. B. Marković and V.Z. Cvijić, 'Huligani sa stadiona pravo u zatvor', *Blic*, November 3, 2009. For a wide-ranging debate on hooliganism and violence in Serbian society, see the panel discussion sponsored by the Friedrich Naumann Foundation, available in *Vreme*, October 29, 2009.
19. *Danas*, 'Novi derbi – stara priča', November 29, 2009.
20. *B92*, 'Šutanovac: Borba protiv huligana', December 13, 2009.
21. Predrag Paunović, 'Džaba vam zakon', *Kurir*, November 30, 2009.
22. Ibid.; M. Derikonjić, 'Tadić: Neću više da nazdravljam na stadionima', *Politika*, December 2, 2009.
23. Dragan Šormaz quoted in 'Nasilje i stranke', *NIN*, October 1, 2009.
24. Ivana Tošović, 'Brankica Stanković', *Danas*, December 7, 2009; Jovo Bakić, 'Država i sportski klubovi', *Politika*, December 29, 2009; Momir Turudić, 'Navijači protiv Insajdera', *Vreme*, December 17, 2009.

25. *B92*, 'Pravda novinare na kraju zaobiđe', July 12, 2011. The lawyers of Uroš Mišić, who was convicted of a brutal attack on an undercover police officer at a football game in December 2007, tried unsuccessfully to block the emission of the *B92* documentary. The lawyers argued that the broadcasting of the documentary threatened the independence of the judiciary. M. Derikonjić, 'Advokati Uroša Mišića traže zabranu Insajdera', *Politika*, December 24, 2009.
26. *B92*, 'Navijaču Rada 30 godina zatvora', December 10, 2009.
27. *B92*, 'Dačić: Pola klubova vodi mafija', December 31, 2009. See also A. Ž. Adžić and B. Marković, 'Kriminalci se bore za status vođe navijača', *Blic*, May 31, 2010.
28. Vuk Z. Cvijić, 'Odugovlače istragu protiv Svetlane Ražnatović', *Blic*, February 13, 2010.
29. Lazar Delić, 'Sever opasan po život', *Politika*, April 16, 2010. See also Slobodan Georgijev, 'Zahuktala mašina mržnje', *Vreme*, April 22, 2010.
30. A.Ž.A. and B.M., 'Zvezdin sever zna ko je pucao ali svi ćute', *Blic*, April 17, 2010.
31. A.Ž.A. and B.M., 'Razrešiti sudiju koja je oslobodila huligane', *Blic*, April 23, 2010. A disciplinary committee was later formed to examine the conduct of the same judge, Jelena Milinović, after a controversy surrounding another controversial case unrelated to football.
32. D. Pušonjić, 'Sudija mora da odgovara za sramno obrazloženje', *Blic*, June 26, 2010; R.D., 'Sukob izvršne i sudske vlasti', *Politika*, April 25, 2010. In August 2010, Miloš Radisavljević 'Kimi', one of the leaders of the 'Alcatraz' group accused in the case, was sentenced to 16 months in prison, yet the court simultaneously released Radisavljević until such time as the conviction was confirmed by the court of appeals. In July 2011, the court of appeals confirmed part of the original conviction, but annulled another part, reducing the sentence to six months and ordering a retrial of the most substantial count of the indictment. M. Dudvarski, 'Dok su vođu uhapsili, druge već oslobodili', *Press Online*, May 23, 2010; *Blic*, 'Navijaču ukinut deo presude za ugrožavanje Brankice Stanković', July 11, 2011.
33. M. Derikonjić and V. Dugalić, 'Olako odbačena optužnica za pretnje novinarki', *Politika*, April 25, 2010; M. Derikonjić, 'Sud oslobodio navijače koji su vređali Brankicu Stanković', *Politika,* April 25, 2010.
34. Interview with Brankica Stanković, 'Kažiprst', *B92*, May 19, 2010.
35. Tamara Skrozza, 'Zakon između mišića i mozga', *Vreme*, September 16, 2010.
36. P.Z. Veličković, 'Izbo mladiće jer je mislio da su gej', *Blic*, August 13, 2010; Danijela Vukosavljević, 'Huligansko nasilje ne bira naciju', *Politika*, August 16, 2010.
37. R.D., 'Postavljena spomen-ploča Brisu Tatonu', *Danas*, September 18, 2010.
38. Boris Delić, 'Može li dobar Srbin biti gej', *Danas*, September 18, 2010.
39. Portions of the discussion of Gay Pride 2010 appeared previously in my post for *Nationalities Blog*. Christian Axboe Nielsen, 'After 20 Years Will the "Culture of Violence" Finally End in Serbia?' *Nationalities Blog*, October 16, 2010.
40. Andrew Rettman, 'EU Ambassador to Attend Gay Pride in Serbia', *euobserver.com*, October 6, 2010.
41. Mikuš, 'State Pride', 835.
42. Jelena Ilić and Lana Gedošević, 'Organizovano nasilje', *Blic*, October 11, 2010; Jovana Gligorijević, 'Teror nad Srbijom', *Vreme*, October 14, 2010.
43. V.Z.C. and T.M.S., 'Obraz nije sam mogao da organizuje nasilje', *Blic*, October 12, 2010; 'Vođa Obraza Mladen Obradović ostaje u pritvoru', *Politika*, March 5, 2011.
44. Mary Beth Sheridan, 'Clinton Praises Serbia's Progress, New Leaders', *Washington Post*, October 12, 2010.
45. *B92*, 'Ko "diriguje" hiljadama huligana', October 11, 2010.
46. Svetlana Lukić, 'Varvari među nama', *e-Novine*, October 15, 2010.
47. Dačić, State Secretary Homen and Dubravka Filipovski, a member of the opposition New Serbia party participated on 11 October 2010 in the RTS talk show 'Upitnik'.
48. *Blic*, 'Delević: EU nije tražila održavanje gej parade', October 14, 2010.
49. Slobodan Georgijev, 'Linč u Đenovi', *Vreme*, October 14, 2010.
50. S.B., 'Prekid u Genovi bio najavljen', *24 Sata*, October 13, 2010.
51. *Blic*, 'Dačić: Italijanska policija napravila veliki propust', October 13, 2010; *B92*, 'FSS: Odgovornost na Italijanima', October 15, 2010.
52. Danijela Vukosavljević, 'Huliganima za nerede plaćeno 200.000 evra', *Politika*, October 16, 2010; Vuk Z. Cvijić, 'Vođa novobeogradskog klana platio divljanje huligana', *Blic*, October 18, 2010.

53. Zoran Milosavljević, 'Serbia Paying Price for Ignoring Hooliganism: Milošević', *Reuters*, October 13, 2010.
54. *B92*, 'Milošević: Problem mnogo opasniji', October 13, 2010.
55. Tatjana Tagirov, 'Srbija i huligani', *Vreme*, October 21, 2010.
56. Bruno Vekarić, 'Ko zaliva korov u Srbiji', *Danas*, October 13, 2010. For a well-articulated, similar argument in English, see Ian Traynor, 'Serbian Thugs Are the Toys of Nationalist and Neo-Fascist Leaders', *Guardian*, October 13, 2010.
57. *Politika*, 'Đelić najavio zabranu ekstremističkih grupa', October 16, 2010; *B92*, 'Huligani tretirati kao kriminalce', October 16, 2010; I. Pejčić, 'Pritvor i za nasilničko i nedolično ponašanje', *Danas*, October 15, 2010; D.Č., 'Blage presude ekstremistima', October 17, 2010; *B92*, 'Država spremila stroži ZKP', October 17, 2010.
58. Interview with Čedomir Jovanović, *Press Online*, October 12, 2010.
59. *Danas*, 'Ko je jači – država ili huligani', October 15, 2010; Aleksandar Rodić, 'Vlast ne želi da se obračuna s huliganima', *Blic*, October 17, 2010.
60. Interview with Ivan Čolović, *e-Novine*, October 17, 2010.
61. Interview with Ivan Čolović, *e-Novine*, October 5, 2009.
62. *B92*, 'Izmena zakona pred derbi', October 20, 2010; *B92*, 'Izmene zakona stupile na snagu', October 23, 2010.
63. Tatjana Tagirov, 'Još jedan krivični bumerang', *Vreme*, November 4, 2010.
64. Ivan Janković, 'Bumerang zakon', *Danas*, October 20, 2010.
65. Aleksandar Radonić, 'Derbi pod opsadom', *Kurir*, October 23, 2010.
66. M. D. Milikić, 'Dogovor navijača i države loše rešenje', *Danas*, October 25, 2010.
67. Ž. Babović, 'Ili će Srbija proterati huligane sa stadiona ili neće igrati u Evropi', *Blic*, February 25, 2011; 'Pravda za stadione', *Vreme*, March 3, 2011.
68. M. Derikonjić, 'Nema zabrane navijačkih grupa', *Politika*, March 19, 2011.
69. V.Z. Cvijić, 'Zabranjen Nacionalni stroj', *Blic*, June 3, 2011.
70. Miroslava Derikonjić, 'Vođi Obraza dve godine zatvora', *Politika*, April 21, 2011.
71. O. Milanović, 'Kako je osuđen Uroš Mišić', *Politika*, May 3, 2011.
72. Momir Ilić, 'Huligan za sud postao karakteran mladić', *Blic*, May 3, 2011.
73. *Danas*, 'Udri novinara', May 12, 2011.
74. Jovo Bakić, 'Pravda u Srbiji', *Politika*, May 17, 2011.
75. *Politika*, 'Dačić: Za policiju bolje da ne bude gej parade', September 24, 2011; Jovana Gligorijević, 'Kako su nasilnici postali politički faktor', *Vreme*, September 29, 2011.
76. Branislava Gigović and Tamara Marković Subota, 'Dačić bi sada da održavanje Parade obezbede Evropljani', *Blic*, September 28, 2011.
77. Jovana Gligorijević, 'Neslaganje oko parade i ponosa', *Vreme*, August 25, 2011.
78. I. Pejčić, 'Sukobi na severu Kosova otkazuju Paradu ponosa', *Danas*, September 28, 2011.
79. *Blic*, 'Zabranjeni svi skupovi za vikend, kao i Parada ponosa', September 30, 2011.
80. *B92*, 'Brisel pritiskao da se održi Parada', October 3, 2011.
81. In a bid to prove that he was not against the LGBT movement, Dačić also claimed that his party was the only one in Serbia with a gay activist in its leadership. *Blic*, 'Dačić: Možda je bio crn dan za ljudska prava, ali je bio divan za Beograđane', October 3, 2011.
82. Press release of Dveri srpske, 'Pobeda porodične Srbije: U Srbiji neće biti gej parade', October 2, 2011.
83. *e-Novine*, 'Fašisti slave, imaju i zašto', September 30, 2011; *e-Novine*, 'Policijska parada srama', October 2, 2011; 'Cinizam i zabrane', *Danas*, October 2, 2011.
84. Ljubiša Rajić, 'Danas se stidim', *Danas*, October 3, 2011.
85. *B92*, 'Gde su oni koji bi da pale Beograd', October 9, 2011.
86. Filip Švarm, 'Ko je ispao peder', *Vreme*, October 6, 2011.
87. *Politika*, 'Dačić: Odluka o zabrani nije poraz i slabost države', October 1, 2011; *B92*, 'Dačić: Država nije kapitulirala', October 1, 2011.
88. *Danas*, 'Kapitulacija', September 20, 2009.
89. Svetislav Basara quoted in *Danas*, 'Kako da ih zovemo: Banditi, huligani …', October 15, 2010.
90. Aleksandar Miletić, 'Političari i huligani – neporeciva veza', *Politika*, October 4, 2009; V.Z. Cvijić and M. Maleš, 'Vođe navijača u službi stranaka', *Blic*, October 6, 2009; S. Čongradin and I. Živanović, 'Amnezijom zamenili amnestiranje ekstremista', *Danas*, October 2, 2009.
91. V.Z. Cvijić and M. Maleš, 'Vođe navijača u službi stranaka', *Blic*, October 6, 2009.

92. Koković, *Naličje takmičenja*, 119.
93. Dušan Telesković, 'Ko štiti klubove', *Politika*, September 27, 2009.
94. Vuk Z. Cvijić, 'Umesto u sudnici sedi u upravi Zvezde', *Blic*, October 16, 2010; *B92*, 'Ostavka vođe navijača u C. zvezdi', October 20, 2010.
95. Spaaij, *Understanding Football Hooliganism*, 30.
96. Ibid., 47.
97. On the connection between right-wing extremism and the Serbian Orthodox Church, see Byford, 'Christian Right-Wing Organisations', 43–60; Vukomanović, 'The Serbian Orthodox Church as a Political Actor', 237–69.
98. Lidija Kujundžić, 'Instrumentalizacija nasilja', *NIN*, October 1, 2009.
99. Miša Vacić quoted in Jovana Gligorijević, 'Hronologija događaja koji se nije desio', *Vreme*, September 24, 2009.
100. Interview with Radović, *B92*, October 22, 2010.
101. Vladan Glišić, 'Dveri nisu ekstremna organizacija', *Danas*, December 22, 2010.
102. Vladan Glišić, 'Elementi ideologije homoseksualizma', *Nova srpska politička misao*, September 16, 2009.
103. Mikuš, '"State Pride"', 845.
104. D. Bukvić, 'Prećutno podržavanje "dobrog" nasilja', *Politika*, September 27, 2009.
105. Zoran Dragišić quoted in Lidija Kujundžić, 'Instrumentalizacija nasilja', *NIN*, October 1, 2009.
106. Boško Jakšić, 'Kapitulacija, ponovo', *Politika*, October 8, 2012.
107. Nebojša Trajković quoted in T. Tagirov, 'Amnezija, ne amnestija', *Vreme*, November 29, 2012.

References

Byford, Jovan. 'Christian Right-Wing Organisations and the Spreading of Anti-Semitic Prejudice in Post-Milošević Serbia: The Case of the Dignity Patriotic Movement'. *East European Jewish Affairs* 32 (2002): 43–60.
Garland, Jon, and James Treadwell. '"No Surrender to the Taliban": Football Hooliganism, Islamophobia and the Rise of the English Defence League'. *Papers from the British Criminology Conference* 10 (2010): 19–35.
Koković, Dragan. *Doba nasilja i sport*. Novi Sad: OKO, 1990.
Koković, Dragan. *Naličje takmičenja: Sport – između olimpijada i iluzijada*. Novi Sad: Prometej, 2008.
Mikuš, Marek. '"State Pride": Politics of LGBT Rights and Democratisation in "European Serbia"'. *East European Politics and Societies* 25 (2011): 834–51.
Nielsen, Christian Axboe. 'The Goalposts of Transition: Football as a Metaphor for Serbia's Long Journey to the Rule of Law'. *Nationalities Papers* 38 (2010): 87–103.
Spaaij, Ramón. *Understanding Football Hooliganism: A Comparison of Six Western European Football Clubs*. Amsterdam: Amsterdam University Press, 2006.
Vukomanović, Milan. 'The Serbian Orthodox Church as a Political Actor in the Aftermath of October 5, 2000'. *Politics and Religion* 1 (2008): 237–69.

Football, hooliganism and nationalism: the reaction to Serbia's gay parade in reader commentary online

Tamara Pavasovic Trost[a] and Nikola Kovacevic[b]

[a]Department of Sociology, Harvard University, Cambridge, MA, USA; [b]Department of Sociology, University of Belgrade, Belgrade, Serbia

Recent events in Serbia, particularly the murder of a French football fan in 2009, hooligan violence in response to the gay parade in Belgrade and riots during the Serbia–Italy UEFA football game in 2010, have brought renewed attention to the issue of hooliganism in Serbia. Apart from vehemently opposing the gay parade, the main actors in these riots – football hooligans and members of radical nationalist groups – have made far-reaching appeals about the nature of Serbian identity, morality and the 'true' Serbian nation, have called for toppling of the current government and a clear anti-EU stance. This paper simultaneously explores the overlap between football hooliganism and the extreme-right movement, as well as the reaction of everyday people to the activities of the groups' participants. Discourse analysis of 2700 reader comments in response to the events surrounding the 2010 gay parade provides rich information on the major themes in everyday people's reactions to hooliganism.

Recent events in Serbia, particularly the murder of a French football fan in 2009, hooligan violence in response to the gay parade in Belgrade and riots during the Serbia–Italy UEFA football game in 2010, have brought renewed attention to hooligans and the ultra-right movement in Serbia. Apart from vehemently opposing the gay parade, the main actors in these riots – football hooligans and members of radical nationalist groups including *Obraz* and *1389*, dubbed the 'renegade elements of Serbia's nationalist past' – have made far-reaching appeals about the nature of Serbian identity, morality, the 'true' Serbian nation, have called for toppling of the current government and a clear anti-EU stance. While these groups are admittedly supported by only a small fraction of the mainstream Serbian population, and despite the connection of these two events to specific occurrences (gay rights and football), these events have triggered a widespread debate on the issues around hooligans and their 'mission' to create a truer, 'healthier' Serbia.

The interplay between football, nationalism and violence is certainly not new, nor is it unique to the Serbian case. 'Sport in general, and football in particular, have been proven to be significant theatres for the working up and expression of national identity, and its mobilized form, nationalism'.[1] The connection between sports and nationalism has been demonstrated time and again.[2] Sports fans are described as a sort of 'proxy warriors'[3] and sport remains one of the most valuable weapons at the disposal of nationalists.[4] Particularly well-known are the violence at the Argentina–Peru Olympics qualifying match in 1964, which included 300 deaths and 500 injuries, the 1969 'football war' between El Salvador in Honduras prompted by a football World Cup qualifying game including several deaths and rapes, and many others:

A sport such as soccer provides opportunities for thousands of spectators to collectively reaffirm their commitments to beliefs, values, and myths that underlie their cultural identity. It allows people to make public declarations about what they stand for and what they stand against. Although ideologically neutral, sport often reflects and reinforces national rivalries and age-old grievances that emanate from sources far beyond the playing field. Because of this, sport has been used effectively as a tool for political manipulation.[5]

A particularly relevant role in the relationship between sports and nationalism can be played by football hooligans,[6] and indeed, scholarly work on all aspects of hooliganism has proliferated in the past several decades.[7] In the Serbian context, hooliganism generally refers to not only football hooligans but also members of radical groups or individuals engaged in delinquent activities. Indeed, the two groups – football fan groups and far-right organizations – draw upon a similar demographic, to some extent, have overlapping membership, and frequently draw upon common rhetoric and imagery. The actors in these groups tend to be aligned in their stance towards several issues – homosexuality, minority rights, Serbia's future in the EU, opposition towards The Hague – and as such, represent a formidable 'powder keg', which can be easily manipulated for national or political gains. The case of the 2010 Belgrade gay parade represented one such incident when hooligans of otherwise warring football clubs and extreme organizations allied in their mission to violently threaten and jeopardize the gay parade.[8] Most worryingly, their violent actions are increasingly being justified by members of mainstream society who share their patriotic sentiments and disillusionment with Serbia's democratic and pro-European path: 'Social poverty and working class are being instrumentalized through the propaganda identifying masses of hooligans and aggressively chauvinistic parties as natural allies of impoverished citizens'.[9] As a result, violent football hooligans and extreme radical groups are becoming a legitimate, integrated part of Serbia's society.[10]

The 'ethnification' of sports fans in Serbia was already clear in the 1990s, as the atmosphere at inter-republic games became more about nationalism than about sport – chants of the football team emphasized allegiance to Serbia, Milosevic and Kosovo, and the two Serbian rival teams would establish ethnic solidarity in outside matches.[11] A similar situation unravelled in Croatia, where the Croatian teams Dinamo and Hajduk, otherwise fierce rivals, would forget internal conflicts and sing about Croatian pride together, and indeed, Croatian football is seen as an exemplar for the utilization of football for intensifying nationalist sentiments.[12] Particularly relevant was a 1990 football game between Croatian Dinamo and Serbian Red Star at the Maksimir stadium in Zagreb, which included heavy political-laden chants and threats, and evolved into full-scale riots with hurled stones, violence and subsequent helicopter evacuation of the Serbian players, and continued on Zagreb's streets, including burned cars, smashed shop windows and demolition of kiosks and buildings. This game is considered a kind of planned political campaign,[13] and both the Red Star's fan club *Delije* and Dinamo's *Bad Blue Boys* were 'as much paramilitary organizations as they were fan clubs and had a fairly clear political agenda'.[14] The Dinamo fans later constructed a monument in the stadium to 'all of the fans of Dinamo, for whom the war started on May 13 1990 at Maksimir stadium, and ended by laying their lives on the altar of the homeland of Croatia'. As the 1990s progressed, both the Croatian and Serbian football teams sunk deeper and deeper into nationalist logic:

> On both sides, members of football fan clubs were among the first recruits of the new fighting groups and paramilitary forces that were at the fore of hostilities. On frontlines and in war ruins, the names of football clubs were mingled with symbols of nationalistic extremists: swastikas, the 'U' used by Ustashas, and the symbol of the cross employed by Serbian paramilitary groups.[15]

The most obvious link between Serbian sports and nationalism was apparent in 1990, as Zeljko Raznjatovic 'Arkan' gained influence among the Red Star fans and eventually emerged as the head of the official Red Star club *Delije*, a move believed to have been purposefully orchestrated by the Serbian State Security (Drzavna bezbednost).[16] During the wars of the 1990s, Arkan's Serbian Volunteer Guard, known as the *Tigers*, committed major war crimes in Bosnia including murder, torture and rape,[17] and the core of the guard is known to have been made up of *Delije* members.[18] The blurry line between football fans and extremist groups continues today: pro-Kosovo chants and Mladic and Karadzic support can frequently be seen at football games, and despite their enmity, football fans from opposing teams 'unite' in struggles against 'bigger' evils, such as their collaboration in opposing the gay parade. 'Ever since the late 1980s when nationalism exploded, violence has been spiraling at sports grounds [. . .] As a rule, these fan groups are aggressively nationalistic'.[19] Many leaders and members of the groups belong to both football and nationalist groups, effectively creating overlap in membership. The Helsinki Committee for Human Rights has identified neo-Nazi and 'patriotic' organizations and football fans as both the main promoters and executioners of escalating chauvinistic violence,[20] explicating the relationship between football fan clubs, ultra-right and patriotic organizations, and anti-democratic forces in Serbia:

> Clubs and movements of fans are not, in fact, spontaneous social phenomena. Even less so are they spontaneous nuclei of pure patriotism. They are backed not only by clubs but also by certain social and political groups, which in the energy, numbers, and aggression of football fans see not only a certain human potential, but also the possibility to send political messages most quickly and directly with the help of football fans.[21]

While extreme nationalistic logic and hooliganism are usually considered to take place in the margins of society, their prominence in many recent events has brought them to the forefront of public debate. This paper utilizes an innovative approach in discourse analysis to consider the issues debated by mainstream society, by considering reader commentary to news online. In this way, we explore the reactions, 'practical categories, situated actions, cultural idioms, cognitive schemas, and discursive frames'[22] utilized by ordinary people in discussing issues of hooligan violence, arguing that the way issues of nation and identity are discussed on the ground plays an important role in constructing identity itself. Over two decades ago, Hobsbawm argued that nationalism 'cannot be understood unless analyzed from below, that is in terms of the assumptions, hopes, needs, longings, and interests of ordinary people'.[23] Studies have shown that how people talk about the nation becomes a consequential idiom in everyday life, and thus the focus is on examining how understandings of nationhood are negotiated through acts of discourse.[24] The social construction of identity occurs, among other means, by *discourse*, or discursive formations or symbolic or cultural systems that have their own logic and agency, acting like 'cultural scripts'.[25] In Bourdieu's words, acts of discourse are not merely descriptions of social reality; they actually constitute the reality.[26] It is this discourse that produces identity '[. . .] by the way of talking and thinking and acting that realities on these sorts of claims to produce collective identity, to mobilize people for collective projects, and to evaluate peoples and practices'.[27] A similar strand of research on 'everyday identity' has focused on everyday individuals as agents of construction, positing that identity 'responds to the logics, imperatives, and concerns of the everyday contexts in which it is embedded'.[28] Scholars have begun to describe ordinary people's understandings of identity, finding that these understandings 'do not simply mimic those variants traded in elite discourse, but more often resonate with the currents and rhythms of their everyday concerns and predicaments'.[29]

The contribution of this paper is twofold. First, it explores the intersection between football fans and the far-right movement, which is particularly relevant considering the blending between hooliganism and ethnic war in Serbia's past, when these young sports fans and their aggression became 'a valuable capital of hatred for the state of war, and the fans themselves welcome as "cannon fodder"'.[30] Second, while not offering a statistical study of attitudes, it explores the reactions of everyday people to hooliganism, using discursive analysis of thousands of reader comments, ascertaining which themes and logic are most prominent. This type of analysis is particularly fruitful in online commentary where people are honest and uncensored, and even more so in the Serbian context, where:

> the opportunity to comment . . . is the best option for free speech . . . The only way that ordinary web users can have their say in the media/public sphere is by posting comments in online editions of the most popular media.[31]

In the following section, we first overview the most important events concerning hooligan violence in Serbia in the past several years, followed by an overview of the major known hooligan groups in Serbia, including both football fan clubs and extreme nationalist organizations. Particularly relevant are the commonalities in the participants in hooligan violence towards events as diverse as football matches, political manifestations and the organization of the gay parade in Belgrade. We then turn to an analysis of the reactions of readers to the hooligan violence in response to one of the major incidents of hooligan violence, the 2010 gay parade, which is selected because of the collaboration of hooligans from various groups in its opposition. Finally, we present the results of the analysis, consider sources of the predominant discourse and discuss implications of the findings for further research as well as for the future of democracy in Serbia.

The events

Several recent events have brought hooligan violence to the forefront of attention in Serbia. Public debates about the actions of football fans were particularly strong in 2007, when during a Red Star–Hajduk match, one of the Red Star sports fans, Uros Misic (18 at the time), attacked a plain-clothes police officer by trying to force a lit flare down the policeman's throat. He was later sentenced to 10 years in jail, the minimum for charges of aggravated attempted murder. This event sparked an outcry among the football community, as well as extreme-right groups, and Belgrade was covered in graffiti and posters demanding 'Justice for Uros', to reduce his sentence.[32] The following year, two events received particular attention: first, at the protests organized in response to the declaration of independence by Serbia's southern province Kosovo titled 'Kosovo is Serbia' in February, groups of hooligans interrupted the peaceful assembly by attacking the embassies of Croatia, Turkey, the UK and several others, while they managed to enter and set on fire the embassy of the USA, leading to the death of one Partizan fan trapped in the burning building. The protests continued in downtown Belgrade, which was virtually demolished, resulting in the wrecking of around 100 objects, restaurants, cars, street lights, 130 wounded, and widespread store looting.[33] Later the same year, in response to the arrest of Hague indictee Radovan Karadzic, several political parties organized an 'all-Serbian assembly' in support of Karadzic and against President Boris Tadic. The speakers included politicians from the Serbian Racial Party, the Democratic Party of Serbia and New Serbia, while the attendees included most rightist organizations including *Obraz* and several fan groups.[34] The meeting was interrupted by a group of hooligans believed to be Partizan and Rad fans, who attacked police and journalists and demolished downtown Belgrade.[35]

The most extreme case occurred a year later, when a French Toulouse football fan was killed in Belgrade. Brice Taton came to Belgrade for the Toulouse–Partizan match in September 2009, and was sitting with a group of friends in a cafe in downtown Belgrade, when around 30 Partizan fans attacked the French fans. One of the Toulouse fans and a cafe waiter were injured, while Taton sustained injuries he died from 12 days later. Fourteen Partizan fans were charged with his murder, mostly members of the *Alkatraz* and *Iriducibili* groups.[36] Later that year, the *B92* investigative journalism show 'Insider', led by Brankica Stankovic, broadcast an episode on football and hooligans, including the identities of the hooligan group leaders, their involvement in criminal activities, connections with politicians and corruption in the courts preventing accountability for those convicted of heavy crimes.[37] After the broadcast, the journalist was the subject of numerous death threats, most notably at a Partizan match when the group *Alkatraz* brought a blow-up doll representing the journalist, which they subsequently stabbed through with a stake, kicking and hitting the doll in the head, and via Facebook and YouTube pages calling for her rape, 'slaughter' and murder. Eleven Partizan fans were arrested in connection with the death threats.[38]

These events led up to the organization of the gay parade in 2010. Previously, there was an attempt to hold the country's first gay parade in Belgrade in 2001, but the participants were violently attacked by large numbers of opponents, without adequate police protection, and the march was stopped quickly after it started. The second gay parade was supposed to be held in 2004 but it was cancelled due to the organizers' inability to guarantee participant safety.[39] A similar thing happened in 2009 – the parade was scheduled to take place in September, but due to heavy threats and calls to violence from the side of several extreme-right organizations, several days before the parade, the Serbian Ministry of Internal Affairs requested that the parade be moved away from the city centre, effectively cancelling the parade. In 2010, the parade (called the Pride Parade) was organized in downtown Belgrade, albeit under similar circumstances: threats to call off the parade including graffiti such as 'Faggots, we're waiting for you' [Pederi, cekamo vas], 'Blood will flow in Belgrade, but there will be no gay parade' [Beogradom krv ce liti, gej parade nece biti] and 'Kill, slaughter, so there are no faggots' [Ubi, zakolji, da peder ne postoji] – an adaptation of the same chant normally directed at Albanians. The day before the parade, an anti-march called 'Family Walk' was held, in which around 2500 people participated, supported by various church officials. On the day of the parade, there were around 1000 participants, protected by a police force of over 5000. The police were able to effectively protect the parade participants, but in the riots that followed, around 140 people were hurt, downtown Belgrade was demolished, including the centre of the Democratic Party, several public transportation vehicles and a public mammography machine, with a total damage of over one million euros. After the parade, investigations were held against 124 hooligans, of which 83 faced charges. The leader and two members of the nationalist group *Obraz* were convicted for organizing the parade, including a meeting several days prior to the parade when they determined which hooligan group leaders would instigate violence in particular parts of the city.[40]

Only a few days after the gay parade in 2010, football fans rioted at the Serbia–Italy UEFA game in Genoa. The game was cancelled in the sixth minute due to the actions of several Serbian fans, including throwing fire torches in the field, cutting the protective netting and climbing the fence separating fans from the court. The fans were armed with saws and metal poles, had placards stating 'Kosovo is Serbia' and burned an Albanian flag. The leader of the fans, Ivan Bogdanov (dubbed 'Ivan the Terrible'), said that their wrath was directed against the Serbian Football Association, and particularly at Vladimir Stojkovic, a player who had recently switched from the Red Star to the Partizan team. Bogdanov is a member of the Red Star group *Ultra Boys*, and also of the nationalist organization *1389*; his clothing and tattoos include Nazi symbols, including the number 28, which is a symbol of the neo-Nazi group *Blood and Honor*.[41]

In 2011 and 2012, the highlight on hooligan violence continued to be omnipresent in Serbian media, most notably in response to the arrest of Hague indictee Ratko Mladic, when protests were organized in Belgrade and Novi Sad. Hooligans displaying markings of *National Formation*, *1389*, *Obraz* and several football teams displayed signs and yelled slogans of 'Knife, wire, Srebrenica' [Noz zica Srebrenica], 'Save Serbia and kill yourself Boris' [Spasi Srbiju i ubij se, Borise] and 'Ratko Hero', although more serious incidents were avoided by strong police presence in both cities.[42] The gay parade 2011 was cancelled because of threats of renewed violence and the government's decision that another parade would 'seriously jeopardize national safety', thus signalling to many the victory of hooligans in their threats, bullying and intimidation.[43] Hooligan violence continued in the latter half of 2011 with the Red Star–Partizan derby, before and during which fans yelled malicious slogans and threw burning torches, leading to 18 arrests and several injured fans[44] and the violence towards Croatians during European Handball Championship, when Croatian fans were attacked and several Croatian cars demolished and set on fire in early 2012.[45]

The actors

The two major football clubs in Serbia are Red Star (Crvena Zvezda) and Partizan. Red Star fans, or *'Delije'* (official name of all Zvezda fans since 1989), include various subgroups (*Brigate, Heroes, Hijene, Kenjaj, Orthodox Boys, North Army, Lunatics*), although the most well known for their hooliganism are *Belgrade Boys*, *Ultras* and *Ultra Boys*. The various subdivisions of *Delije* are not organized and official as is the case with Partizan fans. *Delije* members formed the base for the Serbian paramilitary force under Arkan (Arkan's *Tigers*), which, as mentioned previously, was implicated in genocidal acts during the Bosnian war in the 1990s.[46] Partizan fans, or *'Grobari'*, include three official groups: *Južni Front*, *Grobari 1970* and *Grobari Beograd*, with various subgroups, of which *Alkatraz* is most infamous, as well as *Ludaci Padinska Skela*, *Anti-Roma*, *South Family* and *Headhunters*. In addition, the football club Rad has been identified as harbouring currents of extreme hooligans, particularly its subgroup *United Force*, which is particularly well known as a 'concentration of extremism' and 'nationalistic nucleus'[47] including slogans such as 'Knife, wire, Srebrenica' [Noz zica Srebrenica], and 'Kill, slaughter, so there are no more Shiptars [Kosovo Albanians]' [Ubi, zakolji, da siptar ne postoji].[48]

When speaking of Serbia's extremist organizations, several currents can be identified: 'patriotic' groups appealing to mainstream Serbian population and enjoying open support from several politicians and academics, including *Dveri* and *Nasi*, extreme 'patriotic' groups such as *Obraz* and *1389*, which have played an explicit role in organizing hooligan violence at events deemed to be of national significance, and finally openly neo-Nazi or fascist groups, including *National Formation* and *Blood and Honor*. While precise membership is not known, it is estimated that there are around 1000 members of extremist groups, in addition to around 2500 to 3000 extreme football hooligans.[49]

The *Dignity Patriotic Movement Obraz* [Otacastveni Pokret Obraz] is an Orthodox clero-fascist organization. Prior to a crackdown in 2001, their website listed as Serbia's enemies 'Zionists – Jewish racists', ustashe, poturice (converts to Islam), Albanians, democrats, pacifics, homosexuals ('perverts'), drug addicts, criminals, etc. They advocate the return of all Serbian lands and Eastern-Orthodox piety.[50] Their leader, Mladen Obradovic, was arrested prior to the gay parade due to the instrumental role he played in organizing hooligan activity against the parade. The *Serbian National Movement 1389*

[Srpski narodni pokret 1389] was founded in 2004 and is dedicated to 'defending sovereignty and territorial integrity of Serbia, which especially means keeping Serbian south province Kosovo and Metohija inside national borders', in alliance with 'Nasi' Russian organization, against the EU and NATO and pro-Russian alliance.[51] It significantly differs from the *National Formation* in its anti-fascist views. The *Serbian National Movement 'Nasi'* [Srpski narodni pokret 'Nasi'] grew out of a collaboration with 1389, with similar anti-EU, anti-NATO and pro-Russian views, except with the explicit goal to become a political party and achieve its programme 'through Serbian institutions'.[52] The *Serbian Assemble 'Dveri'* [Srpski Sabor 'Dveri'] is a religious rightist group, focused on propaganda activism and with aspirations to participate in the coming elections. Members consider themselves the only real Orthodox Christians and are against Serbia joining the EU. Their projects include *Movement for Life*, which advocates homophobia and anti-abortion views, *Assembly of Serbian Youth* [Sabor srpske omladine] and *Serbian Network* [Srpska mreza]. They are particularly well connected to the Serbian Orthodox Church and many politicians and academics: they organize seminars at the University of Belgrade, receive government funding for some of their projects and similar, leading to the perception of *Dveri* as a mainstream group, despite its radical views.[53]

Apart from these groups, there are two explicitly neo-Nazi organizations that operate in secrecy due to the illegal nature of several of their activities. *National Formation* [Nacionalni stroj] was banned by the Serbian government in 2011, and most of the leadership and many members are currently on trial for activities, including anti-Semitic desecrations and celebrations of Srebrenica. The group is dedicated to reunification of all Serbs into one unique Serbian territory. According to their statute, 'Full civil rights . . . can be held only by loyal citizens of our country who are members of the white Arian race'; the group stands for geographic segregation of races, believes that physical, mental, moral and racial characteristics are 'hereditary and unchangeable', that any kind of racial mixing should be forbidden and that any form of human 'perverseness' (drug addicts, homosexuals, etc.) should be strictly punished. The group is also anti-abortion (except in cases of racial mixing, or if the foetus is physically defective), and strict national control of print and media, and their foreign policy is pro-white-European.[54] Finally, *Blood and Honor* [Krv i cast] is a branch of the international *Blood and Honor* movement, propagating national socialism and the survival of the white race, openly propagating eugenics. According to their website, being 'under the boot of Zionist oppression', they want to motivate people to take on 'radical activities' to save the 'white racial identity and Arian culture', which had dwindled to only 8% of the six billion people in the world. Most of the members are 'comrades' in the wars in Bosnia, Croatia and Kosovo.[55]

Several court proceedings have been taking place to combat the more extreme of both the football and nationalist groups. First, in 2009, State Prosecutor Slobodan Radovanovic filed a recommendation to the Constitutional Court to ban 13 football fan subgroups of Partizan, Red Star and Rad football clubs[56], due to their 'actions aimed at the violent overthrow of Constitutional order, violation of human and minority rights, and encouragement of racial, ethnic and religious hatred': 'Participants in these groups only have the prefix "fans". These are fans of crime and groups with characteristics of gangs. They have nothing in common with sports, but with crime'. The document outlines the purpose of the ban to 'protect youth of this society from pollution by hatred, intolerance, violence and xenophobia', and that the groups have become 'private armies', functioning like 'wolf packs, looking for victims of their unrestrained passion, hatred and intolerance'[57]; however, the application was rejected in March 2011. Second, amendments to the Law on Prevention of Violence at Sporting Events, to the Law on Misdemeanors and to the Criminal Code in 2009 and 2010 have provided for more strict and efficient proceedings, including an increased sentence for criminal acts committed in a group (2–8 years in prison; 3–12 years for the ring leader), the obligation of sports clubs to install video cameras in stadiums and an increased maximum period of detention from 8 to 30 days.[58] Third, the group *National Formation* was banned by the Constitutional Court in June 2011.[59] Proceedings to ban the groups *Obraz* and *1389* due to their 'violent destruction of Constitutional order, violation of human and minority rights, and instigation of racial, ethnic and religious hatred and intolerance' are still ongoing.[60]

Methodology

In this section, we analyse three of the main Serbian newspapers' stories about the gay parade on 10 October 2010, performing a discourse analysis on the themes that reappear in reader comments. Studying reader comments to online news is a relatively underutilized research approach, despite the proliferation of studies focused on the potential for interactive technologies to enable new avenues for citizen participation in the political process and for promoting diverse and authentic public deliberation.[61] Since the internet provides cheap, fast, geographically unbound, free, egalitarian and uncensored interaction, communication can in turn be void of social cues, offering peer-to-peer interaction as well as many-to-many communication, and increase participants' issue knowledge, political efficacy and willingness to participate in politics.[62]

Of course, studying online commentary has several inherent limitations. Since participation is unstructured and unmoderated, questions of participation access abound. Studies have pointed to the fact that online discussions frequently include only a small core of very active users[63]: participants must have both the ability to handle mass amounts of information, be technologically savvy and have time and attention for participation.[64] Due to the absence of social control, online debate is frequently accompanied by conflictive behaviour, and particularly the tendency for the occurrence of flaming or outraging conflict, coupled with offensive language and personal attacks.[65] Indeed, scholars of social identity/deindividuation (SIDE) theory have shown that online opinion tends to polarize easily due to in-group and out-group discrimination, as online discussion participants remain anonymous and develop a strong group identity, resulting in enhanced polarization of attitudes.[66] In addition to stereotyping of out-group members, studies have found that debates are often characterized by aggressiveness, insult, ideological abstraction and the attempt to humiliate opponents[67], as well as fake identities, frequent insincerity and purposeful dramatization. Finally, it is difficult to develop a sound methodology for online content analysis because outcomes largely depend on the specific technology utilized as well as the policies and social contexts of the particular online forum.[68]

Nonetheless, analysing reader commentary has several significant advantages over other avenues of research. The 'combined effects of immediate response, unlimited space, and minimal censorship'[69] provide a unique space for vigorous exercises in free speech, and a 'rare opportunity for free participation in a political forum where one may meet widely divergent views'.[70] In addition, the absence of social cues allows for greater participation, allowing in people who would otherwise be too shy to participate, as well as helping to keep debate centred on rational-critical argumentation instead of person-oriented thus allowing people to interact as equals.[71] Online commentary allows for a true glimpse into the minds of ordinary people, allowing for honest and open thoughts void of political correctness which would otherwise afflict in-person interviews or surveys.

The newspapers analysed include *Blic*, a popular daily newspaper, *Kurir*, a right-wing daily tabloid, and *B92*, a liberal broadcaster. While sales of print editions of all newspapers have been steadily declining, online news portals are increasing in popularity: it is estimated that 42% of all internet users in Serbia read online news regularly.[72] *Blic* is one of the three most popular non-tabloid dailies, and its online edition has an estimated 1.5 million unique visitors every month,[73] making it among the top five most frequently visited websites in Serbia (after *Google*, *Facebook* and *YouTube*).[74] *B92* is a radio–television broadcaster with national coverage, so it does not have a print edition. Its online edition has an estimated 1.3 million unique users every month, and is currently the sixth most frequently visited website in Serbia. It is mostly read by a young, urban and pro-Western liberal audience. *Kurir* is one of the five most widely read tabloids and its online edition is the fifteenth most frequently visited website in Serbia. *Kurir* runs mostly sensational stories, relying mostly on celebrity gossip and rumours, but with considerable political influence.[75]

Blic and *B92* each had one article about the gay parade, which was updated throughout the day; the *Blic* article[76] garnered 1714 reader comments, while the *B92* article[77] had 548 reader comments. *Kurir* published five smaller articles,[78] garnering a total of 445 reader comments. In total, the number of reader comments analysed for this paper is 2706. The average comment length was 51 words, the longest being *B92* comments (average of 59 words per comment) and the shortest in *Kurir* (average of 47 words per comment).

When content analysing the reader comments, we first considered the central focus of the comment, and three broad categories appeared, concerning (1) homosexuality or the gay parade broadly (24%); (2) the actions of the hooligans and violence following the parade (40%) and (3) the reaction of the police/government (15%). Comments on other topics (21%) were grouped into a fourth category. The comments that did not convey an attitude (11% of original) were discarded,[79] leaving 2433 comments that were then analysed on the qualitative position advanced (Table 1).

Overall, the most noticeable differentiation was in the difference in attitudes of *Kurir* and *B92* readers, albeit unsurprising given the readership of these media: almost half of *Kurir*'s comments were negative about the gay parade or homosexuality in general, as opposed to only 6% of *B92* comments; and even more telling, only 12% of *Kurir* comments condemned hooligan violence, as opposed to over half of *B92* comments (Figure 1).[80]

Given the focus of this paper, during the discourse analysis we paid particular attention to the category of comments regarding the hooligan violence itself (40%): how hooligans were considered by ordinary people, in what way were their actions justified, and which cognitive categories and idioms were invoked when discussing this particular event. Two sub-types of hooligan-supporting comments could be observed: first, those that specifically dealt with the hooligans, commenting the actors and their actions, and

Table 1. Distribution (%) of reader comments by focus and opinion.

		Blic	B92	Kurir	Overall
Homosexuality, parade	Positive	8.3	5.8	5.2	7.3
	Negative	13.7	6.2	41.8	16.4
Hooligan violence	Support	10.6	5.7	10.4	9.5
	Condemn	27.6	51.7	11.5	30.3
Police reaction	Positive	3.4	4.1	1.1	3.2
	Negative	12.1	14.4	9.0	12.1
Other		24.4	12.2	21.0	21.3
Total		100.0	100.0	100.0	100.0

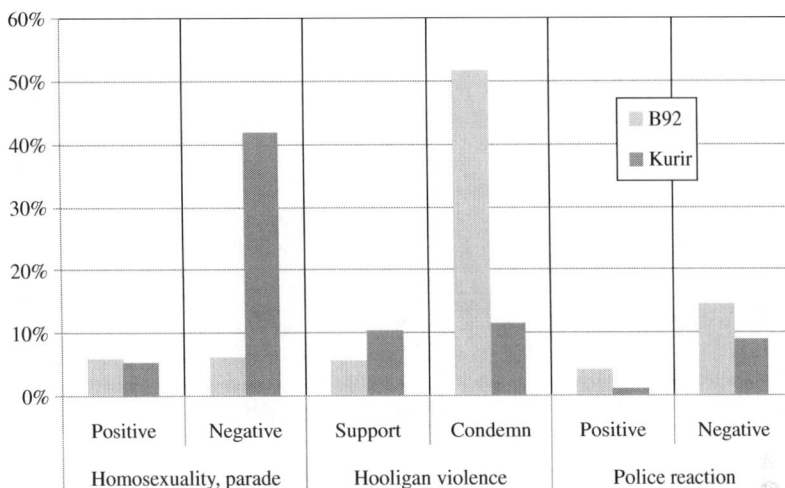

Figure 1.   Distribution (%) of reader comments by focus and opinion in *B92* vs. *Kurir*.

second, comments that considered other societal problems, only tangentially mentioning the violence as a symptom or consequence of other factors.

In the first sub-type, comments focusing on the hooligans themselves, several arguments surfaced. First, that hooligans are 'kids', young people, 'children of Serbia', in some variants even 'heroes' and 'fighters for freedom', simply standing up for what they believe is right. In this type of arguments, the hooligans were seen as defending the needs of the majority of Serbs, which is typically supported by the fact that the majority of Serbs had been against the parade taking place.

> I ask all creative people to print T-shirts with the text I AM ALSO A HOOLIGAN or I AM PROUD TO BE A HOOLIGAN; I will buy one for myself and for my wife, children. I am nearly 50 years old and have nothing, I work for a meagre salary and I feel crushed, while these pieces of shit sell out and give away the land for which our fathers bled. (*Kurir*)

> Who are you thinking of arresting? Our children! Our children who no longer want to listen to your lies. Arresting our children who no longer want to look at you stealing and destroying the state of Serbia. No, you will not arrest our children, we will arrest you and bring you to justice, so that you can return every penny you've robbed and go to prison. (*Blic*)

> But these are 15–16 year old kids, with no weapons or equipment, with just hearts in their chests and rage in their lives, kids who struck at the professional, superbly equipped praetorian guard of 'democratic' tyrants ... I would rather say that these kids are foolishly brave because they faced 1 on 1 the most powerful opponent they could find here! (*Blic*)

> Today in Belgrade were 50 gay men and thousands of gays in blue uniforms and hummers who beat and trampled on Serbian children who do not want to see sick gays touching each other and walking through streets. And the government even dares to call them hooligans. Thank you, Heroes of Serbia for showing the world and these degenerates what Serbia thinks about these sick people. (*Kurir*)

> ... Dacic's police is armed to the teeth, attacking our Serbian children who are shedding blood for our national interests. (*Kurir*)

Similarly, in many comments, hooligans are equated to the anti-Milosevic protesters in October 2000, when the protesters used similar methods (stoning police, setting property on fire, etc.), yet were considered revolutionaries. These commenters typically equate the 'hooligans' of 2000 and the current ruling democratic political parties:

> And when they burned Belgrade on October 5th, then it was OK and heroic . . . who was held accountable for that? I do not support city destruction, but I guess someone has to be accountable for October 5 also??! What a disaster happening to us . . . elections urgently!!! (*Kurir*)

> We should not overblow this. Belgrade was in a far worse shape on October 5th. The hooligans then, today's democrats, didn't throw roses around Belgrade. They burned, demolished, stole, chanted, beat the police, beat the army, even the security of the then president. The great democrats even used bulldozers! Have the hooligans of yesterday, today's democrats and rulers, been held accountable for that? No! They were even rewarded and pardoned [. . .] Hooligans at the parade were not hooligans. They were the revolted citizens and children of those same people who brought to power the great democrats, hooligans from 10 years ago. Is Serbia, while presenting itself as a democratic country, a country of double standards? It seems to be. (*Kurir*)

> Well, people fought using the same and even worse methods against Milosevic when they had no way out anymore, but then they (THESE WHO CAME TO POWER WITH HIS HELP) were not called hooligans but freedom fighters, and now these same people who are fed up with these politics are satanized on every step AND NAMED HOOLIGANS??? (*Blic*)

A related type of comment was also prominent: that hooligans are youth who have no perspective and hope because they live in poverty; they are frustrated with the current Serbian political and economic system. This type of argument included those that considered violence as a natural and understandable outcome of frustration with the current economic situation, unrelated to the actual gay parade, as well as those that considered the gay parade as the 'cherry on top' of the frustration of youth, which they could not be expected to tolerate.

> Hooligan behaviour is the only thing left for these children, after everything that they are served through the media. For anyone to FIND A JOB, you need a CONNECTION, and not of expertise and skills; you should sell that story somewhere else, this is Serbia. And as to the school system, from personal experience I know that for passing some courses you must bribe the professor. You talk as if you do not live here, it's easy to romanticize everything, 10% of people live in a way befitting an honest worker, and this 10% are people from the ruling system and workers in the public sector. (*Kurir*)

> This is not the right; these are kids with no prospects, no education and no money to see the world and to have a wider view of themselves and others. This is the outcome of everyone – of the EU and its visas, and all of the governments since the 90s. Before asking for draconian punishments, think about this . . . (*B92*)

> These so-called hooligans took to the streets because they are frustrated by the distorted conditions in this country, which was created by bad government policy. This is not an anti-gay protest, but a political protest. That's why the DS [Democratic Party] building is burning. And unfortunately, the same will happen in the future, since a peaceful voice is not worth a penny in Serbia. (*Blic*)

> These 'hooligans' are our youth, and they are what we made them to be. Generations of young people have no prospects or jobs; they are watching the injustice all around them, and cannot live normal lives. To run away as far away as possible, or stay and in desperation watch as the state rots. This parade was just a drop in the bucket; I think that something a lot bigger is brewing. The set of people who have been destroying us for years has to go. And I will support them in this. (*Blic*)

Apart from dealing with the hooligans or their actions, many readers commented on other unrelated societal problems, and the majority of hooligan-supporting comments fall into this category. In this sub-type of comments, the fact that someone actually deliberately participated in the destruction in response to the gay parade is typically overlooked, and instead, the actions of the police and response of the government are taken as a starting point. Thus, hooligan violence is seen as the outcome of a variety of factors, most typically the failure of the government, and is therefore justified. The government is blamed for a variety of reasons; foremost for the poor economic state of the country:

> This demolition has nothing to do with the parade . . . People are frustrated by bad life, and, logically, they need only an excuse to behave like this. I blame the incompetent government and their economic policies. Therein is the root of all problems in the country. (*B92*)

> If people had jobs and regular salaries to support them, they would not use every opportunity to express their dissatisfaction, instead they would be occupied by planning. Thus, it will be no wonder if they get to the Parliament today. (*B92*)

> This parade is a trigger, against this government which does not care about anything except when forced by Brussels, a government which tramples its citizens most brutally, and which holds nothing as sacred. (*B92*)

> These conflicts should be recognized as the protests of dissatisfied people against the government. The parade is just a trigger. They [the government] have come to power by force. They will leave in the same way. (*Blic*)

> What were they expecting! People are sick of this regime, and they have to put up with the gays as well! I'm sorry I was prevented to join in expressing my anger against the state. They ask: how can you demolish the country you love? They were demolishing because of frustration and anger. This state is killing people's minds. This is only the beginning. There will be more riots. I love this country, but things cannot be changed in a nice way, this is the only way. (*Blic*)

While the government is mostly blamed for the poor state of the country, another frequent criticism is its subordinate acceptance of the EU's relentless demands for membership. The connection between the gay parade and the EU comes from various sources, including the media's exaggeration of the EU's support of the parade, as well as the public's perception that homosexuality is a Western affliction, which is now also threatening Serbia.

> I do not want this Europe in Serbia . . . I will not have my child looking at gays and lesbians on the streets, end of story!! Is there something else in that 'rich, unattainable and shiny Europe' apart from twistedness? Why didn't our politicians wish us higher standards, higher salaries, better protection of the mother and child, for pregnant women receive salaries on time, just as they do in their beloved European Union . . . not this! with faith in God, Family, and our Holy Orthodox Faith, thank these guys for a wonderful day . . . (*Kurir*)

> If this is freedom, then I'm a rhinoceros. But when someone from the EU tells these guys in DS [the Democratic Party] that this is normal and that it has to happen, then that's how it is. If they told the DS that they all had to come naked to parliament sessions, they would get naked, because this is what the EU says. This kind of world must end. (*Kurir*)

> The state was aware that this was going to happen. Everywhere there's crookedness and robbery. That is why people are angry. Because they will not go into the European Union and you keep persistently trying to convince them that they do! They are sick of these kinds of values and new conditions! (*Kurir*)

> This is a horror and a disgrace [. . .]. These are the European values that our state wants to, at all costs, force upon our people. Down with the gay government that finances gays. Down with the government who meets with and smiles to the biggest enemies of this country, while it tears of pieces of our country with no anesthetic. Unlike you Europeans, people are in pain because of the injustice. The Serbian people have never tolerated traitors, and it won't tolerate you either. (*Kurir*)

As seen in the previous comments, the connection between the EU, the 'gay lobby' and the idea that the government somehow profited or was paid by the EU/the West to hold the parade also appeared in several comments:

> Well, we don't want to be part of deviant Europe where the gay lobbies rule!!! Period! It [Europe] did not bring anything good to anybody; don't fool yourself any more. Europe is a group put together by force and held in place by force. Very similar to the old Yugoslavia. Germans cannot stand the Mediterraneans, Belgians the Dutch; everybody (these developed democracies) is deporting gypsies from everywhere, and we are forced to build houses for them. Yuck, I'm disgusted by it (Europe) . . . it will break down sooner or later and I don't see what will we be doing there, except that all those who became rich stealing will legalize the stolen [. . .] So, you asked for it – watch it, and enjoy together with the faggots, all of you who are modern and European-oriented. (*Kurir*)

> Shameful! Does this 'train' on which you're taking us to Europe, contain only cattle wagons for Serbs? This is you treat your people who you call hooligans, because it opposes sickness and betrayal of national interests. How much money did you get for organizing the parade of shame? (*Kurir*)

> It seems to me like no one is realizing that it was ordered by the West, most likely America, that the parade has to be held at all costs. Well, from 'Dynasty' on they put at least one faggot into each motion picture, and try to make it seem quite normal and common. Well, I don't expect one Serb to tell them that it is deviant? (*Kurir*)

In addition, the gay community in Serbia is also blamed for 'provoking' the violence by holding the parade:

> Let the gays pay the damage of one million euros! Those whose cars were smashed should sue the organizers of the parade, these gays, and seek compensation! The city also needs to sue the gay parade organizers, and gays should pay all damages to Belgrade. Why is Djilas [Belgrade mayor] changing theses? Belgrade will pay? The gays asked for a gay parade, and now the gays should pay the damage of EUR 1,000,000. (*Kurir*)

> This is not about beating up homosexuals, but about their extreme arrogance and insolence, because they knew perfectly well that there is a general outcry against the parade and they knew what awaited them and yet they disregarded it all, and went to streets to express their sick ways; and how then can a normal human being understand them. (*Blic*)

Finally, 15% of the comments focused on the police reaction to the hooligans, not on the hooligans themselves. In the majority of these comments, the police are either seen as an extension of the government, invoking similar blame, or as independent actors who somehow 'chose' to be against the hooligans after the gay parade. Accordingly, the police are faulted for standing up for the wrong causes, for not being on the side of the people, for being crooked, and so on. The police are also frequently faulted for being in the wrong place, assaulting youth instead of, for instance, defending Serbs in Kosovo.

> Last winter the police with military equipment beat hungry workers [protesters] who laid on the railroad at −10 degrees, today that same police beats citizens, supposedly protecting the gay population. Under the pretext of democracy. The citizens of Serbia, regardless of political and sexual orientation, will live in a democracy when somebody tells us where they are spending our money and when the police understand that they exist for the citizens and not vice versa. The police are paid by deductions from our salaries, and they, in addition of taking from the salaries of the hungry, ask for an increase in their salaries, beat the poor and befriend the criminals. Every ten days a police officer is arrested as part of a criminal group. It is not easy when you have no bread to eat, and when you go out to protest, they rupture your kidneys, break your arms and legs and you have no insurance to go to the doctor. Let the government decide and publicly announce whether it will take care of its citizens and families and fight the white plague, or is it more important to it to protect the rights of gay people who are not threatened at all. (*Blic*)

And the city burned because of 1000 faggots. Well, let them pay the taxes... Kosovo has been burning for years, Serbs down there are disappearing, and nobody does anything about it. Why didn't you send 5600 turtles [police officers] to Novi Pazar to fight those who burned flags and staged protests against Serbia? (*Kurir*)

Where was this police when the Serbian flag was burned and Serbian police stoned in Raska?? (*Kurir*)

This is a catastrophe. Because a thousand people who want to walk the city and promote their distorted sexual orientation, to mobilize so many police to protect them! Why don't you jerks go to Kosovo to save those poor families who can't dare to poke their heads out of their homes, instead of beating normal people in our capital. This is how you are courting Europe? Shame on you! (*Kurir*)

Discussion

Content analysis of the reader comments point to two important considerations. First, while reader commentary analysis does not provide a way to determine the prevalence of these ideas in the broader population, it nonetheless shows that at least among some segments of Serbian society, the discourse of the hooligans and the ultra-right movement has been adopted, pointing to a certain degree of normalization of this type of discourse. When coupled with the fact that many citizens are similarly disheartened by poverty, unemployment, Serbia's slow progress forward and the European Union's never-ending demands, the issues the hooligans and the ultra-right movement advocate are becoming increasingly mainstream, leading to the prospects that their actions might begin to be seen as a means to a shared goal. Certainly, hooligans themselves would not be able to forge anti-democratic discourse on their own, and indeed, their narrative is an echo of statements given by several politicians, representatives of the Serbian Orthodox Church, and supported by tabloid media, all of which have inadvertently or directly provided legitimacy to the actions of the hooligans.

The relationship between the Serbian Orthodox Church and several ultra-right organizations is particularly interesting, and this was nowhere more obvious than in the actions of the Church and some of its representatives in regard to the gay parade. Although the Serbian Orthodox Church declined to officially comment on the parade, the rhetoric used by several bishops and priests was strikingly similar to the rhetoric of the hooligans. Bishop Amfilohije Radovic especially stands out in his statements and de facto calls for violence: he frequently referred to the parade as the 'parade of shame' or 'parade of Sodom and Gomorrah', and has said that 'the tree that doesn't bear fruit [reproduce] should be cut and thrown into the fire',[81] culminating in his statement after the parade: 'Yesterday we watched the stench poisoning and polluting the capital of Serbia, scarier than uranium...'. Instead of condemning violence, he attributes the blame to the participants of the gay parade ('wrongheaded infidels'), and says 'Now they are wondering whose fault it was, and they are calling our children hooligans'.[82] Apart from Bishop Radovic, other representatives of the Church were also open in their positions on homosexuality, calling transsexuality a mental disorder, interests of homosexuals 'frivolous', the parade as a violation of the right to family life and an insult to the dignity of believers[83] and the 2009 Anti-Discrimination Law 'malignant'.[84] In addition to statements about the gay parade, the Serbian Orthodox Church has played a particular role in providing credibility to right-wing movements, most notably by its reverence of Bishop Nikolaj Velimirovic, an anti-Semite, xenophobe and zealous nationalist. This provides members of *Obraz* and other radical organizations legitimization: 'By assimilating their extremist political views within the ideology of an esteemed religious figure, organizations such as *Obraz* are able to present themselves as reasonable and respectable'.[85]

Aside from the Church, discourse found in reader comments is also fuelled by the media, which had with their coverage de facto given ultra-right organizations a voice. Leading up the parade, many daily newspapers published interviews with representatives of the Church and of ultra-right organizations, with headlines such as 'The Church is only defending morality' (*Vecernje Novosti*), 'Gay parade represents imposing a new ideology on Serbia' (*Pravda*) and 'After faggots, sodomists and necrophiliacs will want to parade' (*Alo*). These texts were frequently published without comment or context to the views represented, the organizations were frequently labelled as 'patriotic' and the participants in threats and intimidation called football supporters or merely 'youths'.[86] A few days before the parade, even non-tabloid media such as *Politika* and *Vecernje Novosti* published stories practically calling for the lynch of the gay population, by citing the strategies for assault and quoting messages by *Obraz* and *1389*.[87] The media also played an important role in making the connection between the parade and other nationalist concerns such as the status of Kosovo, so it is unsurprising that so many readers made similar connections. For instance, *Kurir* published an article titled 'Faggot Seceding Kosovo' in response to one of the activists elsewhere supporting Kosovo independence and other 'anti-Serbian' activities.[88] In this way, the media propagated the view that the parade participants were not people fighting for their human rights, but instead also enemies of the Serbian state and traitors.

In addition to uncritically reporting messages of the ultra right, tabloid media often talk about hooligans in a personal way that gives them legitimacy – by publishing interviews with their family members, unfair treatment by the police, or simply by using discourse that represents them as youths of the country with legitimate political needs. Tabloid media in particular avoid criticizing actions of football fans or of members of extreme organizations, likely because of their readership, although this avoidance can also be found among many politicians for similar reasons:

> Certain politicians try very hard to avoid direct answers about fan hooliganism because they frequently use fans as a direct threat against their political opponents. Because of this, they frequently try to relativize various forms of aggression and violence as youthful excesses, or as a response to direct provocations from the other side. In this political code, fans are represented as the most patriotic part of the nation which as, by its very nature, the most sensitive to injustice and threats to national interests.[89]

One example of such politician 'courtship' of hooligans can be found in statements of several politicians following the hooligan violence in response to Kosovo independence in 2008: Velimir Ilic of the New Serbia Party said hooligans were warranted in their breaking of windows on foreign embassies, since [foreigners] did much worse to us; that *B92* should 'beware' what it says about these 'young people' – and later even threatened the Minister of Youth and Sports with the words 'you should be watch out, sports fans will come and get you'.[90] Most extreme was a statement from the Primer Minister Vojislav Kostunica himself: 'Those hooligans, as you call them, only reacted to the violation of international law'[91] – thus indicating that the participants of violence and looting should not be considered hooligans, and that they were righteous in their demands. Apart from relativizing hooligan violence and justifying their demands, some politicians utilize discourse, which is later explicitly mimicked by hooligans. For example, Dragan Markovic Palma, head of the political party United Serbia, has called homosexuality 'sick' and stated that he cannot stand gays and has elaborated on how disgusted he is by their effeminate mannerisms,[92] and similarly, the Serbian Progressive Party (SNS) said of the gay parade that it will 'lead to a situation in which one day sodomy and pedophilia will be protected as personal preferences'.[93]

Intellectuals and political analysts also play an important role in forging discourse readily used by hooligans, but more importantly, by providing hooligans with legitimacy via the credentials and educational background behind their otherwise ultra-nationalistic writings. For instance, Slobodan Antonic, a sociology professor at the University of Belgrade and political analyst, has said that tolerance of homosexuals in a few years 'will become a new, much more comprehensive and far-reaching violence'[94] and that the parade demonstrated Boris Tadic's 'capitulation before Ashton' and 'turning Serbia into a vassal state'.[95] Djordje Vukadinovic, editor of the conservative magazine *Nova srpska politicka misao* [New Serbian Political Thought] and philosophy lecturer at University of Belgrade, argued that the parade was forced upon Serbia from the West and justified the violence of hooligans by comparing the rights of homosexuals to the 'right to work and a decent life', which 'disenfranchised and unemployed' Serbian workers will not be afforded, saying the parade was 'against historical and political logic', and compared today's hooligans to the 'heroes' in the anti-Milosevic protests a decade earlier.[96] Similarly, Oliver Antic, professor at the Faculty of Law, called members of *Obraz* and *1389* 'kids who like having their own political idea and political path' and said they were no different from the anti-Milosevic Otpor movement in the late 1990s.[97] Branko Radun, another esteemed political analyst, also clearly propagates the idea that the hooligans, nationalistic organizations and mass society are on the same side, while the 'Euro-Atlantic' government and foreigners are on the other: ('[...] the potential of the cooperation between football fans, nationalistic organizations and patriotic forces on the one hand, and growingly embittered victims of a failed transition and the global economic crisis on the other'). He has called the pro-European government 'domestic European transvestites', and frequently furthers the idea of a Western conspiracy against Serbia, turning post-Milosevic Serbia into a 'vassal state' of the West.[98]

On a similar note, this analysis supports the argument of the triumph of what Michael Rossi has coined the 'illiberal' national identity narrative in Serbia and the further bipolarization of discourse surrounding Serbian identity: on one side are 'true' Serbians who value history, religion, family, honest work, Kosovo, the military and the Church (and as such, are defended by football hooligans and ultra-right groups), and on the other side are pro-Western, pro-EU and gay rights-supporting 'democrats' (seen by the former as traitors of the true Serbian nation). This bipolarization has been documented by several recent studies, noting the divide between the former ('First Serbia', with a populist vision of citizenship) and the latter ('Other Serbia', with an elitist vision of citizenship), and the inherent class differences in the two groups.[99] Rossi points to the failure of democratically minded political and cultural elites to take advantage of symbolic material in Serbian history to provide an alternative set of symbols and narratives, leading to a situation where symbolic imagery and historical ideas of the nation are completely co-opted by nationalists. Reader commentary to hooligan violence confirms this binary, both in discourse and in the difference in distribution of comments in *Kurir* (populist readership) and *B92* (elitist readership). The class dimension is certainly of particular significance and represents a fruitful direction for future research.

Finally, a relevant factor worth further consideration is the particular context in which hooliganism surfaced in Serbia, including the utilization of football fans by warmongers like Arkan and the Serbian State Security, as well as the socialization of entire generations of youth during the poverty, crime and corruption of the late 1980s and 1990s. The connection between some groups of football fans and their leaders with the criminal underworld began in this context in the 1990s and these connections continue to exist today. While certainly not all football fans are members of extremist organizations, nor are all football fans involved in criminal activities, the connections between fan leaders, who have at their disposal large numbers of impressionable youth, and criminal and extremist enterprises continue. Indeed, the issue of the connections between hooligans, the football 'mafia' and various crime groups is a topic that warrants further attention. As far as the extreme-right movement is concerned, scholars had previously concluded that the recent emergence of aggressive organizations reflects the 'marginalization of radical political options' and 'signals the retreat of extremism to the periphery of politics'.[100] While this might be true, and is certainly supported by the recent ban of *National Formation*, our analysis above points to an alarming parallel between slogans utilized by hooligans and mantras of the extreme-right movement on the one hand and writings of mainstream and 'sensible' actors such as academics and members of the Serbian Orthodox Church on the other.[101] This is further compounded by the fact that, while the government has officially taken a firm stance in denouncing hooligan violence, the judicial system has remained tenuous and irresolute in the actual sentencing of hooligans. In this way, Serbian hooliganism differs significantly (and becomes more difficult to deal with) than the more conventional forms of football hooliganism endemic to many societies.

However, it is important to note that nevertheless, mainstream society in Serbia remains in condemnation (and to some extent, fear) of hooligans, even while they might relate to the purported goals of the hooligans. The qualitative analysis in this paper focused on the subset of comments that supported hooligan violence (10% of all comments), while the number of comments expressing condemnation was three times higher (30% of all comments; highest in *B92* with 52% and lowest in *Kurir* with 12%). In other words, while many citizens in Serbia might be disillusioned with the current economic and political situation in the country and share the grievances of the hooligans, the number of those who consider violence an acceptable means of realizing social change remains relatively low. Unfortunately, online reader commentary does not provide a way of ascertaining the percentage of mainstream society empathetic with hooligan violence, nor is it possible to conclude which segments of society actually participate in online debates, so caution should be utilized in overgeneralizing on the basis of the comments analysed above.

Notes

1. Sugden and Tomlinson, *Hosts and Champions*.
2. Arbena, 'Sport, Development and Mexican Nationalism'; Duke and Crolley, *Football, Nationality and the State*; Guilianotti, Bonney, and Mepworth, *Football Violence and Social Identity*; Hargreaves, 'Olympism and Nationalism'; and Sugden and Tomlinson, *Hosts and Champions*.
3. Hoberman, 'Sport and Ideology'.
4. Bairner, *Sport, Nationalism and Globalization*.
5. Sack and Suster, 'Soccer and Croatian Nationalism', 306.
6. While hooliganism typically refers to a specific form of spectator violence at football matches, used to cover a variety of actions taking place in football-related contexts, the term 'hooliganism' is largely a media construct rather than a specific concept relating to football violence, and is frequently used in a 'cover-all' umbrella term including various forms of minor and more serious 'violence', referring broadly to football fans who cause 'damage' to society. See Spaaij, *Understanding Football Hooliganism*.
7. Studies of football hooliganism are too plentiful to mention here. For an excellent overview of the field, see Spaaij, *Understanding Football Hooliganism*. Also see Dunning, 'Towards a Sociological Understanding'; King, 'Outline of a Practical Theory'; and Guilianotti, Bonney, and Mepworth, *Football Violence and Social Identity*.

8. Stakic, 'Homophobia and Hate Speech in Serbian Public Discourse'.
9. Helsinki Committee for Human Rights in Serbia, 'Radicalization'.
10. Ivan Colovic, as quoted in Stankovic, 'Insajder: (Ne)moc drzave' [Insider: Power(less) of the state].
11. Colovic, *Politics of Symbol in Serbia*, 273–4.
12. Gasser and Levinsen, 'Breaking Post-War Ice', 459.
13. Marcus Tanner, 'Yugoslavia's Ethnic Hatred Boils over in Soccer Violence', *The Times*, May 10, 1990, 10.
14. Sack and Suster, 'Soccer and Croatian Nationalism', 311–2.
15. Gasser and Levinson, 'Breaking Post-War Ice', 459.
16. Arkan himself was a member of the State Security (Drzavna bezbednost) branch of the Serbian Ministry of Interior, a post he filled due to his propensity for criminal activities as well as the relationships with his father, general of the Yugoslav National Army, and Stane Dolanac, Minister of Interior and later member of the presidency. See Shentov, Todorov, and Stoyanov, *Partners in Crime*, 41–2; and Stewart, *Hunting the Tiger*, 145–6.
17. A summary of the charges against Arkan by the International Criminal Tribunal for the former Yugoslavia can be found here: International Criminal Tribunal for the Former Yugoslavia, 'Zeljko Raznatovic "ARKAN"', United Nations International Criminal Tribunal for the Former Yugoslavia, http://www.icty.org/x/cases/zeljko_raznjatovic/cis/en/cis_arkan_en.pdf.
18. While Arkan initially recruited *Delije* members for his Volunteer Guard, he later selected 'volunteers' from Serbian prisons as well as members from criminal circles in Serbia. For a thorough account of the recruitment of Tigers and their activity, see Australian Government Refugee Review Tribunal, 'Country Advice Serbia'. See also Sack and Suster, 'Soccer and Croatian Nationalism', 312.
19. Helsinki Committee for Human Rights in Serbia, 'Hooliganism Spills from Political', 3.
20. Helsinki Committee for Human Rights in Serbia, 'Radicalization', 1.
21. Kazimir, 'Nasilje u sportu i mediji' [Violence in sport and the media], 2 (our translation).
22. Brubaker, *Ethnicity without Groups*.
23. Hobsbawm, 'Invention of Tradition', 10.
24. Wodak et al., *Discursive Construction of National Identity*.
25. Fearon and Laitin, 'Violence and the Social Construction of Ethnic Identity', 851–2.
26. Bourdieu, 'Identity and Representation', 223.
27. Calhoun, *Nationalism*, 5.
28. Fox and Miller-Idriss, 'Everyday Nationhood', 538.
29. Ibid., 539.
30. Colovic, *Politics of Symbol in Serbia*, 280.
31. Surculija, Pavlovic, and Padejski, 'Mapping Digital Media'.
32. His sentence was reduced in 2011, because the Appeals Court decided there was insufficient evidence that Misic tried to stick the torch down the police officer's throat, since the burn injuries were not on his mouth but on his back and the left side of his face only. See FoNet, 'Preinacena presuda Urosu Misicu' [Judgment revised for Uros Misic], *Vecernje Novosti Online*, May 4, 2011, http://www.novosti.rs/vesti/naslovna/aktuelno.69.html:329209-Prei nacena-presuda-Urosu-Misicu.
33. *Elektronske Novine*, 'Otkriveni napadači na ambasade i policiju?' [Embassy and police attackers discovered?] *Elektronske Novine*, August 25, 2011, http://www.e-novine.com/srbija/vesti/50293-Otkriveni-napadai-ambasade-policiju.html.
34. Rade Stanic, 'Moc desnice' [The power of the right], *Politika Online*, August 3, 2008, http://www.politika.rs/rubrike/Tema-nedelje/Moch-desnice/Moc-desnice.lt.html.
35. *Blic Online*, 'Huligani ponovo lomili Beograd' [Hooligans smashing Belgrade again], *Blic Online*, July 30, 2008, http://www.blic.rs/Vesti/Politika/51112/Huligani-ponovo-lomili-Beograd; and *Glas javnosti*, 'Huligani opet ruse' [Hooligans destroy again], *Glas javnosti*, July 30, 2008, http://www.glas-javnosti.rs/clanak/tema/glas-javnosti-30-07-2008/huligani-opet-ruse.
36. In January 2011, the main organizer Djordje Prelic was sentenced to 35 years in prison, while the other accomplices received between 4 and 32 years. See *Blic*, 'Huligani nasrtali na novinare i vređali sud' [Hooligans attacked/journalists and insulted the court], *Blic Online*, January 26, 2011, http://www.blic.rs/Vesti/Hronika/231597/Huligani-nasrtali-na–novinare-i-vredjali-sud. In January 2012, the Appeals Court reduced their sentences by half, including Prelic's from 35 to 15 years; see Vuk Cvijic, 'Prepolovljene kazne ubicama Brisa Tatona' [Penalties halved for

the killers of Brice Taton], *Blic Online*, January 26, 2012, http://www.blic.rs/Vesti/Hronika/303657/Prepolovljene-kazne-ubicama-Brisa-Tatona.

37. Stankovic, 'Insajder: (Ne)moc drzave' [Insider: Power(less) of the state].

38. *Beta Agency*, 'Potvrdjena presuda za pretnje Brankici Stankovic' [Judgment confirmed for the threats to Brankica Stankovic], *Blic Online*, September 16, 2010, http://www.blic.rs/Vesti/Hronika/207487/Potvrdjena-presuda-za-pretnje-Brankici-Stankovic.

39. K. Djordjevic, 'Datum i marsuta gej parade' [Date and route for the Pride Parade], *Politika Online*, July 21, 2009, http://www.politika.rs/rubrike/vesti-dana/Datum-i-marshruta-gej-parade.sr.html.

40. Ognjen Zoric, 'Vodji "Obraza" dve godine zatvora za nerede na Paradi ponosa' [Two years in prison for the leader of 'Obraz' for rioting at the Gay Parade], *Radio Slobodna Evropa*, April 20, 2011, http://www.slobodnaevropa.org/content/vodja_obraza_osudjen_na_dve_godine/9500255.html.

41. Helsinki Committee for Human Rights in Serbia, 'Pride Parade'.

42. 'Neredi zbog hapsenja Mladica' [The riots over the arrest of Mladic], *Vreme*, May 27, 2011, http://www.vreme.com/cms/view.php?id=993035; and 'Protesti zbog hapsenja Mladica, privedeno 35 osoba' [Protests against the arrest of Mladic, 35 persons detained], *Vecernje Novosti Online*, May 26, 2011, http://www.novosti.rs/vesti/naslovna/aktuelno.69.html:332054-Protesti-zbog-hapsenja-Mladica-privedeno-35-osoba.

43. 'Zabranjena "Parada ponosa" i svi skupovi' ['Pride Parade' and all assemblies prohibited], *Vesti Online*, September 30, 2011, http://www.vesti-online.com/Vesti/Srbija/168166/Zabranjena-Parada-ponosa-i-svi-skupovi.

44. 'Fudbal, incidenti i pobeda Partizana' [Football, incidents and Partizan victory], *Tanjug*, November 25, 2011, http://www.tanjug.rs/novosti/25371/fudbal–incidenti-i-pobeda-partizana.htm.

45. '"Delije" i "Firma" tukli hrvatske navijače, kod 13 uhapšenih nađeno oružje' ['Delije' and 'Firma' beat Croatian fans, 13 arrested with arms], *Blic*, http://www.blic.rs/Vesti/Hronika/303537/Delije-i-Firma-tukli-hrvatske-navijace-kod-13-uhapsenih-nadjeno-oruzje.

46. Colovic, *Politics of Symbol in Serbia*, 276. For more background information, see 'Football, Blood and War', *The Observer, Observer Sport Monthly*, January 18, 2004, http://observer.guardian.co.uk/osm/story/0,6903,1123137,00.html.

47. Kazimir, 'Nasilje u sportu i mediji' [Violence in sport and the media], 5 (our translation).

48. *Kurir*, 'Zatvor zbog Srebrenice' [Prison for Srebrenica], *Kurir*, October 19, 2006, http://arhiva.kurir-info.rs/Arhiva/2006/oktobar/19/SP-03-19102006.shtml.

49. According to the show 'Insider' and several newspapers (e.g. *Glas javnosti*, August 1, 2006, 12), this figure comes from official evidence on the basis of criminal court proceedings of the police.

50. Official site of *Obraz*, http://www.srb-obraz.org.

51. Official site of *1389*, http://www.1389.org.rs.

52. Official site of *Nasi Srbija*, http://nasisrbija.org.

53. Official site of *Dveri*, http://www.dverisrpske.com.

54. Official site of *Nacionalni stroj*, http://www.nacionalnistroj.com.

55. Official site of *Blood and Honor*, https://www.bhserbia.org/.

56. The 15 groups included Partizan sub-groups Brigate, Ludaci Padinska Skela, Alkatraz, Anti-Romi, South Family, Shadows, Head Hunters, Extreme Boys, Brain Damage, Iriducibili New Belgrade and Cuvari casti; Zvezda subgroups Ultra Boys, Belgrade Boys and Ultras and Rad subgroup United Force.

57. M. Derikonjic, 'Nema zabrane navijačkih grupa' [No ban for fan groups], *Politika Online*, March 19, 2011, http://www.politika.rs/rubrike/Hronika/Nema-zabrane-navijackih-grupa.lt.html.

58. Helsinki Committee for Human Rights in Serbia, 'Annual Report, Serbia in 2010', 75.

59. V. Cvijic, 'Zabranjen Nacionalni stroj' [Nacionalni stroj banned], *Blic Online*, June 2, 2011, http://www.blic.rs/Vesti/Hronika/257679/Zabranjen-Nacionalni-stroj.

60. *Beta Agency*, 'Ustavni sud trazi dodatne dokaze za zabranu "Obraza"' [The Constitutional Court asks for further evidence for the prohibition of 'Obraz'], *Blic Online*, December 14, 2011, http://www.blic.rs/Vesti/Hronika/295552/Ustavni-sud-trazi-dodatne-dokaze-za-zabranu-Obraza.

61. Manosevitch and Walker, 'Reader Comments to Online Opinion Journalism'; and Dimaggio et al., 'Social Implications of the Internet'.

62. Albrecht, 'Whose Voice is Heard?'; and Min, 'Online vs. Face-to-Face Deliberation'.
63. Rojo and Ragsdale, 'Participation in Electronic Forums'; and Dahlberg, 'Internet and Democratic Discourse'.
64. Dahlberg, 'Internet and Democratic Discourse'; and Albrecht, 'Whose Voice is Heard?'.
65. Kollock and Smith, 'Managing the Virtual Commons'.
66. Postmes, Spears, and Lea, 'Breaching or Building Social Boundaries?'; and Min 'Online vs. Face-to-Face Deliberation'.
67. Benson, 'Rhetoric, Civility, and Community'.
68. Albrecht, 'Whose Voice is Heard?'.
69. Manosevitch and Walker, 'Reader Comments to Online Opinion Journalism'.
70. Benson, 'Rhetoric, Civility, and Community'.
71. Albrecht, 'Whose Voice is Heard?'; and Dahlberg, 'Internet and Democratic Discourse'.
72. Marija Drajic, 'Stampani mediji u Srbiji. Zuto nam se pise' [Print media in Serbia. Yellow is written for us], *Preko ramena – Online casopis*, November 23, 2010, http://www.prekoramena.com/t.item.75/stampani-mediji-u-srbiji-tabloidna-stampa.html.
73. Surculija, Pavlovic, and Padejski, 'Mapping Digital Media'.
74. 'Top Sites in Serbia', *Alexa, The Web Information Company*, http://www.alexa.com/topsites/countries/RS.
75. The top five non-tabloids are *Blic*, *Vecernje Novosti*, *Politika*, *B92* and *RTS*, while the top five tabloids are *Kurir*, *Press*, *Alo!*, *Pravda* and *Svet*. See Surculija, Pavlovic, and Padejski, 'Mapping Digital Media'.
76. *Blic*, 'Parada ponosa zavrsena, huligani pljackali grad, uhapsen vodja "Obraza"' [Gay Parade finished, hooligans loot city, leader of Obraz arrested], *Blic Online*, October 10, 2010, http://www.blic.rs/Vesti/Drustvo/211212/Parada-ponosa-zavrsena-huligani-pljackali-grad-uhapsen-vodja-Obraza.
77. 'Demoliranje Beograda, jos jednom' [Demolishing Belgrade, once again], *B92*, October 10, 2010, http://www.b92.net/info/vesti/index.php?yyyy=2010&mm=10&dd=10&nav_category=16&nav_id=464314.
78. The five *Kurir* articles are Sasa Stajic, 'Dan kada je grad goreo' [The day the city burned], October 10, 2010, http://www.kurir-info.rs/vesti/dan-kada-je-grad-goreo-54033.php; 'Parada ponosa u Beogradu istorijski dogadjaj' [Gay Parade in Belgrade a historical event], October 10, 2010, http://www.kurir-info.rs/vesti/drustvo/pavlovic-parada-ponosa-u-beogradu-istorijski-dogadjaj-54006.php; *News Agencies*, 'Gay Parade Held, Police Drive Participants Home', October 10, 2010, http://www.kurir-info.rs/vesti/drustvo/odrzana-parada-ponosa-policija-ucesnike-razvozi-po-kucama-53968.php; 'Parada ponosa – sredjji prst za monahinje' [Gay Parade: Middle finger for nuns], October 13, 2010, http://www.kurir-info.rs/vesti/gej-parada-haos-u-beogradu/parada-ponosa-srednji-prst-za-monahinje-54435.php; and *Beta Agency*, 'Uhapsen vodja Obraza Mladen Obradovic' [Leader of Obraz Mladen Obradovic arrested], October 13, 2010, http://www.kurir-info.rs/vesti/gej-parada-haos-u-beogradu/veljovic-uhapsen-vodja- obraza-mladen-obradovic-54025.php.
79. For example, 'The Democratic Party Headquarters Are Burning!'; response to a previous comment 'What Are You Trying to Say?', a one word response only, or similar. *Kurir* had the most unusable comments (17.8%), followed by *Blic* (9.4%) and *B92* with the least (6%).
80. The difference in attitudes towards the reaction of the police is more difficult to interpret, because a negative reaction in *B92* comments mostly reflected dissatisfaction that the police were not doing more to crack down on hooligans, while *Kurir*'s reflected disapproval that the police were protecting the parade in the first place.
81. 'Drvo koje ne rađa se siječe i u vatru baca'. See *Press*, 'Skandalozno: Amfilohiju sude zbog gej parade?!' [Scandalous: Amfilohije is tried due to Gay Parade], *Press Online*, September 24, 2009, http://www.pressonline.rs/sr/vesti/vesti_dana/story/80702/Skandalozno%3A+Amfilohij.
82. *B92*, 'Govor mrznje: Parada kao uranijum' [Hate speech: The Parade as uranium], *B92 Online*, October 14, 2010, http://www.b92.net/info/vesti/index.php?yyyy=2010&mm=10&dd=14&nav_id=465324.
83. Holy Assembly of Bishops, 'Saopstenje Svetog Arhijerejskog Sinoda povodom najava gej parade u Beogradu' [Statement of the Holy Synod of Bishops on the occasion of the announcement of the Gay Parade in Belgrade].

84. Bishop of Backa Irinej Bulovic, as quoted in *Blic*, 'Vladika sazvao sednicu Vlade' [Bishop summoned the meeting of the government], *Blic Online*, March 6, 2009, http://www.blic.rs/Vesti/Politika/82119/Vladika-sazvao-sednicu-Vlade.
85. Byford, 'Christian Right-Wing Organisations', 50.
86. Labris Organization for Lesbian Human Rights, *Godišnji izveštaj o položaju LGBTIQ* [Annual report on the position of the LGBT].
87. Helsinki Committee for Human Rights in Serbia, 'Radicalization'.
88. *Kurir*, 'Peder odstranjuje Kosovo!' [Faggot removes Kosovo!], *Kurir*, July 14, 2009, http://www.kurir-info.rs/vesti/peder-odstranjuje-kosovo-25339.php.
89. Kazimir, 'Nasilje u sportu i mediji' [Violence in sport and the media], 96 (our translation).
90. Part of the transcript of the parliament session following the violence in response to Kosovo independence: *Blic*, 'Kostunica: Mladi su samo branili medjunarodno pravo' [Kostunica: Young people were just defending International Law], *Blic Online*, February 22, 2008, http://www.blic.rs/Vesti/Politika/31371/Kostunica-Mladi-su-samo-branili-medjunarodno-pravo-.
91. Ibid.
92. *Press*, 'Palma za Press: Znam ko su homici u skupštini Srbije!' [Palma for Press: I know who is gay in the Serbian Parliament], *Naslovi Net*, March 17, 2009, http://www.naslovi.net/2009-03-17/press/palma-za-press-znam-ko-su-homici-u-skupstini-srbije/1078628.
93. P. Vasiljevic, 'Opozicija brani stavove Crkve' [Opposition defends the views of the Church], *Vecernje Novosti Online*, March 16, 2009, http://www.novosti.rs/vesti/naslovna/aktuelno.289.html:234550-Opozicija-brani--stavove-Crkve.
94. Slobodan Antonic, 'Tolerancija nije dovoljna' [Tolerance is not enough], *Politika Online*, March 19, 2009, http://www.politika.rs/pogledi/Slobodan-Antonic/TOLERANCIJA-NIJE-DOVOLJNA.lt.html.
95. Slobodan Antonic, 'Reakcija drzave ce biti jeziva!' [The reaction of the State will be dreadful!], *Pecat*, Internet portal slobodne Srbije, October 13, 2010, http://www.pecat.co.rs/2010/10/slobodan-antonic-reakcija-drzave-ce-biti-jeziva/.
96. Djordje Vukadinovic, 'Od parade do poraza' [From the parade to the defeat], *Politika Online*, October 12, 2010, http://www.politika.rs/pogledi/DJordje-Vukadinovic/Od-parade-do-poraza.lt.html.
97. *B92*, 'Oliver Antic o "Otporu" i "1389"' [Oliver antic about Otpor and 1389], *B92*, September 24, 2009, http://www.b92.net/info/vesti/index.php?yyyy=2009&mm=09&dd=24&nav_category=11&nav_id=383024.
98. See biography and posts by Branko Radun, Fond Slobodan Jovanovic, http://www.slobodanjovanovic.org/author/Branko/?lang=lat.
99. See Rossi, 'Resurrecting the Past'; Mikus, 'State Pride'; and Pavasovic Trost, 'Construction and Contestation of Ethnic Identity'.
100. Byford, 'Christian Right-Wing Organisations', 44
101. The success of *Dveri* at the upcoming elections will be indicative of the prevalence of these views in mainstream society.

References

Albrecht, Steffen. 'Whose Voice is Heard in Online Deliberation? A Study of Participation and Representation in Political Debates on the Internet'. *Information, Communication & Society* 9 (2006): 62–82.
Arbena, Joseph. 'Sport, Development and Mexican Nationalism 1920–1970'. *Journal of Sport History* 18 (1991): 350–64.
Australian Government Refugee Review Tribunal. 'Country Advice Serbia'. Australian Government. March 2010. http://www.mrt-rrt.gov.au/ArticleDocuments/152/SRB36154.pdf.aspx
Bairner, Alan. *Sport, Nationalism and Globalization: European and North American Perspectives*. New York: State University of New York Press, 2001.
Benson, Thomas W. 'Rhetoric, Civility, and Community: Political Debate on Computer Bulletin Boards'. *Communication Quarterly* 449 (1996): 359–78.
Bourdieu, Pierre. 'Identity and Representation: Elements for a Critical Reflection on the Idea of Region'. In *Language and Symbolic Power*, ed. Pierre Bourdieu, 220–8. Cambridge, MA: Harvard University Press, 1991.
Brubaker, Rogers. *Ethnicity without Groups*. Cambridge, MA: Harvard University Press, 2004.

Byford, Jovan. 'Christian Right-Wing Organisations and the Spreading of Anti-Semitic Prejudice in Post-Milošević Serbia: The Case of the Dignity Patriotic Movement'. *East European Jewish Affairs* 32 (2002): 43–60.

Calhoun, Craig. *Nationalism*. Minneapolis: University of Minnesota Press, 1997.

Colovic, Ivan. *The Politics of Symbol in Serbia*. London: Hurst, 2002.

Dahlberg, Lincoln. 'The Internet and Democratic Discourse: Exploring the Prospects of Online Deliberative Forums Extending the Public Sphere'. *Information, Communication & Society* 49 (2001): 615–33.

DiMaggio, Paul, Eszter Hargittai, W. Russell Neuman, and John Paul Robinson. 'Social Implications of the Internet'. *Annual Review of Sociology* 27 (2001): 307–36.

Duke, Vic, and Liz Crolley. *Football, Nationality and the State*. New York: Addison Wesley Longman, 1996.

Dunning, Eric. 'Towards a Sociological Understanding of Football Hooliganism as a World Phenomenon'. *European Journal on Criminal Policy and Research* 8 (2000): 141–62.

Fearon, James D., and David D. Laitin. 'Violence and the Social Construction of Ethnic Identity'. *International Organization* 54 (2000): 845–77.

Fox, Jon, and Cynthia Miller-Idriss. 'Everyday Nationhood'. *Ethnicities* 8 (2008): 536–83.

Gasser, Patrick, and Anders Levinsen. 'Breaking Post-War Ice: Open Fun Football Schools in Bosnia and Herzegovina'. *Sport in Society* 7 (2004): 457–72.

Guilianotti, Richard, Norman Bonney, and Mike Mepworth, eds. *Football Violence and Social Identity*. London: Routledge, 1994.

Hargreaves, John. 'Olympism and Nationalism: Some Preliminary Considerations'. *International Review for the Sociology of Sport* 27 (1992): 119–37.

Helsinki Committee for Human Rights in Serbia. 'Hooliganism Spills from Political onto Sports Terrains'. *Helsinki Bulletin*, 52 (2009): http://www.helsinki.org.rs/doc/HB-No52.pdf

Helsinki Committee for Human Rights in Serbia, 'Radicalization: A Constant Threat to Democratic Forces'. *Helsinki Bulletin* 44 (2009): http://www.helsinki.org.rs/doc/HB-No44.pdf

Helsinki Committee for Human Rights in Serbia. 'Annual Report, Serbia in 2010: Human Rights Reflect Institutional Impotence'. http://helsinki.org.rs/doc/Report2010.pdf

Helsinki Committee for Human Rights in Serbia, 'The Pride Parade – "Violence Culture" and the Offensive from the Right'. *Helsinki Bulletin* 72 (2010): http://www.helsinki.org.rs/doc/HB-No72.pdf

Hoberman, John. 'Sport and Ideology in the Post-Communist Age'. In *The Changing Politics of Sport*, ed. L. Allison, 15–36. Manchester: Manchester University Press, 1993.

Hobsbawm, Eric. 'The Invention of Tradition'. In *The Invention of Tradition*, ed. Eric Hobsbawm and Terence Ranger, 1–14. Cambridge: Cambridge University Press, 1983.

Holy Assembly of Bishops. 'Saopstenje Svetog Arhijerejskog Sinoda povodom najava gej parade u Beogradu' [Statement of the Holy Synod of Bishops on the occasion of the announcement of the Gay Parade in Belgrade]. Belgrade, Serbian Orthodox Church. 2010. http://www.spc.rs/sr/saopstenje_svetog_arhijerejskog_sinoda_povodom_najava_gejparade_u_beogradu

Kazimir, Velimir Curgus. 'Nasilje u sportu i mediji' [Violence in sport and the media]. Ebart Media documentation research paper prepared for the Serbian Center for Free Elections and Democracy (CeSID) and the Serbian Ministry of Youth and Sport. http://www.b92.net/info/download.phtml?398238

King, Anthony. 'Outline of a Practical Theory of Football Violence'. *Sociology* 29 (1995): 635–51.

Kollock, Peter, and Marc Smith. 'Managing the Virtual Commons: Cooperation and Conflict in Computer Communities'. In *Computer-Mediated Communication: Linguistic, Social and Cross-Cultural Perspectives*, ed. S.C. Herring, 109–28. Amsterdam: John Benjamins, 1996.

Labris Organization for Lesbian Human Rights. *Godišnji izveštaj o položaju LGBTIQ populacije u Srbiji, za 2009. godinu* [Annual report on the position of the LGBT population in Serbia in 2009]. Belgrade: Labris Organization for Lesbian Human Rights. 2010. http://www.labris.org.rs/images/npublikacije/izvestajSR.pdf

Manosevitch, Edith, and Dana Walker. 'Reader Comments to Online Opinion Journalism: A Space of Public Deliberation'. Paper presented at 10th International Symposium on Online Journalism, Austin, TX, April 17–18'. 2009. http://online.journalism.utexas.edu/2009/papers/ManosevitchWalker09.pdf

Mikus, Marek. '"State Pride": Politics of LGBT Rights and Democratisation in "European Serbia"'. *East European Politics and Societies* 25 (2011): 834–51.

Min, Seong-Jae. 'Online vs. Face-to-Face Deliberation: Effects on Civic Engagement'. *Journal of Computer-Mediated Communication* 12 (2007): 1369–87.

Pavasovic Trost, Tamara. 'Construction and Contestation of Ethnic Identity: Identity Discourse among Serbian and Croatian Youth'. PhD diss., Harvard University, 2012.

Postmes, Tom, Russell Spears, and Martin Lea. 'Breaching or Building Social Boundaries? Side-Effects of Computer-Mediated Communication'. *Communication Research* 25 (1998): 689–715.

Rojo, Alejandra, and Ronald G. Ragsdale. 'Participation in Electronic Forums: Implications for the Design and Implementation of Collaborative Distributed Media'. *Telematics and Informatics* 14 (1997): 83–96.

Rossi, Michael. 'Resurrecting the Past: Democracy, National Identity, and Historical Memory in Modern Serbia'. PhD diss., The State University of New York, 2009.

Sack, Allen, and Zeljan Suster. 'Soccer and Croatian Nationalism: A Prelude to War'. *Journal of Sport and Social Issues* 24 (2000): 305–20.

Shentov, Ognian, Boyko Todorov, and Alexander Stoyanov, eds. *Partners in Crime: The Risks of Symbiosis between the Security Sector and Organized Crime in Southeast Europe.* Sofia: Center for the Study of Democracy, 2004. http://www.my-world-guide.com/upload/File/Reports/Bulgaria/Organised_Crime_Southeast_Europe.pdf

Spaaij, Ramon. *Understanding Football Hooliganism: A Comparison of Six Western European Football Clubs.* Amsterdam: Amsterdam University Press, 2006.

Stakic, Isidora. 'Homophobia and Hate Speech in Serbian Public Discourse: How Nationalist Myths and Stereotypes Influence Prejudices against the LGBT Minority'. Master's thesis, University of Gothenburg, 2011.

Stankovic, Brankica. 'Insajder: (Ne)moc drzave' [Insider: Power(less) of the state]. *Radio Television B92.* 2009. http://www.b92.net/tv/site.php?nav_category=644&nav_id=315475

Stewart, Christopher S. *Hunting the Tiger: The Fast Life and Violent Death of the Balkans' Most Dangerous Man.* New York: St. Martin's Press, 2008.

Sugden, John and Alan Tomlinson, eds. *Hosts and Champions: Soccer Cultures, National Identities and the USA World Cup.* Surrey: Ashgate, 1994.

Surculija, Jelena, Biljana Pavlovic, and Djurdja Jovanovic Padejski. 'Mapping Digital Media: Serbia'. A Report by the Open Society Foundations. 2011. http://www.opensocietyfoundations.org/publications/mapping-digital-media-serbia

Wodak, Ruth, Rudolf de Cillia, Martin Reisigl, and Karin Liebhart. *The Discursive Construction of National Identity.* Edinburgh: Edinburgh University Press, 1999.

Football after Yugoslavia: conflict, reconciliation and the regional football league debate

Shay Wood

Department of History, University of Kansas, Lawrence, KS, USA

Twenty years after Yugoslavia began breaking apart into new states, former Yugoslavs have re-established many of their commercial, professional and cultural ties. This network of renewed connections extends to most team sports, but not to football. Advocacy for a regional football league is a decade old, and there have been several concrete proposals. Despite all this, the idea remains intensely controversial. This article provides an argument for the controversy's depth and persistence, which is that football, unlike other sports, had a role in Yugoslavia's dissolution and continuing post-war inter-ethnic animosities and conflicts. This article also pays attention to challenges and alternatives to this legacy, as expressed in the league debate. Given the intolerance and violence in post-Yugoslav football, the increasing openness to football reunion is noteworthy.

Introduction

Twenty years after Yugoslavia began breaking apart into new states, which today number seven, former Yugoslavs have re-established many of their commercial, professional and cultural ties. Bosnians shop at Slovenian-owned supermarkets; Croatian, Montenegrin and Serbian police cooperate in criminal investigations; Kosovars import a significant proportion of their goods from Macedonia; and thousands of the region's young people assemble at a large annual music festival in Vojvodina, the autonomous province in northern Serbia.[1] This network of renewed connections also extends to sports. Since the turn of the twenty-first century, sports officials have created and expanded a number of international leagues, which include teams from multiple Yugoslav successor states. The first was the Adriatic Basketball Association's Goodyear League, founded in 2001 with headquarters in Slovenia. Its original teams came from the host country as well as Bosnia and Herzegovina, Croatia and Montenegro (then still united with Serbia); clubs from Serbia joined a year later. Since then the league, now called NLB rather than Goodyear, has consisted almost entirely of teams from these five formerly Yugoslav republics. Beyond basketball, men's clubs from no fewer than two successor states now belong to leagues in water polo, handball, ice hockey, volleyball, rugby, field hockey and American football. Women's teams compete in volleyball, handball and field hockey. Reintegration, it appears, has become the norm in post-Yugoslav sports.

The glaring exception is football, which at the local level continues to be organized solely into national leagues. This is not due to a lack of interest in reuniting former Yugoslavs in a football league. In fact, the first proposal appeared no less than a decade ago, around the time of the founding of the Goodyear League, and since then, preliminary talks involving football officials and potential sponsors have taken place on occasion. The first concrete attempt occurred in 2004 in Slovenia at a conference organized by a sports rights marketing firm. The Slobodan Vujčić-Red Star Agency brought together representatives of national football federations, clubs and potential sponsors to lay the foundation of the Central European Football League (CEFL). The CEFL was to consist 20 teams, approximately two from each of the Yugoslav successor states, then numbered five, and the same proportion from five of their neighbours – Austria, Hungary, Slovakia, Bulgaria and Romania. The list of proposed clubs was impressive. It comprised Yugoslavia's 'Big Four' – Red Star Belgrade, Dinamo Zagreb, Hajduk Split and Partizan (Belgrade) – and storied clubs such as Rapid Vienna, Ferencvaros (Budapest), Steaua Bucharest and Levski Sofia. Managements of the top Croatian and Serbian clubs gave their support. Dinamo's representative said, 'The future is in the creation of a regional league. Dinamo wishes to be involved in that process from the start'. Red Star's director spoke similarly on behalf of his club: 'We are absolutely for this idea'. All the details of the CEFL were to be worked out in 2005, and the league was to begin later that year.[2] In the end, however, the CEFL never happened.

Between 2005 and 2011, additional proposals for an international football league involving teams from the former Yugoslavia have likewise come and gone. In 2006, according to one optimistic report, 'A regional football league, with Croatian clubs as its integral part, will finally, judging by the latest developments, become reality'.[3] In 2009, the president of the Serbian Football Federation announced plans to continue negotiations.[4] In 2010, the president of the Slovenian Football Federation suggested a tournament of national champions as a test run for an amalgamated league.[5] Federation officials decided to postpone this discussion until after the World Cup that summer in South Africa, but they never resumed it.

Even if the advocates have changed over the years, the stated reasons for forming a regional football league have remained consistent. Advocates consider such a venture, with well-paying sponsorships and lucrative television deals, the best solution to the major financial problems facing federations and clubs. At present, clubs rely largely on government contributions and the sale of young and talented players to richer clubs. A consequence of this latter practice is the lack of parity in the various national leagues.[6] As of 2012, Partizan and Red Star have won the Serbian national championship 19 out of 20 times, a feat that Dinamo and Hajduk have matched in Croatia. Even these statistics mask the recent dominance of only two teams: Partizan has won five consecutive national championships, while Dinamo has taken seven straight. This superiority at home has not, however, translated into much success 'in Europe', as European competitions are referred to locally. In 2010–2011, Partizan gave one of the worst performances ever in the group stage of the Champions League, losing all six matches. The following year, Dinamo gave arguably the worst performance, not only dropping all six contests but also finishing with the league's worst-ever goal difference. Such poor showings abroad by the pre-eminent teams in the successor states are ammunition for proponents of an international league, who claim that regular matches between the region's top teams will be a better preparation for European contests.[7] Proponents also suppose that higher quality of play on the pitch and the revival of old rivalries will bring back spectators.[8] Using a familiar phrase among advocates, Ivica Osim, the last manager of the Yugoslav national team, exclaimed, 'A regional league is the salvation for all the [formerly Yugoslav] countries'.[9]

What is fascinating about the regional football league idea is that it remains deeply controversial locally, despite 10 years of circulation and the increasing renewal, even in sports, of old connections. As one Croatian radio–television reporter puts it, 'While everyone cooperates, from politicians and businessmen to cultural figures and even criminals, the most hell gets raised over the question of a united football league'.[10] Why is this so? The answer does not lie simply in disagreements about the alleged benefits of an amalgamated league, or in worries about the fate of clubs not selected for participation – or even in the scepticism regarding its feasibility. 'I want answers', Dejan Savičević, the president of the Montenegrin Football Federation, told the press in 2010, 'who will delegate referees, who will lead the league, where will its headquarters be, what will the champion get, and what will be with the national leagues?'[11] As Savičević's request for details demonstrates, the controversy is due to lingering strains from the break-up of Yugoslavia. But this explanation is not yet sufficient because general post-Yugoslav tensions do not fully account for the controversy's depth. Multiple regional sports leagues have come into existence in these same conditions without this kind of uproar.[12]

Rather, the idea of a football league reuniting clubs from the Yugoslav successor states remains incredibly contentious because football itself was entangled in the dissolution of Yugoslavia and the creation of its successor states, and, what is more, continues to serve as one of the main vehicles for inter-ethnic conflict among the peoples of the ex-Yugoslav republics. In short, football is where the antagonism lives on. The undying resistance to football reunion stems as much from this legacy of Yugoslav club football as from concern for the sport itself. At the same time, many in the league debate have raised challenges and proposed alternatives to this legacy, encouraging a move towards reconciliation. Given the intolerance and violence in post-Yugoslav football, this increasing openness to football reunion is all the more remarkable.

Football conflicts

During the twentieth century, football clubs competed for more than six decades in a statewide Yugoslav championship, which was interrupted by the country's partition during World War II and dissolved by the country's partition during the Yugoslav Wars. From 1923 to 1940, teams vied for the title of state champions in the Kingdom of Yugoslavia (from 1918 to 1930, the Kingdom of Serbs, Croats and Slovenes). Akin to the current regional league debate, the central tension in football then existed between Croatian and Serbian officials. Disagreements over which competition format to use precipitated the cancellation of the 1933–1934 season and later the withdrawal of Croatian teams from the 1936 contest. A few years later, in 1940, football officials set up separate Croatian, Slovenian and Serbian leagues, with the top three teams from each qualifying for the First League. These leagues were dismantled in 1941 when the Axis Powers invaded and divided Yugoslavia. Many football clubs remained active during the war, though, playing in leagues and matches sponsored by Nazi Germany, Fascist Italy, or their puppet states or allies.

This wartime activity spelled doom for many clubs when the People's Liberation Army of Yugoslavia, known as the Partisans, expelled the Axis forces, and Marshal Josip Broz Tito's Communist Party established a new Yugoslav state. In 1945, the new authorities swiftly disbanded many 'collaborationist' clubs, including the two greatest clubs in the interwar kingdom: the Belgrade Sports Club and Zagreb's Croatian Citizens' Sports Club. That same year, Red Star (Belgrade) and Dinamo (Zagreb), whose names were inspired by the country's new communist vision, took their place. Hajduk Split, another successful club before World War II, survived because it had refused to join an Italian league – Split had been seized by Fascist Italy – and had spent the final years of the war travelling through Allied territory as the Partisans' team. When Hajduk was demobilized at the war's end in 1945, the Yugoslav Army, based in the capital city of Belgrade, established its own club, Partizan. These four clubs – Red Star, Dinamo, Hajduk and Partizan – soon became known as the Big Four, and in the 45 years of the Yugoslav First League (1946–1991), they collectively won 41 state championships and 33 Yugoslav cups. But there were many other clubs that competed, and occasionally triumphed, in the Yugoslav First League. These included FK Sarajevo and Željezničar in Sarajevo, Vardar in Skopje, Budućnost in Titograd, FK Vojvodina in northern Serbia, NK Rijeka on the north Croatian coast, Velež in Mostar and Olimpija in Ljubljana. These clubs have played in separate national leagues since the early 1990s, when state disintegration and war broke up the Yugoslav league once again.[13]

Club football played a significant role in this dissolution. By the second half of the 1980s, amid economic troubles and political instability, cheering for a football club became a way to declare one's national loyalty and political preferences.[14] Ivan Čolović, a Serbian ethnographer, has noted the introduction of ethnic politics into football:

> In the years that preceded the outbreak of armed conflict in Croatia, supporters at sports stadiums, and most of all at football grounds, began carrying placards bearing political messages, portraits of national leaders and saints, national coats of arms and flags.[15]

Red Star Belgrade became one of the pillars of Serbian national identification among Serbs throughout Yugoslavia, and fans from all walks of life rooted for the club to express support for Serbian national politics and Serbia.[16] Partizan was also seen by many to be a Serbian club. Serbian fans, akin to participants at the political rallies in the late 1980s in Serbia and Montenegro, voiced support for communist-turned-nationalist Slobodan Milošević, often chanting, 'Serbian Slobo, Serbia is with you'.[17] Dinamo and Hajduk were for Croats what Red Star was for Serbs. Fans groups in Croatia, especially the Bad Blue Boys (Dinamo supporters) and Torcida (Hajduk supporters), offered the first mass support for Franjo Tuđman and his nationalist Croatian Democratic Union. According to the Croatian sociologist Benjamin Perasović, 'Fans looked like a specific avant-garde group of a social movement for national rights or even a "National Liberation Front"'. In the absence of political rallies in Croatia, these fan groups 'strived more and more to transform the stadium into a place of worthy response and political (and mono-national) gatherings'.[18] Unlike anything seen before in Yugoslav fan culture, groups of supporters united and clashed on the basis of national identification.[19]

Such politically charged inter-ethnic tensions culminated into a significant riot on May 1990 in Zagreb before a Dinamo–Red Star match, which was ultimately called off. Two weeks earlier, Franjo Tuđman and the Croatian Democratic Union had defeated the Communist Party (renamed the Social Democratic Party) in the republic's parliamentary elections. As spectators were still entering the stadium, several incidents broke out. Whatever the initial cause (controversial then and now), Red Star's fans, called the Delije (Braves), scuffled with some spectators and tore down stadium billboards. The Bad Blue Boys, located at the other end of the stadium, eventually broke through the retaining fence and invaded the pitch, steaming towards the Red Star supporters. At this point, the Zagreb police, whose ranks were allegedly dominated by Serbs, clashed with the invading fans and thereby prevented an all-out war between the Delije and the Bad Blue Boys. The riot then moved outside the stadium. The Croatian and Serbian media blamed the other side for causing the incidents.[20] In hindsight, the Bad Blue Boys interpreted this event as the opening salvo of the so-called Homeland War.

Relations and attitudes were more complicated in multi-ethnic Bosnia and Herzegovina, and Montenegro. Many fans in Sarajevo and Mostar initially expressed support for Yugoslavia, as this was the greatest insurance of cohesion in a multi-ethnic republic full of the so-called mixed marriages. But as many Croats and Serbs rallied around the ethnic flag, so did many fans of Muslim background. At election time in Bosnia in the early 1990s, many members of the Horde Zla, or Hordes of Evil (supporters of FK Sarajevo), recognized the Party of Democratic Action as representative of the Muslim nation.[21] In Titograd (now Podgorica), Budućnost's fan group, the Varvari, or Barbarians, fractured over the issue of national identification and politics. A small number of Varvari remained pro-Serbian, while the New Barbarians advocated an intact Yugoslavia or, in the event of its break-up, an independent Montenegro. Accordingly, these two groups supported different political parties. During the election campaign at the end of 1990, the Varvari endorsed Novak Kilibarda and the pro-Serbian People's Party, while the New Barbarians supported Ante Marković's Union of Reform Forces of Yugoslavia.[22]

When war began in Croatia in 1991, members of football fan groups were some of the earliest volunteers, and thereby carried their violent inter-ethnic rivalries to the battlefields. Members of the Bad Blue Boys and Torcida joined the military units of the emerging Croatian army. The latter fought, for example, in the Fourth Brigade. These fan-soldiers wore their team scarves at the front, and there were inscriptions of Torcida and BBB (Bad Blue Boys) on some of their tanks. NK Rijeka fans, known as the Armada, fought close to home in Croatia on the Lika front.[23] Supporters of Sarajevo's two main clubs joined the ranks of the Bosnian army. The rivalry between the Manijaci, or Maniacs (supporters of Željezničar), and Horde Zla (supporters of FK Sarajevo) turned into alliance with the coming of the Bosnian Serb military and the division of the city. 'For the first time', the Bosnian journalist Ozren Kebo explains, 'the Horde Zla and Manijaci stood side by side – in the ranks of the Territorial Defense, which later evolved into the Army of Bosnia and Hercegovina'.[24] In Montenegro, the pro-Serbian Varvari served in the Serbian-led Yugoslav People's Army, while the pro-Yugoslav, pro-Montenegrin New Barbarians turned down the call.[25]

Most famously, the Delije of Red Star formed the core of the Serbian Volunteer Guard, or Tigers, a paramilitary led by the international criminal Željko 'Arkan' Ražnatović. Arkan, who became the leader of the amalgamated group of Red Star fans around 1990, later boasted that the military training of Delije started immediately after the May 1990 riot in Zagreb (at which he was present): 'I insisted on discipline from our very beginning...I made them cut their hair, shave regularly, stop drinking and – it took its own course'.[26] The Tigers fought in Slavonia (eastern Croatia), including the city of Vukovar, and in Bosnia. They, like other fan-soldiers, adapted their songs to the conditions of wartime.[27] Srđan Vrcan and Dražen Lalić, two Croatian sociologists, reported that 'the first armed clashes were frequently described by those participants as a direct continuation of the clashes between Croatian and Serbian fan groups'.[28] They add that 'some of the most brutal and criminal war actions in the early stages of the civil war were committed by units full of football fans'.[29] The Serbian ethnographer Čolović makes a sweeping argument about the dissolution of Yugoslavia, which he says can be understood as:

> the story of the evolution of violence in Yugoslav sport, especially among football hooligans, and the gradual transference of that violence, at the end of the 1980s and the beginning of the 1990s, into the domain of inter-ethnic conflicts and 'greater-nation' politics, and thence onto the battlefield.[30]

Football fan groups did not only join the war; they acted as 'a war vanguard'.[31]

Some football clubs were directly targeted in the conflict. A good example is Velež, the club of Mostar, a city of Muslims, Croats and Serbs in western Bosnia and Herzegovina.

Velež, seen as representing the communist state's official ideology of the brotherhood and unity of the country's various national groups, became the target of nationalists during the fighting in Bosnia (1992–1995).[32] In 1992, Croat nationalists established their own club, Zrinjski, and fan group; Velež came to be labelled as the 'Muslim' club.[33] According to historian Richard Mills, Zrinjski was 'resurrected solely in the pursuit of ethnic separation, or in other words, as another vehicle from which Croat nationalists could challenge the inclusive and multiethnic values of brotherhood and unity which Velež had always claimed to uphold'.[34] Velež's stadium, which is located in the divided city's Croat area, was appropriated and leased to Zrinjski. One member of Velež's fan group, the Red Army, mentioned that the cross-town football rivalry perpetuates the inter-ethnic strife: 'Now all of the confrontation actually takes between the football clubs – due to the war'. Velež management and fans, for their part, have tried to strip the club of any ethnic designation.[35]

As the case of post-war Mostar football illustrates, the war has remained a part of football fans' narratives and identifications. Writing in 1999, Vrcan and Lalić observed that 'Serbian and Croatian clubs now meet only in international competition, and their matches have so far been seen as an extension of the war', even if played in front of nationally homogenous audiences.[36] In the early years of Croatian independence, it was possible to see posters in the stadiums declaring fans' military units, such as 'Torcida – IV. Brigada'.[37] Football fan groups, often in coordination with club managements, still commemorate the role of fellow supporters in the military conflicts. The Bad Blue Boys, Torcida and Armada have erected monuments in honour of fans who died in battle. The plaque outside Dinamo stadium, erected in 1994, reads, 'To all Dinamo fans for whom the war began 13 May 1990 at Maksimir Stadium and ended with the laying down of their lives on the altar of the Croatian homeland'. For Croatian fans, the city of Vukovar – where Arkan's Tigers fought and pillaged – remains a site where they exercise their national identification and 'defence' of the Croatian nation. In 2008, for instance, the Bad Blue Boys, Torcida and other Croatian fan groups, including some from Bosnia and Herzegovina, organized a protest in Vukovar after an attack on a student's home. The attackers were reported to be youth of Serbian background wearing Red Star scarves and chanting 'This is Serbia', as they broke over 20 of the home's windows. During the protest march, the Croatian fans chanted, among other things, 'O Mother Croatia, We'll Slaughter the Serbs' and 'Kill the Serb'.[38] Serbian fans, for their part, have been heard yelling anti-Croatian slogans, as during a Red Star–Rad match in May 2011, when some fans also burned a Croatian flag.[39] Chants and banners promoting inter-ethnic intolerance are still common throughout the former Yugoslavia, and, as the Vukovar march demonstrates, they do not always take place in a football context.

There have also been numerous incidents of inter-ethnic physical violence. Only a small fraction are listed here as illustrations. In 2007, Serbian fans clashed with Hajduk fans as the latter were in Podgorica, Montenegro, for a match against Budućnost. In 2008, NK Osijek's fan group, the Kohorta, or Cohort, assaulted local Red Star fans near Vukovar. In 2008, Partizan was expelled from the UEFA Cup because of fan disorder during a match against Zrinjski Mostar, even though Partizan won 11-1. (UEFA [Union of European Football Associations] is the governing body of European football.) In late 2011, Torcida and Željezničar fans engaged in a massive brawl on the streets of Sarajevo on the occasion of a friendly match. The inter-ethnic incidents among football fans would be difficult to total, but it is certain that many fans view them as a continuation of the Yugoslav Wars. Taken together, the lasting inter-ethnic intolerance and violence is a powerful legacy of Yugoslav club football.

Legacy's impact on the debate

Given this record of inter-ethnic intolerance and violence among football fans, security is understandably the pre-eminent concern both for advocates and critics. This worry comes up in the hundreds of conversations about the idea of an amalgamated league. Some propose to ban visiting fans for a number of years. Beyond security, though, the legacy of Yugoslav club football influences the football league debate in at least three important ways. One is the perpetual belief that the time for reunion is premature. Another is the widespread anxiety over the possibility of reviving the *Yugoslav* league. The final aspect is related to this loathing for all things Yugoslav. In the post-Yugoslav period, as successor peoples have emphasized (and invented) distinctions among themselves, they have tried to position themselves, and others, on the cultural map of Europe.

With continued intolerance and violence, there is a common view that it is too early for a regional football league, especially one that comprises Croatian and Serbian teams. Igor Štimac, not yet speaking as the coach of the Croatian national team, does not back such a league because 'we live in hooligan times'.[40] Velimir Zajec, a former Dinamo player, believes that a regional league is premature for several reasons, including lingering post-war animosity. In 2010, he told the Serbian news agency *Blic*, 'War wounds from the nineties have not yet healed'.[41] For those who oppose a regional league, this is an easy card to play. This outlook is rather noteworthy too because football is a key site where war wounds are kept fresh.

Unsurprisingly, fan groups are the most vehement opponents of reunion of formerly Yugoslav football clubs. Supporters of the Red Star, Partizan, Dinamo and Hajduk have openly declared their resistance to a regional league involving clubs of 'enemy' nations. In February 2010, when the idea of an international league re-emerged as a hot topic of discussion, the Bad Blue Boys released a public statement declaring that they 'will never support a single form of competition or regional league in which Dinamo appears together with clubs from Serbia, Montenegro, and the Serbian Republic'. They added the caveat that this excludes UEFA contests.[42] Torcida holds the same stance.[43] Even though fan groups of Red Star and Partizan oppose reunion with Croatian clubs, they have expressed their delight in the chance to come to Zagreb for the first time since the 1990 riot in order to watch Serbia play against Croatia in the group stage of the 2014 World Cup.[44] These protests by fan groups have been influential. Zdravko Mamić, Dinamo's executive vice-president, a long-time advocate for a regional league, began to waver in his advocacy in early 2010 after the boisterous protests of the Bad Blue Boys.[45] Such a response by club management illustrates the sway of fan groups in the successor states.[46]

These sorts of negative narratives of the Yugoslav past have further influenced the debate. Opponents of reuniting former Yugoslavs in football sometimes accuse advocates of 'Yugo-nostalgia', a label intended to discredit one's views and end discussion. In her article on nostalgia for the Yugoslav People's Army, Tanja Petrović explains the successor states' demonization of favourable attitudes towards Yugoslav state and society. As she succinctly puts it, 'Any positive stance toward the Yugoslav past is seen as a lack of patriotism and is pejoratively marked as "Yugo-nostalgia"'.[47] Midway through the first decade of the twenty-first century, Zdravko Mamić, Dinamo's executive vice-president, was labelled a 'Yugo-nostalgic and opponent of Croatia' for advocating an amalgamated league with other former Yugoslav countries.[48] Red Star's president, Vladan Lukić, said in early 2010 before he changed his mind that 'nostalgics pine for an ex-Yugo league'.[49] In 2004, the then president of Hajduk, Branko Grgić, revealed the common fear of reviving Yugoslavia. 'None of those interested, and especially Hajduk and Dinamo, want the new regional league to overlap with the territory of the former Yugoslavia. Hajduk's management has clearly said that we are against restoring the Yugoslav league'.[50] Later, in 2009, Hajduk's president, Mate Peroš, illustrated the patriotic nature of opposition: 'We have our Croatia and our [national league] is entirely sufficient for the development of our clubs'.[51] Press coverage of the televised conversation noted that Hajduk opposed a regional league because 'they see a danger of an attempt at a revival of former political connections between the former republics'.[52]

Most of the concrete proposals have encompassed clubs from countries that never belonged to Yugoslavia – Austria, Hungary, Czech Republic, Slovakia, Romania, Bulgaria and Greece – but the media are partly responsible for playing on the widespread loathing for the former state. Reporters often refer to the 'Yugo league' and 'SFRY league' (the official name of the state was the Socialist Federal Republic of Yugoslavia), and have called its possible creation the 'return of SFRY football', 'nogoslavija' (foot-slavia) and 'football Yugo-resurrection'. Unlike the Yugoslav People's Army, some sort of Yugoslav football league is revivable, and this is what creates an anxiety for those who detest the Yugoslav past; and it also makes for sensationalist copy in the press.

This aversion to the Yugoslav past informs current cultural identifications, that is, who is Central European and who is Balkan. The person who brings this up the most is Vlatko Marković, until recently the president of the Croatian Football Federation. Marković, like many Croats, will not countenance a Balkan football league, insisting instead on a Central European one,[53] a cultural identification somewhat reflected in the membership of amalgamated leagues in other sports.[54] In response, the president of the Serbian Football Federation, Tomislav Karadžić, says that a regional league can be formed without Croats. 'We can do it, of course, without Croats', he retorted in 2009. 'If they do not want to play, for whatever reason, that should not slow down the rest from trying to take a European step forward'.[55] In the former Yugoslavia, Central Europe trumps the Balkans, but Europe trumps them all.

Alternative memories and visions

The intent of accusations of Yugo-nostalgia is to stifle discussion, but for some others, nostalgic reflection is a goad for future collective action. The achievements of clubs in the Yugoslav era remain a standard by which performance in the national leagues is judged. And many observers are dissatisfied with what they see as the comparatively low quality of play throughout the successor states. Darko Pančev, the Macedonian-born striker who starred for the European champion Red Star side in 1991, is one of them. In an interview in 2009, he expressed his desire for federations and clubs to work together to return football's 'former glory'.[56] In terms of international results, the Yugoslav First League was indeed much stronger – many locals even claim that it was among the best five in Europe. The greatest success was achieved by the Big Four. Dinamo triumphed in the 1967 Inter-Cities Cup, having lost in the final in 1963. Partizan won the Mitropa Cup in 1978 and was placed second in the 1966 European Cup. Red Star, the most successful club abroad, won the 1991 European Cup – it lost in the 1979 final – and the 1991 Intercontinental Cup, the contest between Europe's and South America's respective champion. Hajduk was the strongest Yugoslav team never to have won a European competition, reaching the semi-finals of major European tournaments in 1973 and 1984.

By comparison, these same clubs, since the break-up of Yugoslavia, have not won a European title, and their performance has dropped since the end of the 1990s. Partizan's greatest success came in the 2004–2005 UEFA Cup, when the club made it to the 16th round. Hajduk reached the quarter-finals of the Champions League in 1994–1995. 'Did Star become what it is today playing a Serbian league or the other one?', Pančev's former teammate and now director of the Serbian club Napredak (Progress) Dragiša Binić asked Red Star's president, Vladan Lukić, another member of that side. Binić pressed further, 'Did we become world champions as champions of Serbia or Yugoslavia?'[57] Those, like Pančev and Binić, who reflect wistfully on Yugoslav club football are not simply selectively remembering the past: the claim that the quality of play in the Yugoslav First League was much higher than any successor league is accurate.[58] And their reflections are directed at the future, not the past.

Because positive attitudes towards the Yugoslav past have been deemed unpatriotic, some football officials have been trying to reformulate patriotism. In early 2010, Dragiša Binić, Napredak's director, said, 'I am for forming a united league with those who lived with us in SFRY! That is how every Serbian patriot who loves football ought to think'.[59] His argument was that a regional league would benefit Serbian football and was therefore in the nation-state's best interests. Ivica Osim, the last coach of Yugoslavia's national team, contends that it is time to move beyond remaining ethnic divisions, most pronounced in football. In an interview, he said:

> there has been much investment in violence and misfortune for years and years. There are too many who supported the wars, destructive people who profited from another's misery and misfortune. I think the time of these people, who divided people on a religious and national basis, and now on a fan basis, has passed.[60]

The loud resistance of the organized fan groups disguises the support of other fans for an amalgamated league. In March 2010, the Croatian sports paper *Sportske novosti* teamed up with the Serbian daily *Politika* to conduct an online opinion poll. There were more than 1700 respondents, and more than 1200 of them favoured the creation of a regional league.[61] In another online poll, this time organized by the Croatian newspaper *Jutarnji list*, 52% of the 2430 respondents indicated support, while 30% expressed opposition, with the remaining 18% finding the league interesting but unviable because of security concerns.[62] Fans in online forums have debated the issue for years, and many have also expressed a fair amount of support.[63]

A few even hold that a regional league is a pathway to reconciliation. Otto Barić, a former coach, argues that it is time to put an end to all the tensions and look to a common future, 'which is best built through football'. He says that the danger of fan violence should not be the decisive factor against forming a league. 'It is time we move on and outgrow those things'.[64] The former coach of the Croatian and Bosnian national teams, Miroslav 'Ćiro' Blažević, akin to Osim, sees Robert Prosinečki's hiring at Red Star as a sign that relations between Serbian and Croatian sports and society have entered a new, good-neighbourly phase. He told the Belgrade newspaper *Dnevnik* that 'we are on a good path to soon having a regional football league. It's hard to say when that will be, but if Prosinečki is at Star, then why couldn't the club play safely in Zagreb?'[65] But Prosinečki, a star on the 1991 championship Red Star side and the son of mixed Croat–Serb parentage, does not see it as his task to make peace between Serbs and Croats. 'I didn't come to be an ambassador, peacemaker or mediator', he said in an interview with a Belgrade newspaper. 'I came to be the coach of my Red Star and become first in the city'.[66] The other 'soldiers of reconciliation' that Blažević has singled out are the respective presidents of Croatia and Serbia.[67] Croatian President Ivo Josipović and the then Serbian President Boris Tadić jointly expressed support for the project of a regional football league.[68] Josipović's endorsement is a far cry from the stance of one of his predecessors, Franjo Tuđman, who saw sports, football in particular, as war by other means and a way to legitimize the new Croatian state.

Conclusions

The enduring memory of club football's entanglement in the Yugoslav conflicts, combined with the sport's lasting position as a refuge for inter-ethnic antagonism, keeps the question of a regional league highly controversial. But, as is clear, coaches and players, particularly those who achieved great success in the time of Yugoslavia, have spoken out against the inter-ethnic intolerance and violence that remains one of the characteristics of post-Yugoslav football culture. They have also proposed alternatives to this legacy, advocating more tolerant patriotism and even reconciliation. This apparently increasing capacity, notably on the part of politicians, to envision a regional football league with ex-Yugoslav clubs is quite significant.

UEFA president Michel Platini has repeatedly stated his openness to the idea of a regional league in the former Yugoslavia. But he admits that his organization's statutes do not currently allow for such an arrangement. Before UEFA discusses changes, however, he wants to see united political desire, that is, 'an agreement of several states on holding such a competition'.[69] Platini reasons that such a project is up to politicians. For their part, Serbian politicians are more open to the idea than their Croatian counterparts.[70] As noted above, the two country's presidents endorsed the project in 2010, though they passed the responsibility to the national football federations. The federations have been unable to reach any agreement, with some federations in fact opposed to the idea of associating again in football.

With this lack of leadership, clubs have recently taken matters into their own hands. In November 2011, representatives of clubs from Serbia, Bulgaria, Romania, Ukraine, Turkey and Azerbaijan met at the invitation of CSKA Sofia to discuss the creation of the East European Football League (EEFL).[71] The legacy of Yugoslav football is evident in these latest talks. For Serbian clubs, there is much less fear of violence at matches against teams from countries that did not belong to Yugoslavia.[72] Time will tell whether the EEFL will follow the fate of the CEFL, proposed back in 2004, or whether something will actually materialize. If the latter, a possible scenario for ex-Yugoslav football clubs is the creation of two regional leagues, as in water polo, with Serbian teams in one and Croatian clubs in the other; or perhaps Croatian and other ex-Yugoslav teams would join the EEFL later, as Serbian basketball clubs joined the ABA prior to that league's second season. The future is unforeseeable, but it is probable, considering all the renewed connections between the Yugoslav successor states and peoples, that some form of football reunion will happen someday.

Acknowledgements

Funding for this research came from the Oswald Backus Memorial Award (2010) and a U.S. State Department Fulbright grant for Croatia (2011–2012). I am deeply grateful to the University of Kansas History Department and the U.S. State Department for their generous funding.

Notes

1. Judah, 'Entering the Yugosphere'.
2. Rogošić, 'Hajduk i Dinamo'.
3. Hudelist and Španović, 'Ujedinjenje nogometnih gubitnika'.
4. 'Regionalna liga dobra ideja' [Regional league a good idea], *Večernje novosti*, March 14, 2009.

5. 'Regionalna liga tudi v nogometu?' [A regional league in football too?] *Delo*, February 18, 2010; 'Zagrijavanje za regionalnu ligu bit će turnir prvaka?' [Tournament of champions will be warm-up for regional league?] *Dnevnik*, February 18, 2010.

6. Dragiša Binić, the current director of a small Serbian club, Napredak, explained this practice in a 2010 interview: 'Small clubs sell players to Star or Partizan, and then we wait for them to further sell them abroad, and all the titles belong to them [Red Star and Partizan]', Petković, 'Patriotski u SFRJ ligu'.

7. While advocating for an amalgamated league in early 2010, Zdravko Mamić, Dinamo's executive vice-president, called the region's clubs 'cannon fodder' for west European teams – and this was before his club set the Champions League record for worst-ever goal difference. See 'Mi smo braća, a UEFA je naša majka' [We are brothers, and UEFA is our mother], *Jutarnji list*, February 12, 2010.

8. The average match attendance in 2009–2010 in Croatia's league, UEFA's highest-ranked national league in the former Yugoslavia, was 2031; Lalić, 'Umro je hrvatski nogomet'. The only matches that draw large audiences in the former Yugoslavia today, apart from European (and national team) contests, are the two big derbies, Partizan–Red Star and Hajduk–Dinamo.

9. 'Ivica Osim: Regionalna liga, sad ili nikad' [Ivica Osim: Regional league, now or never], www. index.hr, March 10, 2011.

10. 'Je li moguća regionalna liga?' [Is a regional league possible?] *Hrvatska Radio-Televizija*, February 17, 2009.

11. 'Dejan Savičević: Prosinečki i ja smo nosili Zvezdu do europske titule' [Dejan Savičević: Prosinečki and I carried star to the European title], www.index.hr, March 12, 2010.

12. The founders of the Adriatic basketball league staved off much controversy in Slovenia and Croatia by not speaking publicly about their interest in Serbian clubs. Roman Lisac, one of the founders, admitted that 'the idea of having both Red Star and Partizan in the league was there from the very beginning, but we avoided talking about it publicly because of politics' (quoted in Raić, 'An Ex-YU Football League').

13. Bosnia and Herzegovina initially had three separate leagues, one for each major nation (Bosnian Muslims, Serbs and Croats), but since 2002, there has been a statewide Premier League. Montenegro established its own league in 2006, the year it severed union with Serbia.

14. Lalić, 'Nasilništvo nogometnih navijača'.

15. Čolović, 'Football, Hooligans and War', 373–4.

16. Ibid., 379–81.

17. Ibid., 376.

18. Perasović, 'Navijačko pleme', 65.

19. Lalić, *Torcida*, 69, 202.

20. Mihailović, 'Rat je počeo 13. maja 1990'.

21. Kebo, 'Horde zla i manijaci'.

22. Marojević, 'Varvari i New Barbarians'.

23. s.v. 'Armada'; Kramer and Klemenčić, *Nogometni leksikon*, 18.

24. Kebo, 'Horde zla i manijaci', 56.

25. Marojević, 'Varvari i New Barbarians'.

26. Quoted in Čolović, 'Od Delija do Tigrova', 60–1.

27. Čolović, 'Od Delija do Tigrova', 61.

28. Vrcan and Lalić, 'From Ends to Trenches', 177.

29. Ibid.,181.

30. Čolović, 'Football, Hooligans and War', 373.

31. Vrcan and Lalić, 'From Ends to Trenches', 177.

32. Mills, 'Velez Mostar Football', 1107.

33. Ibid., 1120–21.

34. Ibid., 1122.

35. Ibid., 1131.

36. Vrcan and Lalić, 'From Ends to Trenches', 181.

37. Lalić, 'Bad Blue Boys i Torcida', 52.

38. Butigan and Obrenović, 'Razbijali stakla doma'; Lesički and Španović, 'BBB-i i Torcida idu u pohod'; 'Navijači u Vukovaru pjevali "Ubij, ubij Srbina"' [Fans in Vukovar sang 'Kill, Kill the Serb'], *Jutarnji list*, March 2, 2008.

39. Medo, 'Na Marakani gorjela "šahovnica"'. Marakana is the nickname of Red Star's stadium.

40. 'Štimac o regionalnoj ligi: Nema šanse, živimo u huliganskom vremenu' [Štimac on regional league: Not a chance, we live in hooligan times], www.index.hr, November 17, 2010.
41. 'Zajec: Jednoga dana igrat će se YU-liga, ali još je prerano' [Zajec: Yugoslav League will be played one day, but it is still too early], *Jutarnji list*, February 25, 2010.
42. 'BBB: Nikada nećemo prihvatiti natjecanje sa klubovima iz Srbije, Crne Gore i Republike Srpske' [BBB: We will never accept a competition with clubs from Serbia, Montenegro or the Serbian Republic], www.index.hr, February 18, 2010. An irony here is that the violent acts of fans have brought several successor states closer together: Croatian and Serbian governments have met several times to discuss 'football hooliganism', and they even have an agreement on police cooperation in preventing and controlling football fan excesses.
43. Private correspondence, June 2011.
44. 'Grobari i Delije stižu u Hrvatsku: "Ne postoji sila koja bi nas spriječila da dođemo na utakmicu"' [Grobari and Delije coming to Croatia: 'No Power Can Stop Us from Coming to the Match'], www.index.hr, August 2, 2011. Grobari, Partizan's fans, means gravediggers.
45. Židak, 'Dopredsjednik NS Srbije'.
46. For a discussion of the Delije's clout in Red Star affairs, see Pašalić, 'Teror Delija nad Crvenom zvezdom'.
47. Petrović, 'Nostalgia for the JNA?', 63.
48. Breber, 'Mamić'.
49. Krušelj, 'Regionalna liga'.
50. Rogošić, 'Hajduk i Dinamo'.
51. 'U Otvorenom o regionalnoj ligi' [About a regional league on Otvoreno], *Hrvatska Radio-Televizija*, February 17, 2009. Otvoreno is a television programme in Croatia.
52. 'Je li moguća regionalna liga?' [Is a regional league possible?], *Hrvatska Radio-Televizija*, February 17, 2009.
53. 'Marković: Želim Srednjoeuropsku ligu, Balkanska ne dolazi u obzir!' [Marković: I want a Central European League, a Balkan one is out of the question], *Sportske novosti*, February 15, 2009.
54. 'Central European' Croatia and Slovenia compete with other such countries (i.e. former Habsburg territories) in the Erste Bank Ice Hockey League, Middle European Volleyball Zonal Association and field hockey's Central European Interleague. Slovenia and Croatia also remain separate from Serbia in water polo, where two separate leagues have been established, the Adriatic and the Euro-Inter. Yet, Serbia and Slovenia currently participate in the Central European (American-style) Football League along with Hungary and Turkey. And most of the formerly Yugoslav republics are members of the Adriatic Basketball Association's NBL League as well as the men's and women's handball leagues (Southeast European Handball Association and Women's Regional Handball League).
55. 'Regionalna liga dobra ideja' [Regional league a good idea], *Večernje novosti*, March 14, 2009.
56. Milanović, 'Jadranska liga u'.
57. Petković, 'Patriotski u SFRJ ligu'.
58. In 2010, sociologist Dražen Lalić even pronounced the strongest successor league, the Croatian Football League, dead; see Lalić, 'Umro je hrvatski nogomet'.
59. Petković, 'Patriotski u SFRJ ligu'.
60. 'Ivica Osim: Regionalna liga donijela bi novac i plasman u Ligu prvaka' [A regional league would bring money and a spot in Champions League], *Nacional*, November 12, 2009.
61. 'Facebook anketa Sportskih novosti: Regionalna liga pitanje je vremena' [*Sportske Novosti*'s Facebook poll: Regional league is a question of time!] *Sportske novosti*, March 10, 2010.
62. *Jutarnji list* conducted the opinion poll on its website (www.jutarnji.hr) and the cited figures were taken on March 2, 2010, by which time responses were no longer coming in.
63. See the following online forum discussions throughout the former Yugoslavia (their years are noted in parentheses): (2004) http://forum.b92.net/topic/16171-regionalna-liga-u-nogom etufudbalu/page__st__15; (2006) http://www.nkmaribor.com/forum/sporocila.asp?id_sporoci la=207952&res=1; (2006) http://www.sarajevo-x.com/forum/viewtopic.php?f=14& t=29258; (2008) http://www.mycity.rs/Fudbal/Regionalna-liga-diskusija.html; (2008) http://forum.b92.net/topic/48047-jadranska-liga-u-fudbalu/; (2010) http://www.footytube.com/forums/the-stands-general-footy-banter/balkan-affairs-15042/; (2010) http://fcinter.forum akers.com/lige-svijeta-f9/regionalna-liga-ex-yu-liga-t567.htm; (2011) http://forum1.orbis.hr/s howthread.php?t=592067&page = 231

64. Deželić, 'Regionalna liga'.
65. 'Blažević o Prosinečkom i regionalnoj ligi' [Blažević on Prosinečki and regional league], *Hrvatska Radio-Televizija*, December 25, 2010; 'Ćiro: Odnosi Hrvatske i Srbije nikad bolji, sve bliže je regionalna liga!' [Ćiro: Relations of Croatia and Serbia never better, regional league is ever closer], *gol.dnevnik.hr*, December 25, 2010.
66. 'Moj posao nije miriti Srbe i Hrvate' [My job is not to reconcile Serbs and Croats], *Hrvatska Radio-Televizija*, December 31, 2010. The Belgrade newspaper was *Press*.
67. 'Ćiro Blažević: Josipović, Tadić i Prosinečki su "vojnici" pomirenja' [Ćiro Blažević: Josipović, Tadić and Prosinečki are 'soldiers' of reconciliation], *dalje.com*, December 25, 2010.
68. 'Tadić and Josipović podržali regionalnu fudbalsku ligu' [Tadić and Josipović endorsed regional football league], *Blic online*, July 18, 2010; Ivan Gojčeta, 'Josipović i Tadić složni: Podržavamo regionalnu ligu' [Josipović and Tadić in Unison: We support a regional league], www.index.hr, July 19, 2010.
69. 'Nisam protiv "balkanske lige", ali to ne znači i da sam pobornik iste' [I am not against a 'Balkan League', but that does not mean that I am an advocate of it], *Sportske novosti*, March 3, 2009.
70. 'Srpski mediji: Naši političari žele regionalnu ligu, ali HDZ i SDP su vrlo skeptični' [Serbian media: Our politicians want a regional league, but the HDZ and SDP are very skeptical], www.index.hr, November 18, 2010.
71. 'Pao dogovor, rađa se Istočnoevropska liga (EEFL)' [Agreement made, East European League is born], www.sportske.net, November 15, 2011.
72. Ivelić, 'Balkanska liga'.

References

Breber, Matko. 'Mamić: Na SP-u ću navijati za Srbiju!' [Mamić: I'll be cheering for Serbia at the World Cup!] *Jutarnji list*, February 4, 2010.
Butigan, Sanja, and Mladen Obrenović. 'Razbijali stakla doma, vrijeđali Tuđmana i vikali: Ovo je Srbija' [They broke home windows, insulted Tuđman and yelled: This is Serbia]. *Jutarnji list*, February 14, 2008.
Čolović, Ivan. 'Od Delija do Tigrova'. *Erasmus* 10 (1995): 60–2.
Čolović, Ivan. 'Football, Hooligans and War'. In *The Road to War in Serbia*, edited by Nebojša Popov, 373–96. Budapest: Central European University Press, 2000.
Deželić, Vanja. 'Regionalna liga koristila bi samo Dinamu i Hajduku' [A regional league would benefit only Dinamo and Hajduk]. *dalje.com*, February 19, 2009.
Hudelist, Darko, and Sanjin Španović. 'Ujedinjenje nogometnih gubitnika' [Unification of football's losers]. *Globus*, October 13, 2006.
Ivelić, Ante. 'Balkanska liga za početak ide kao kup, Hajduka ni ne zovu' [Balkan League will start as cup, Hajduk did not even get a call]. *Slobodna Dalmacija*, October 12, 2011.
Judah, Tim. 'Entering the Yugosphere'. *The Economist*, August 20, 2009.
Kebo, Ozren. 'Horde zla i manijaci'. *Erasmus* 10 (1995): 56–8.
Kramer, Fredi and Klemenčić, Mladen, eds. *Nogometni leksikon* [Football lexicon]. Zagreb: Leksikografski zavod Miroslav Krleža, 2004.
Krušelj, Dražen. 'Regionalna liga: Mamuzanje mrtvog konja' [Regional league: Spurring a dead horse]. *Jutarnji list*, February 19, 2010.
Lalić, Dražen. 'Nasilništvo nogometnih navijača: geneza fenomena u Jugoslaviji' [Football fan violence: Genesis of the phenomenon in Yugoslavia]. *Kultura* 88–90 (1990): 111–32.
Lalić, Dražen. 'Bad Blue Boys i Torcida'. *Erasmus* 10 (1995): 51–5.
Lalić, Dražen. 'Umro je hrvatski nogomet' [Croatian football has died]. *Slobodna Dalmacija*, May 5, 2010.
Lalić, Dražen. *Torcida: pogled iznutra.*, 2nd and exp. ed. Zagreb: Profil International, 2011.
Lesički, Alen, and Sanjin Španović. 'BBB-i i Torcida idu u pohod na Vukovar' [BBB and Torcida going on march on Vukovar]. *Jutarnji list*, February 19, 2008.
Marojević, Igor. 'Varvari i New Barbarians'. *Erasmus* 10 (1995): 58–9.
Medo, Ivica. 'Na Marakani gorjela "šahovnica"' [Croatian coat of arms burned at Marakana]. *gol.dnevnik.hr*, May 16, 2011.
Mihailović, Srećko 'Rat je počeo 13. maja 1990' [The war began 13 May 1990]. In *Rat je počeo na Maksimiru: govor mržnje u medijima*, edited by Svetlana Slapšak, 77–124. Belgrade: Medija centar, 1997.

Milanović, Petar. 'Jadranska liga u fudbalu – hitno!' [Adriatic League in football – Urgent!]. www. naslovi.net, January 5, 2009.

Mills, Richard. 'Velez Mostar Football Club and the Demise of "Brotherhood and Unity" in Yugoslavia, 1922–2009'. *Europe-Asia Studies* 62, no. 7 (2010): 1107–33.

Pašalić, Davor. 'Teror Delija nad Crvenom zvezdom' [Delije terrorize Red Star]. *Nacional* 672 September 29, 2008.

Perasović, Benjamin. 'Navijačko pleme: do nacije i natrag' [Fan tribe: To the nation and back]. *Erasmus* 11 (1995): 61–7.

Petković, Dejan. 'Patriotski u SFRJ ligu' [Patriotic into an SFRY League]. *Kurir*, February 20, 2010.

Petrović, Tanja. 'Nostalgia for the JNA? Remembering the Army in the Former Yugoslavia'. In *Post-Communist Nostalgia*, edited by Maria Todorova and Zsuzsa Gille, 61–81. New York: Berghahn Books, 2010.

Raić, Ante. 'An Ex-YU Football League: Will It Ever Happen?' *balkananalysis.com*, October 1, 2011.

Rogošić, Željko. 'Hajduk i Dinamo ponovno u ligi sa Zvezdom i Partizanom' [Hajduk and Dinamo again in a league with star and Partizan]. *Nacional* 473 December 7, 2004.

Vrcan, Srđan, and Dražen Lalić. 'From Ends to Trenches, and Back: Football in the Former Yugoslavia'. In *Football Cultures and Identities*, edited by Gary Armstrong and Richard Giulianotti, 176–85. London: Macmillan, 1999.

Židak, Tomislav. 'Dopredsjednik NS Srbije: Platini ne vjeruje u YU-ligu!' [Vice-president of Serbia's Football Federation: Platini does not believe in a Yugoslav League!]. *Jutarnji list*, February 22, 2010.

Index

Football Supporters and the Commercialisation of Football

Comparative Responses across Europe

Edited by Peter Kennedy and David Kennedy

As football clubs have become luxury investments, their decisions increasingly mirror those of any other business organisation. Football supporters have been encouraged to express their club loyalty by 'thinking business' - acting as consumers and generating money deemed necessary for their clubs to compete at the highest levels. In critical studies, supporters have been portrayed as passive or reluctant consumers who, imprisoned by enduring club loyalties, embody a fatalistic attitude to their own exploitation. As this book aims to show, however, such expressions of loyalty are far from hegemonic and often interface haphazardly with traditional ideas about what constitutes the 'loyal fan'. While there is little doubt that professional football is experiencing commodification, the reality is that football clubs are not simply businesses, nor can they ever aspire to be organisations driven solely by expanding or protecting economic value. Rather, clubs hover uncertainly between being businesses and community assets.

This book explores the implications of this uncertainty for understanding football supporter resistance to, and compromise with, commodification and offers a Euro-wide comparison of supporter reactions to commercialisation.

This book was previously published as a special issue of *Soccer and Society*.

Peter Kennedy and David Kennedy both lecture at Glasgow Caledonian University

October 2012: 246 x 174: 152pp
Hb: 978-0-415-61890-8
£90 / $155

Related titles from Routledge

Governance, Citizenship and the New European Football Championships

The European Spectacle

Edited by Wolfram Manzenreiter and Georg Spitaler

This volume takes the 2008 EUROs hosted by Austria and Switzerland as a case study to analyze the political and cultural significance of the tournament from a multidisciplinary angle. What are the special features and spatial arrangements of a UEFAesque Europe, in comparison to alternative possibilities of a Europe? Situating the sport tournament between interpretations of collective European ritual and European spectacle, the key research question will ask what kind of Europe was represented in the cultural, political and economic manifestations of the 2008 EUROs.

This book was published as a special issue of *Soccer and Society*.

Wolfram Manzenreiter is associated with the Department of East Asian Studies, University of Vienna, where he teaches modern Japanese society.

Georg Spitaler is a part-time lecturer at the Department of Political Science, University of Vienna, as well as editorial board member of Austria's leading football magazine, *Ballesterer*.

July 2011: 246 x 174: 216pp
Hb: 978-0-415-55106-9
£85 / $145